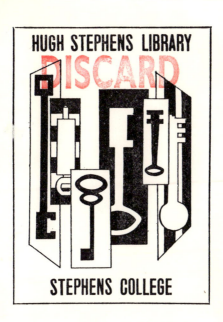

EYEWITNESS: RED CHINA

Here are first-hand, on-the-spot reports from Free World journalists, writers and correspondents on life inside Red China today. They come from many countries and from many walks of life—British Lord, Canadian scientist, Swiss theater critic, Brazilian foreign correspondent, Danish travel writer, Indian population expert, Anglo-American TV commentator. They answer such questions about Red China as:

How do you get a divorce in Red China?
How much does a Chinese film actor earn?
Has the West over- or under-estimated
    Chinese industrial capacity?
Why is there virtually no stealing in Red China?

Are foreign visitors allowed to take photographs?
What is the only raw material Red China must import?
Is there much sexual promiscuity in Red China?
What is a Chinese actor's analysis of Hamlet?
Is forced labor used in Red China?
What subjects are taught in a Chinese school?
Why does the state pay for a young couple's
    wedding reception?
What do Russians think of Chinese communism?
What does an average Chinese apartment look like?
What does the one uniform worn by all Chinese—men and
    women, from coolie to university professor—look like?
What is a typical Chinese breakfast?
Are foreign visitors spied on in Red China?

**THESE QUESTIONS AND HUNDREDS MORE ARE ANSWERED
IN THIS REVEALING, PENETRATING REPORT ON RED CHINA
TODAY!**

REPORT FROM RED CHINA

**Edited by
Robert E. Evans**

**With an introduction by
Tillman Durdin**

BANTAM BOOKS NEW YORK

FOR GEORGE BUSH

REPORT FROM RED CHINA

A Bantam Book / published September 1962

2nd printing

For permission to reprint the selections in this volume by each of the following authors, grateful acknowledgment is made to the holders of copyright, publishers or representatives named below.

LORD BOYD ORR and PETER TOWNSEND; selections from *What's Happening in China?* are reprinted by permission of Doubleday & Company, Inc. and Macdonald & Co. (Publishers) Ltd., London. Copyright © 1959 by Lord Boyd Orr and Peter Townsend.

SRIPATI CHANDRASEKHAR; selections from *Red China; An Asian View* are reprinted by permission of Frederick A. Praeger, Inc. *The Human Inflation of Red China,* from The New York Times Magazine, December 6, 1959, is reprinted by permission of the author and The New York Times.

GERALD CLARK; selections from *Impatient Giant: Red China Today* are reprinted by permission of David McKay Company, Inc. Copyright © 1959 by Gerald Clark.

MICHAEL CROFT; selections from *Red Carpet to China* are reprinted by permission of St. Martins Press, Inc. and A. D. Peters, London. Copyright © Michael Croft 1958.

KARL ESKELUND; selections from *The Red Mandarins* are reprinted by permission of the author and Alvin Redman Limited, London. © Karl Eskelund 1959.

FELIX GREENE; selections from *Awakened China: The Country Americans Don't Know* are reprinted by permission of Doubleday & Company, Inc. Copyright © 1961 by Felix Greene.

LIU SHENG; *Life in a Chinese University,* from the Atlantic Monthly, December 1959, is reprinted by permission of The Atlantic Monthly Company, Agent for Liu Sheng.

ROBERT LOH; *Setting the Stage for Foreigners,* from the Atlantic Monthly, December 1959, is reprinted by permission of the author.

PETER SCHMID; selections from *The New Face of China* are reprinted by permission of George G. Harrap & Company, Ltd., London.

J. TUZO WILSON; selections from *One Chinese Moon* are reprinted by permission of Hill and Wang, Inc. and Longmans Canada Limited, Toronto. Copyright © 1959 by J. Tuzo Wilson.

LOUIS WIZNITZER; selections based on *I Saw Red China from the Inside,* a copyrighted interview in U.S. News & World Report, June 15, 1959, appear in revised form by permission of the author.

Library of Congress Catalog Card Number: 62–19342

Bantam Books are published by Bantam Books, Inc. Its trade-mark, consisting of the words "Bantam Books" and the portrayal of a bantam is registered in the United States Patent Office and in other countries. Marca Registrada. Printed in the United States of America. Bantam Books, Inc., 271 Madison Ave., New York 16, N. Y.

TABLE OF CONTENTS

PREFACE

This book is a compilation of observable facts about life in Red China today, with the emphasis on "observable" and "life." When I began compiling *Report from Red China,* I had no axe to grind—either for or against the Red regime. The same standard, as far as possible, was applied to the contributors.

My method of compilation was straightforward—read everything available in English written about China by people who have been there within the past five years and select the best. My criteria were: 1. the writer had to have seen what he wrote about; 2. he had to leave the conclusion-drawing to the reader; 3. he had to make it interesting.

Because the United States and the mainland Chinese government have had no diplomatic relations for the past twelve years or so, and because U. S. State Department policy forbids Americans to visit Red China, there is an obvious lack in this book of reports by American observers. There have been reports on Red China in the American press, but most of them have not qualified as "eyewitness" material.

In the list of sources you will find each author's name, the book or periodical from which his contribution has been excerpted, the publisher and date of publication. Throughout the book each selection is headed by the author's name and the page numbers of his original work from which the selection has been taken. For example: [CROFT, 23-28]. To preserve the flavor and maintain accuracy we have reprinted the selections exactly as they appeared in the original edition.

We have tried to examine and present the basic forms of the new Chinese society, the major plans, concepts and ideas which are driving the Chinese people, and the way of life in China today. It is an attempt to better understand who the Chinese people are, what they want, and how they live. There is no doubt that we need desperately to understand, regardless of what we would like to believe.

ROBERT E. EVANS
Former United Nations
correspondent for the
Associated Press

INTRODUCTION

When Mao Tse-tung was sixteen he set forth on foot from his peasant home in the Hunan countryside to enroll in a school in the distant city of Siangsiang. Going his way were a small boy and an old man. He liked their companionship but grew impatient at their slow pace. Scorning the boy's tearful protests, he urged them on, saying when they lagged: "Faster! Faster! Faster!"

Similar to this episode has been the encounter between the whole Chinese people and Mao Tse-tung as leader of the Chinese Communist Party. Since the Chinese communists took power in Peking in 1949 they have tried relentlessly to propel the protesting Chinese on the road of revolutionary growth and change. Their aim has been to remake the disintegrating traditional society and the backward economy of the world's second largest nation in just a few decades into a powerful, industrialized communist state capable of reasserting China's former imperial greatness. In the following pages the effects of this transformation on the way-of-life of the Red Chinese is fully described.

Today, under the impact of the communist system, reverence for ancestors, loyalties within the big family group and age-old social codes have been disrupted. Religion, the individual and new communist-style, communist-run groupings are instruments of state policy, and a relentless and constant thought control and official surveillance permit no other focus for loyalties. The prestige of elders has been replaced by emphasis on youth —trained, indoctrinated and given heady official responsibilities. Women have been made the social and legal equals of men, in and out of marriage, and serve alongside men as officials and workers. A new mass culture has reshaped traditional opera, dance, and music, and drawn heavily on Western, especially Russian, forms. Ballet troups and symphony orchestras are now a regular part of cultural life in the cities. Mass sports and mass anniversary-day demonstrations are regular, characteristically totalitarian features of the new order. New boulevards and new Western-style buildings have changed the look of upswept eaves and tiled roofs in ancient Peking. Outside the massive old imperial palace walls before the Gate of Heavenly Peace a vast Red Square has been built for the mass ceremonies of the new regime. Much that is old remains, but huge strides have been made in creating a new China.

In their fanatical haste, the Chinese communists have achieved some remarkable results. By often brutal methods, they have liquidated the old Confucian social order and created a new collectivized and regimented society roughly patterned after communism in Russia but with important purely Chinese variations. For the first time in 200 years the Peiping regime has established centralized authority over all the vast Chinese domain (inhabited today by 700,000,000 people) from the Pacific to the Central Asian territories of Tibet and Sinkiang. Modern industries have been built; steel production has been boosted many times over to a 1960 peak of 18,000,000 metric tons. Road, railway, telecommunication and airline networks have been expanded several fold. Education has been made universal for children and augmented enormously for higher ages. Illiteracy, once 80 per cent, is now less than 20 per cent. A modern military force of more than 2,500,000 men is the strongest in Asia. But it was evident by the end of their first decade in power that the Chinese communists had tried to go too far too fast. Big supercollectives, or communes, organized in 1958 in connection with a new, high-pressure "great leap" production drive in all sectors of the economy, proved unworkable because of mismanagement and peasant resistance, aggravated by periods of flood and drought. Agricultural output showed no increase from 1959 to 1961; severe food shortages developed and malnutrition became widespread.

In 1961, the Peking regime was forced to abandon the "great leap." Priority in the national economic effort was shifted from industry to agriculture. The communes were decentralized and peasant families were allowed private plots.

Even with the more moderate policies, there was general popular discontent accentuated by differences with Russia. (Russia withdrew most technical assistance from Communist China and did not grant new credits.) Differences in the ranks of the Chinese Communist Party itself may bring further disruption; Mao Tse-tung is aging and his mental faculties failing. Population growth of from fifteen to twenty million persons a year is another serious complication.

However, Communist China has the natural and human resources necessary for largescale economic development. The instruments of power—the bureaucracy, the military and the police—are still effective, and loyal to the regime. If experience has now modified the Mao Tse-tung urge for haste it is still possible the Peiping regime can put Communist China's affairs in order and direct the country in a new period of growth.

TILLMAN DURDIN
Far East Specialist for
The New York Times

1. The Cities

PEKING

I am possibly the first traveller to have entered China from the north without seeing the Great Wall. After three hours' flying over the gnarled emptiness of the Gobi desert, where there is nothing to note for a thousand miles but wrinkled tracks running down to lonely oases and a solitary single-line railway fingering its way to the north, I gradually lost interest in the outposts of history and fell asleep. When I woke up we had landed in Peking.

The view confronting me from the starboard window was so startling that I wondered if we had arrived ahead of schedule on somebody else's cue. Bathed in afternoon sunshine, the airport was festooned with flags and banners. In front of the main building stood a vast crowd of young Chinese, smiling, waving and clapping. In front of them a separate group of fifty or more, their arms loaded with chrysanthemum bouquets, surged jubilantly towards the aircraft. When we stepped down the gangway they went mad with delight. A multitude of yellow hands fluttered aloft in feverish unison. Hundreds of yellow faces smiled and bubbled and the bouquet-bearers rushed in to plaster us with flowers as if we had been the vanguard of a liberating army. My typewriter was wrenched from my hand by a beaming Chinese girl, my hand almost wrenched from my arm by a beaming boy, bouquets were thrust in my face, even through the opening of my duffle coat; and while everyone waved and clapped more merrily than before we were swept along on the welcoming tide to the official reception-room.

Toasts were drunk in sweet red wine while a torrent of interpreting broke out all around. What anybody was saying it was impossible to tell. The great thing was to smile and clap and smile again as often as the Chinese did. Sometimes it seemed that they were applauding us and we were applauding them, and at other times we were all applauding each other. They have the curious convention when somebody claps them in public of clapping back, but this device also serves to termi-

1

nate the applause, and if the unwary visitor fails to employ it he may find they will go on clapping indefinitely.

When everyone had said what they wanted to say we pushed our way to waiting coaches, wondering the while how far the reception was genuine, how the crowds had been whipped up, whether any of them actually knew who we were and what the whole thing was about. Looking around more carefully, it seemed to me that some of the welcoming band were a little half-hearted and some of the workmen watching outside the airport indifferent almost to the point of hostility.

It would be good to record my first impressions in compelling tones and brilliant verbal hues. The prosaic truth is that I was driven in a coach for thirty minutes down a long rural road where peasants were at work in the fields and labourers building houses and children playing, into a city of gleaming green roofs and blue walls and golden tiles and bamboo scaffolding and steel girders and red-brick office blocks and slum compounds and people swarming about the streets and a clatter of laughing, singing, shouting, yellow-skinned humanity, but to me nothing registered because it was all too vast and too different from any other city I had arrived in before. So that when Stephen Tripp asked, 'Don't you really feel you're in Asia now?' I replied curtly that I felt no such thing, because at that moment my only wish was to have an hour or two entirely alone, or long enough anyway to feel that my mind had landed along with my legs.

Solitude, in fact, was to prove a physical commodity almost impossible to come by.

The traditional picture of the contemplative Confucian gazing from the stillness of the lake or the peace of the garden into the shadows of eternity bears no relation to life in modern China. From the cradle up six hundred million people must automatically find it difficult to get away from each other's company, but since the Liberation such eccentricity of taste would amount almost to a social crime. How *could* anybody want to be alone when there are cultural palaces and play-centres and youth leagues and women's unions and evening classes for the intelligent use of leisure and when every street has its own committee for ensuring that everyone is on the best of terms with everyone else?

I readily concede that if you visit a country on such an outing as this you should never expect to be left alone. The whole object of the exercise is to meet people from morn till night; but on the other hand you are not a convivial pump: there are times when the mind demands a breathing space between the endless receptions, discussions and expeditions, when you want to sit back to try to digest a morsel or two of the huge, unpalatable hunk; when, in short, you simply want time to think. I concede also that our hosts made no attempt to force China down our throats. If you didn't want to visit a mine or a prison they would gladly arrange something else, but to inform them that you simply wished to do nothing at all seemed a gross impoliteness, an abuse of hospitality, a selfish lack of consideration for people whom you had no occasion to offend.

Let me say at once that I do not understand the Chinese mind: if anything, I was more confused by it at the end of my visit than before; I learnt very little about the Chinese character beyond its surface qualities of reticence, forbearance and reasonableness; but, political considerations aside, I grew to admire without reservation the intense courtesy, tact and generosity which graced all their dealings with me—all except one, and that, unhappily, the one which gave an ironic and ugly significance to their pæans to Peace and Friendship. That, however, was not to come till the end of the trip.

Peking encloses four walled cities, the Inner and Outer, the Imperial City and the Forbidden City. Ch'ien Men is the great tower gate which leads from the Outer to the Inner City, and in front of this had just been completed the latest of Peking's modern hotels, called, appropriately enough, the Front Gate.

Its basic features were similar to those of any good-class, large, western hotel: all modern conveniences, hot and cold, with a private bathroom and telephone to every room; a battery of lifts in excellent working order; several large dining-rooms; and a hairdressing saloon. Its differences, however, were more conspicuous. As with the various Peace Hotels on the route, nobody was ever known to receive or pay a bill. There was no reception desk as such; nobody apparently to whom the guests might address enquiries or lodge complaints. The number of staff, or 'servicemen', often seemed to exceed the number of guests, thereby, no doubt, helping to solve the employment problem. There appeared to be no single rooms— a peculiarity which applied to every Chinese hotel I stayed in: it was always a splendid twin-bedded room to yourself, so that you constantly had the feeling of waiting for someone to arrive, a nocturnal helpmeet, perhaps, to soothe the nerves of the jaded delegate with a generous flourish of oriental hospitality; but no such comforter arrived, and in the People's puritanical Republic, you felt, whatever the strength of the Friendship, there would certainly be no Peace if one ever did. A further peculiarity was that, while all the electrical and mechanical facilities worked admirably, the wireless was always either out of order or had disappeared completely without anybody ever knowing where it had gone. Nothing was left to chance in providing for the delegates' wants. Cigarettes and matches were laid on daily for smoker and non-smoker alike, the cigarettes sharp, slightly bitter-tasting, but very good of their kind. (The matches were a different matter. They tended to snap in two at the slightest pressure and, even if the stick survived, the head was likely to fly away from the body at the moment of ignition; while the boxes themselves, equally fragile, rapidly disintegrated once put into the pocket.)

I shall have more to say about Chinese food later, but at the Front Gate hotel the menu was arranged on the assumption that delegates would prefer the western type, although what that type might be the cooks were not at all sure. True, they faced the insoluble problem of trying to reconcile at once the tastes of Frenchman and Russian, Arab and South American, Swede and Italian. In the event they settled for a polygastric confection, optimistically labelled 'European food', which comprised three kinds of soup (potato, lentil and rice); an assortment of fish (the crayfish, which they knew something about, especially good), and chicken; with blancmanges and chocolate mousses as dessert.

Fortunately Chinese food was served to the interpreters and the Asian contingent and it was possible to attach oneself to their tables, although they regarded this as a further manifestation of English oddity.

The hotel service was not merely efficient, but relentlessly so. Certain things were axiomatic, as they are throughout China. The honesty of the hotel staff made it impossible to lose anything. Throw away an old notebook, cast off a worn-out shirt, and they would inevitably find their way back if the entire hotel had to be turned inside out to trace the owner. There is no tipping. That was abolished with the Liberation and, whether the staff approve the innovation or not, they would never risk degrading themselves by accepting a tip. The campaign of sweeping, brushing and polishing which went on throughout the day ensured a standard of cleanliness that was too near perfection to be comfortable. You could never be laid low by dust germs but you could easily have broken a limb by slipping on the polished floors. There was no such thing as a discourteous servant: if they were sometimes slow to carry out your wishes it was only because they had failed to understand them, not because they didn't want to. For all I know, this is a traditional virtue, but it could equally well be a compulsory, more recent one.

There is a darker side to the picture which it is impossible to define accurately without a working knowledge of the language but evidence of which I was to discover for myself much later. The hotel staff are by implication watchdogs of the State, in which function, although they may not actually spy upon the guests, they certainly miss nothing that goes on. The problem does not arise so long as the guests keep to themselves, but if they form peripatetic relationships about the hotel they will find one or more servicemen patrolling the passages as though by telepathic invitation. To be just, I should add that, as far as I could tell, no check was kept on my movements outside the hotel, and inside it there was no evidence of telephone tapping or hidden microphones. As one of my hosts put it: 'You have a remarkable imagination if you think we have so many interpreters in so many languages that we can listen in to what thousands of foreign visitors are saying all the time.' Journalists who had spent several months in other hotels in Peking confirmed that there was no interference of this kind, but they had all been subject in one degree or another to the restrictive scrutiny of the servicemen.

[SCHMID, 21–28]

In Peking I was just lucky. I was lucky enough to find the most intelligent rickshaw boy in the city. On the evening after my arrival, just as I was taking my first few steps in the city, there was a call of "Hello!" behind me, and when I turned my head to identify the caller I saw a round, open face beaming at me from a bicycle which drew a neat, blue-covered seat behind it. This vehicle, compared with the miserable, ramshackle contraptions which rattle through the city with their passengers, was a real luxury craft, a kind of rickshaw Cadillac.

The rickshaws and the characters pedalling them along are, as you can tell at once, the only visible survival of past decadence on the transformed face of Peking. Everybody else is neatly and properly dressed, in that high-buttoned dark blue uniform which is so obviously modelled on the boiler suit and a peaked cap, rather like a European mechanic—the uniform, in fact, of the Workers' State, or, at any rate, a country regarding itself as such. Everybody wears it without exception, from coolie to university professor. Those who belong to the chosen ruling class—*i.e.*, those who, in this State of equals, to quote Orwell, are "more equal than others"—indicate this fact merely by their choice of a somewhat more expensive material.

I was told that the people loved the new fashion, which

makes even the most attractive girl look like a plumber's mate, and that this wearing of the blue represented a joyful avowal of loyalty to a regime which had liberated them from their old rags and made them a present of this new, revolutionary material.

But to get back to the rickshaws. These bicycle folk have, as if by a miracle, been spared by the 'liberating' revolution. Their vehicles look as if they had been picked up at a scrapyard: rusty, creaking in all the joints, with chains sagging like flabby bellies, held together and patched up with bits of wire, string, and tin—just as if they had been devised by Heath Robinson. The drivers are every bit as tattered in their crudely mended smocks, from which the cotton bursts out from a hundred holes like stuffing. Every minute one expects them to burst their seams, to break their axles, to spill their passengers into the road.

The rickshaws, as I said, are the only remnant of imperfection in this capital which reflects a love of imperial perfection at every step. The reason why these 21,000 youngsters have not yet been abolished or else raised to the same level as the rest is simply that they are doomed to extinction. Handsome Skoda buses, made in Czechoslovakia, have already deprived them of a good part of their business, and in framing its revolutionary measures the Chinese government has so far generally subscribed to the principle of not solving domestic issues by force, but, instead, creating a situation in which the people will be compelled by necessity to act in the way it wants them to act. It applies what one might call indirect compulsion. Thus the tattered figures on their broken-down vehicles (for which spares are no longer available) are still free only because they are already doomed.

In this picture of general decay Ma—that was the name of the young man who had hailed me—represented a marked exception. He had served as a boy at the Peking Hotel for some time, and there acquired some rudimentary English; that was why I decided to hire him on the spot for the whole duration of my stay. From that moment onward I reclined on the airy seat of my rickshaw as if in the lap of luxury. For three Chinese dollars a day I had a creature hanging on my lips like a well-trained dog, calling me Master, galloping up with his vehicle—almost as if wagging his tail—the moment I appeared outside the hotel entrance, wrapping me in a thick blanket, and pedalling off like mad in whichever direction my fancy took me.

Such almost maternal solicitude cannot be overrated in a place like Peking. Especially if a man has spent a whole year in the tropics, as I had done, the icy wind from the Mongolian plains will cut through him like a knife. The climate of Peking is as inhospitable as can be: cruelly cold in winter and hot in summer. True, the cold is made more bearable by the fact that there is a cloudless sky overhead and the air is so crisp it almost crackles, and a washed nylon shirt is dry in no time. Which is just as well. For in no city on earth, not even in London, does a person get dirty as quickly and as thoroughly as here. Because no rain binds the dust down, even the lightest breeze raises a veritable cloud of it, and every evening one's shirt is as black as coal and one's hair is a sticky mess. This excessive dryness has yet another alarming effect: Peking is electrically charged. I have met foreign diplomats who, every time they leave their insulated offices and step out into the street, receive an electric shock upon touching their cars and who—this is no fairy-tale—on arriving home are welcomed by a spark leaping from the lips of their loving wives.

My first visit in mid-winter Peking was therefore to an out-fitter's, where I hoped to buy one of those blue proletarian overcoats. But I had no clothing coupons, and textiles were still rationed. My good Ma came to the rescue. "I can let you have some," he said, and presently we were off to his home.

I do not know whether it was in a popular or a select part of the city. In Peking all houses look much the same from the outside. They all present their grey walls to the narrow, crooked little streets and discourage curiosity even more than the equally grey courts of Andalusia, where a glimpse of the interior can at least be snatched through the gateways. The houses here have gates too, and very fine ones at that, with doors painted a brilliant red and with richly sculptured circular marble stools on the thresholds. But just inside there is a wall running across, to ward off not so much the glances of strangers as the entry of evil spirits. Strictly speaking, the succession of courtyards which open up inside the gateway is not a house, but a whole compound, with countless houses facing inward with blind windowpanes. And behind every single door lives somebody. It is quite incredible the number of people who suddenly appear out of a multitude of holes the moment the alarm is given of a stranger's arrival: children above all, whole hordes of them—no one knows where they come from.

Ma, my rickshaw boy, was evidently a loyal supporter of the regime. Above his door sat a replica of Picasso's dove of peace. As I stepped into the room of his old father my eyes naturally alighted on the over-lifesize portrait of Mao Tse-tung, which is obligatory in every Peking home. But next to it—was I seeing things?—hung the photograph of a good old friend of mine, the Swiss Consul in Singapore!

"How does Professor Hoepli get here?" I asked in amazement.

A radiance filled the old man's face. He had been a servant of his at the time when Professor Hoepli taught bacteriology at one of Peking's universities, and since the professor enjoyed a wide reputation among the people for his good deeds and his courtesy he was now allowed to grace the wall side by side with the great Mao. No doubt this was not quite in line with orthodox Communist practice, since it is strictly forbidden nowadays to accept any present from a foreigner. Every other official announcement declares that the days of feudalism are over for good. And all this, of course, is feudal: the master making a present and the subordinate accepting it, just as the whole pattern of cordial affection and comradeship across the confines of social position characterizes a patriarchal relationship.

The friendship of the feudal Swiss citizen Hoepli for his faithful vassal was, nevertheless, presently repeated in the most heart-warming manner between the feudal Swiss citizen Peter Schmid and the old man's Communist son. Soon Ma would not leave my side. Whenever I had a meal he would join me at once—though with such Stakhanovite sucking and smacking of lips that I could not even hear myself chew. No matter whom or what I met, Ma became my interpreter, invaluable in spite of all his imperfections, and there was only one situation in which he would shamefully abandon me—whenever my photographic zeal attracted the notice of a policeman. True enough, the Chinese police are a curious race; they always reminded me a little of vicious bloodhounds. Without exception they wore the white mask below their military peaked cap, and above it glinted eyes of unparalleled hardness. Many a time have I seen some poor traffic offender beg for mercy in the street—always with a whole crowd of curious passers-by providing an audience—but it was just like a wave breaking against a rock: inexorable.

Not long before these beasts had been trained in Russian traffic drill and issued with red-and-white batons and whistles for controlling the traffic in a rigid and ceremonial manner. Now whenever a road-user committed a minor offence they would shower him with an unceremonial flood of spiteful invective. I did not blame Ma for hating and avoiding these types. As soon as one of the green-uniformed men began to make for us, with that ineluctable certainty which totalitarian power lends to this human species, Ma would suddenly vanish without trace, and only when the danger had been averted by the production of my Press card would his face cautiously reappear behind some corner. I readily forgave him his desertion, especially as his shyness refuted the assertions of my foreign friends that he reported all my movements to the police.

Picasso's dove of peace was enthroned not only above the door of Ma's home. It was multiplied on all roofs: live pigeons, mainly white, fluttering inquisitively down into the courtyard and pacing tamely around us in the hope of some crumbs. A few of them had strange clay instruments like pipes fixed to their tail-feathers. These were a kind of Æolian flute. Some one would scare the little flock, so they would take off and cruise round in wide circles. And now I could plainly hear it: a sound as if of organ music, swelling at one moment and fading at another. The pigeons are one of the elements which give Peking its immortal poetry—apart from filling its cooking-pots. Every compound of houses around its courtyard keeps its own flocks, and a secret, ferocious pigeon war sets neighbour against neighbour. Everybody tries, by means of choice food and other attractions, to steal the next man's best pigeons and to swell his own flock with the stolen birds. And everybody watches their flight with the anxiety of ancient augurs, for the pigeons are the bearers not only of poetry, but also of luck.

Having supplied me with his clothing coupons, Ma now pedalled me to the new State-owned department store, completed barely a year previously and the great attraction of Peking. It seems incredible that a city of three million inhabitants should not have had a department store before—they existed, of course, in Shanghai—but then Peking in many ways had always been aloof from the passage of time, until the Communist revolution abruptly precipitated it into the most contemporary present.

In the past the people bought what they needed in the myriads of small shops and at the even tinier artisans' stalls which sprawled all over the city; now this allegedly uneconomical system of production and distribution was to come to an end. This was the meaning of the department store: it was the symbol of an economic transformation which spelled the doom, sooner or later, of those family businesses where everybody, from the grandfather down to very nearly the babe in arms, made his contribution, a transformation which would supersede them by the co-operative shop and the big State-owned enterprise. But the department store was even more than that: it was an exhibition, a show-piece of the Government's achievements. People did not visit it merely to make purchases. I met there entire groups of Young Pioneers who had presumably come to town from the villages and who were now gaping wide-eyed at the wonderful things around them.

It was, moreover, a playground for street urchins, who were chasing one another round the counters or sliding on the polished marble floor. I also saw an aged peasant woman who had sat down on the floor among the counters and was calmly eating some food she had brought with her. Here and there was a visitor, to judge by his clothes, from the remotest parts —from Tibet or Mongolia—with the wind of the steppe still in his thick fur coat and with heavy melancholia in his eyes. He would rub shoulders with robust, terribly uncouth, white-skinned women roaming the store in packs, having themselves measured for suits by delicate Chinese tailors, and leaving the emporium with armfuls of parcels. These were Russian women, the wives of specialists, investing their unchangeable Chinese money by laying in veritable hoards of merchandise from shops more plentifully stocked than those back home in Russia. They were surpassed in vulgarity only by their East German colleagues, whom I found in the fur department rummaging among leopards and minks, greedily feeling them for softness. Ma dragged me over to near where they stood, and asked for a blue overcoat, lined with long-haired Mongolian lamb and trimmed at the collar with brown beaver, to be shown to me. It cost only 75 yuan—ridiculously cheap at the foreign rate of exchange, but more than a month's earnings of a worker. For the underprivileged there were cotton-padded, quilted jackets and trousers, which lent their wearers a somewhat comical, inflated, sausage-like appearance, but nevertheless kept them warm enough to face the Peking winter.

In the men's underwear department I saw the very same pair of silk pyjamas that I had bought in Hongkong, and I looked curiously at the price. Ought they not to be cheaper here, in their country of manufacture, than abroad? But, strangely enough, they cost as much in yuan as I had paid in Hongkong dollars—in other words, about twice as much. The same was true of other Chinese export goods. And as for imported Swiss watches, German cameras, and British bicycles, their prices soared to about five times the Hongkong figures.

[WILSON, 57–59]

The department-store building was three or four stories tall and appeared to be less than eight years old. Inside it was completely Western but conservative. On the top floor it had a particularly lovely selection of new lacquer work, *cloisonné*, carved wood, woven bamboo, porcelain, bronzes, printed silk and carved ornamental stones. In fact every kind of pleasant

Oriental knick-knack was available. Both the service and the goods seemed to be excellent. Many identical articles can be found for sale in Canada but at ten times the cost.

I bought some little carved goldfish of rosewood in Peking for 17 cents each. After my return my sharp-eyed fourteen-year-old daughter Pat discovered identical goldfish on sale in Toronto for $1.65.

The counters along one whole wall of this floor were devoted to the sale of lengths of silk. I looked at a number of rolls, but with the exception of one wash print, which I later bought, I found them a bit gaudy. The wash print I bought bore the modern design in which the pattern is composed of intricate scribbling—many continuous lines each of a different colour.

On the second floor were ready-made clothes and on a later occasion I bought two silk shirts there, but I chose them too quickly and they were not wholly successful. The fault was mine.

Downstairs, they had, among other things, a lot of simple furniture, pottery, thermos bottles and household goods. It was apparent that most goods in the shop, if not all, were made in China.

There were a few Chinese in the shop, but it would not be considered crowded for a department store in any of our cities of comparable size. So far as I could observe I was the only foreigner among the shoppers. Foreigners of any nation including Russian are rare except in the hotels.

I made a list of the prices of some articles which, at the realistic and legal rate of 2½ yuan to the dollar, were as follows:

Turquoise necklaces	about $25.00
Jade necklaces	$50.00 to $280.00
Large amethyst brooch	$16.00
Jade rings	$10.00 to $75.00
Taffeta silk and silk prints	$2.00 per yard
Blue enamel dishes (15″)	$12.00
Enamel plates	$4.00
Enamel vases	$4.00
Red lacquer cigar boxes	$6.00 to $8.00

Next we went across the street and a block away to the old market. This was much more picturesque. A series of sheds provided cover for a vast bazaar. Innumerable stalls each with its own shopkeeper dealt with a wide variety of commodities. I suppose they all belonged to some Communist trust but the effect was still that of a great group of independent traders. This was undoubtedly how the bazaar had begun.

They sold a most astonishing variety of goods—clothes, paper umbrellas, shoes, pottery, jewellery, stationery, food, fountain pens, electrical appliances, and household furniture and furnishings. The prices were all fixed. Everything had a price tag on it and there was no haggling. I'm not an experienced shopper but everything seemed to be extremely cheap.

I was looking specially for things I might buy as presents. Again I found the silk disappointing. There was lots of jade, lovely turquoise and many kinds of carved stones. Some of these seemed very cheap, and on a return visit I bought several old pendants and buckles in carved moss agate and in rose quartz for prices varying from 25 cents to $1.00.

I looked at the jade with interest but I knew so little about it that I felt it was inadvisable to get any. They also had star sapphires and other expensive gems but it seemed to me that in this market they had only second quality and that the finest gems would be found in more exclusive shops.

The bazaar was thronged with Chinese and all the merchants were polite and attentive. The jewellers in particular looked on me as a hopeful customer and took me into their inner rooms to show me their treasures.

In both shops I furiously noted down prices, but at that time bought nothing. Faced with such a wealth of lovely things at such cheap prices and having only limited funds and still more limited room in my luggage I wanted time to decide.

When we went outside it was getting dark. The lights were coming on as thousands of gentle, blue-clad Chinese were hurrying through the streets. There were strange shouts, strange scents, oriental music and no one in sight but Chinese. I found it all exciting and delightful, but I was not sorry to return to the hotel for a late supper and a long sleep.

[BOYD ORR, 36–41]

In Peking we woke to music every morning. Outside, the noodle seller's cry roused the street. The vegetable seller passed with his wares in baskets hung from a bamboo shoulder-pole, shouting "Turnips!" in a sing-song voice. The vendor of sesame cakes and the pedlar frying dumplings competed for customers. Even the pigeons circling overhead made their contribution, for Chinese pigeon fanciers attach tiny whistles to the tail feathers of their birds.

These village sounds seem to persist in Peking until the trams and buses, the pedicabs and bicyclists (as numerous as in Copenhagen or Cambridge), take over the day. Not only village sounds, but village sights as well. As one sits down for breakfast at the Peking Hotel—which has two restaurants, one for serving Chinese food, the other, with menus in English, Russian, and German, serving European—round the corner groups of pedicab drivers sit at wayside stalls breakfasting off twists of dough fried in deep fat and dunked in bean curd.

There is, in fact, a provincial atmosphere about this capital which makes it homely and intimate. The population has trebled since the new Government came to power, so that it numbers more than two million. Streets have been widened in a way that is only possible when a wealthy ruling class has been swept out and a totalitarian authority can ignore inconvenient delays over compensation for ground rents and demolished buildings. German and Czech diesel buses run on the roads alongside jangling Chinese-made trams. Office blocks and apartment houses have been run up in a great hurry, and on one of the main streets a line of battered dwellings was only waiting for a four-storey block that backed right on to it to be completed so that its inhabitants could move into the new homes and its own life end. Yet in spite of the desperate haste there remains an absence of restlessness, a captivating leisurely quality.

Partly this comes from the old face of the city, from the red and ochre walls, the courtyards with their children and trees, the narrow winding lanes which are being macadamized to lay the Gobi dust which blows in on Peking, the grey-tiled roofs and the hawks floating above them. Chief city of the world's oldest living civilization, and itself a settled community for three thousand years, Peking has preserved enough of history to show the visitor, if not the appearance of Kublai Khan's Cambulac from which the Mongols ruled China, then at least an image of its glory four hundred years ago under the Ming dynasty. There are the encircling walls, punctuated by huge gateways; the moated Forbidden City, the Winter Palace of the emperors; the tower where dawn and dusk were announced with drums and gongs; and looking down from Coal Hill, an artificial mound in the centre of the city where the guide still points out the tree from which one unlucky Ming emperor hanged himself in the agony of defeat, you can survey the marvellous symmetry of streets and buildings. North-south, east-west, run the main arteries. Between them lies the honeycomb of narrow *hutungs* and street markets.

Dominating everything—for nine out of ten houses are single-storey affairs, since the emperors could not tolerate any

building high enough to overlook their private residencies—
are the imperial halls and temples with their roofs of yellow
and green and violet tiles. The planners, and the geomancers
who helped them, did a superb job. Not even the Paris of
Napoleon can compete.

It is also a place easy on the legs, because there are no
steep rises apart from Coal Hill, and in between interviewing
Ministers of State and other officials and attending the various
receptions which Chinese hospitality insists on providing, we
explored these streets and their tributary lanes. They provided
sharp, vivid contrasts—the peasants' mule carts against the
cars from Russia, Britain, France, Germany, America; the
side streets where the houses looked a little bleak because no
windows overlooked the lane, but whose red-painted doors
opened on to courtyards where the shrubs and flowers reminded us of the miniature landscape gardens of Japan; and
the wide thoroughfares, well-surfaced, where traffic flowed
smoothly under the direction of policemen using megaphones
to call any traffic offender over to the middle of the road for
a public lecture on road manners.

There are old business quarters, where shopkeepers and
craftsmen carry on their trade in open-fronted shops, their
families living at the back or in cramped rooms overhead. At
noon they take their meals in public view, and in the evening
we would see them sitting out on the pavements, smoking
pipes with brass bowls so small that they would take no more
tobacco than is in a cigarette butt. Some streets are given over
entirely to one trade—copper and brass beating, or artificial
flower-making—as in the days when the guilds ruled commerce. There are also wholly modern districts, with department
stores whose windows are packed with cloth, Thermos flasks,
toilet articles and bicycles; huge State stores with upwards of
a thousand employees, half of whom, we were told, are apprentices learning the business until new branches open; and
bookshops where students come to browse until a late hour.

And there is the ancient Peking, which has set its seal so
imposingly on the pattern of the city.

Really we had not wanted to see the ancient monuments.
We had come to see what work was being done in certain
directions, work which we were qualified to judge. We were in
a hurry, and we didn't regard ourselves as tourists. Mr. Li,
however, was adamant. He was also very upset by our indif-
ference. "You mean," he said incredulously, "that you don't
want to see the Forbidden City and the Tai Miao and the
Temple of Agriculture and the. . . ?" The list was ominously
long, but we hid our chagrin and went, and in the end neither
we nor Mr. Li were disappointed.

It was impossible not to be struck by the beauty of the Temple of Heaven, its white marble balustrades set amongst thousand-year-old cedars where once the Emperors symbolically ploughed the first furrow of the year; and the Tai Miao, where the emperors had worshipped their ancestors and Peking's citizens now drink tea and beer, crowd the halls to inspect exhibitions of public health and industrial work, and listen beneath the trees to itinerant story-tellers recounting tales of Chinese heroes contemporary with Charlemagne. We walked round the enormous courtyards of the Forbidden City, and admired the porcelains in the museum. We sat in a tea-house overlooking the *Pei Hai,* the North Sea, one of the man-made lakes that wind through the heart of Peking, where on Sundays, the accepted weekly holiday, boys and girls go boating. And when we had visited them all we were worn out. Mr. Li, however, was delighted. Young China, it seems, is as proud of its past as ever its elders were, and it was reassuring to see for ourselves the care lavished on this "feudal" past. The repair of the Lamaist temple tucked away in the north-east corner of the city wall, for instance, had cost the Government a million pounds and a good deal of misplaced criticism on the score of "waste". Its pillars gleamed with lacquer and the delicate little landscapes on the exterior wood-work had been picked out with touching care.

This part of Peking, however, the part that travellers used to call "timeless", is not what holds the present-day observer who wants to see what the descendants of its builders are building now. It speaks for an epoch which has ended, and the epoch that is beginning imposes a striking change.

The change, in fact, is twofold, as we soon discovered, and, in the merchant districts we visited, more than external. Their whole nature was being reshaped. In 1955 there had been some four million private businesses in the country. When we were there the majority had merged with State trading organizations or become "joint State-private enterprises". In the process little shops and big stores alike had come under direct Government guidance, with the smaller concerns selling on behalf of the State on a commission basis. This appeared to bring them about the same profit as they earned before, and private shareholders in the bigger enterprises were getting 5 per cent interest a year, or slightly more.

Doing this had not been too difficult for the Government, as it turned out. The distribution of most important items of trade had been controlled through the wholesalers for some years. Moreover, all prices, whether in private or Government shops, were fixed. Even in the curio shops, or the food markets where housewives bought vegetables and had their fishmonger net them a live fish from a water tub, the old custom whereby the seller started by asking twice what he was prepared to accept and the buyer by offering half what he was willing to pay had dropped into disuse. The transformation was intended to centralize distribution. It had also, we understood, reduced a lot of tax evasion. But it must have resulted in a phenomenal book-keeping problem, for everywhere, whatever one bought, whether a tube of toothpaste, or a writing-pad from a two-man stationery stall, one was given a receipt. Even the taxi-cab driver would take out a receipt book, insert a piece of carbon paper, and hand one a receipt for the exact fare at the end of a journey.

Nevertheless, it was the visible change which made the first big impact on us. The mere catalogue of new buildings was formidable. At the time it ran something like this: six hospitals; many schools; thirteen theatres; six cinemas; several hotels; government offices; department stores; not to mention blocks of apartment houses. All told, according to an official report, new buildings with a total floor space of seventeen million square yards had been built since 1949. By now, the grand total is undoubtedly much bigger, since construction was proceeding at such a pace that there was a well-worn joke concerning two old residents which went thus: First citizen— "What's that big building over there?" Second citizen—"I don't know. It wasn't there yesterday."

The superintendent of a 500-bed hospital we inspected told us that the whole place had been built and equipped in fifteen months, and the three-man committee responsible for putting up a reinforced concrete-and-marble trade exhibition hall with 208,000 square feet of floor space, complete with cinema seating 800 and restaurant seating 400, reported that the job had only taken eleven months from the first ramming-in of earth to the official opening. This trade hall, moreover, was built on a marsh, so that ten feet of earth had had to be rammed down to raise the ground level. These buildings could have been put up in quicker time in a Western country. What was remarkable was that they were going up at this speed in an underdeveloped country, short of equipment, and reputedly lacking in "know-how", despite all the Russian help.

Eventually, if present plans are adhered to, Peking will become a city of ten million people, with main highways a hundred yards wide, and zones outside the walls for government offices, industrial plants, and teaching institutions. In a few decades it may be hard to find traces of yesterday, or even of today.

SHANGHAI

[CROFT, 181–189]

From the uppermost window of the Sino-Soviet Friendship House, the most colossal structure in all China, I looked through the night at the remains of the greatest maritime city in the east with an acute sense of nostalgia. Here were the recognisable symbols of European civilisation: the great banks and commercial palaces, the towering hotels, the wharves and warehouses where the ships of every major port in the world had once plied their trade. Here was the dockside that for almost a century had been a byword among British seamen—the happy haven of the hard-drinking mariner, the garden of paradise for the randy-minded crew, the water-front that opened its welcoming arms to provide the cheapest good time on the Seven Seas.

The symbols were still there—the gay lights glittered along the Bund, dense waves of humanity surged through the streets, the splendid edifices of the Matheson and Sassoon dynasties bulked large in the sky—but the substance was gone; the old Concessions were buried in the limbo of history; the International Settlement was one with Nineveh and Tyre.

In the shadows of the river a convoy of sampans glided towards the shore with their cargoes of rice, flour, vegetables and fruit, but they glided alone. From the harbour sheds the *Vei-ho, Wei-ho* of the labourers lapped the night air: but they were hauling buckets of bricks to build new tenements, not cargo from ships' holds. True, thirty ships had been in during the past month and slowly, they said, life was returning to the docks, but, for all that, the river looked dark and desolate, entombing the empty wharves, and the water-front was a rippling avenue of ghosts.

Shanghai was being expanded as an industrial city, devoted mainly at present to textiles and electrical equipment, but soon it would be producing heavy machinery and rolled steel. 'Gone forever,' proclaimed the Mayor, 'are the days when the workers had to share one pair of trousers between several people. Now the men can afford to buy suits for both winter and summer and the women can buy bright print dresses. Many can even afford to imitate city wear.'

Gone forever were many more grisly memories: corpses rotting nightly in the streets; fortunes piled up from opium;

children lured or bullied into the brothels; the rampant scourge of tuberculosis; the disdainful prohibition outside a European Racing Club: 'Chinese and dogs not allowed.' Without doubt the communists had treated the commercial magnates abominably: had forced them out of business by the rent and repairs racket; accomplished the take-over by rigging the prices of property at their own estimate of its 'deterioration'; cut supplies of raw materials and brought in trade-union restrictions to a point which spelt ruin for those who refused to get out—but equally, without doubt, whatever they had done to the Europeans, they were making Shanghai into a city fit for their own people to inhabit.

It is here that the paradox of capitalism in a communist society has found its most potent expression—a fact which they reiterate with delight on every convenient occasion. 'There are now eighty-three thousand shops and factories working harmoniously under joint State–private enterprise management,' declared the Mayor—and you readily took his word for it. If, however, you were in doubt, you could tour the factories where the old-time capitalists are honourably installed as Directors or Technical Supervisors, drawing their modest State salaries and a steady five per cent on their investments.

In this city at least the capitalist class, far from being extinct, rears its well-groomed head at every reception, and to leave Shanghai without having shaken hands with a millionaire is not to have been there at all. There are still sixty or more in residence and they are preserved and paraded at receptions like prize exhibits, holding court to visiting delegations and elaborating with exquisite conviction upon the virtues of the new dispensation compared with the vices of the old. There was no way of finding out what they really thought and I saw nothing to be gained from asking them. They were *alive*; that was the operative point—not because the State is enamoured of them, but because it needs their skill and experience as well as their foreign holdings; and the Chinese communists, being quicker to learn from their mistakes than any other political party in the world, have rapidly realised they will gain more by buying them out decently than by continuing to harass them as bourgeois reactionaries.

Even so, the survival of bourgeois ideas is still their dominant fear; for although the social and economic landscape has been transformed—wages have increased by forty per cent in five years, goods are cheap and plentiful in the shops, slums are being demolished—the communists know too well that a century of exposure to western influence cannot be cancelled out overnight. It is inconceivable that the present regime will be effectively challenged anywhere in China for some time to come, but if it should be challenged at all they know it will come from here: Shanghai was never a chip off the old China block but a polyglot city with a mind and character of its own; so that although ostensibly the nationalist purge ended three years ago—the People's Courts no longer pass daily sentence on members of 'the traitorous clique'; the sinister red vans are no longer seen en route to the execution grounds—the Security Police continue to search relentlessly for nests of 'saboteurs' and 'counter-revolutionary elements'. Security checks, both on Chinese and foreigners, are stricter than elsewhere in China, and the quaint old-world courtesy of the police in Peking is replaced here by a hard-boiled purposefulness which would do great credit to the stronger armed gentry of the New York Homicide Squad.

The outstanding success of the new regime in what was generally regarded as the Number One cesspool of the east has been the elimination of vice—an achievement about which no visitor—and no Londoner, certainly—can reasonably complain: the communists have accomplished within the span of eight years what the Christian countries of Europe have failed to bring about in two thousand.

Believing this to be of more than ideological significance, I took some pains to find out what methods had been used—to discover, as I should have known, that they were of sound ideological origin.

'Our first task,' said Chun Tse-tsung, head of the Civil Law Bureau, 'was to mobilise public opinion, not against the prostitutes themselves, but against the desire of the people to consort with them. Only when this campaign had been launched could we proceed to the next step, which was to close down the brothels, and then embark upon the programme of re-education through productive labour.'

There were, he explained, after expatiating at length upon the multifarious iniquities of the Kuomintang, eight hundred legally licensed brothels and perhaps four or five times that number unlicensed. Between 1949 and 1951, by mobilising public opinion, the majority of the women in them were persuaded to find other employment as well as to undergo treatment for venereal disease. By the end of 1951, of the licensed houses, only seventy-two remained. These were then forcibly closed down.

'When we started our campaign we found many of these women in an advanced state of syphilis, and many had been destroyed in other ways. These had to be removed to special homes where they will spend the rest of their lives.

'They are not, of course, regarded as criminals. They were driven to practise through their miserable economic plight and fell into the clutches of the brothel owners and gang bosses. Many of these men had criminal records, and were consequently dealt with by the Public Security Bureau' (which is to say, they were shot), 'but those with better records, who showed repentance for their crimes, were accepted for treatment at Reception.'

Reception, which I had no time to investigate, appeared to be a system of corrective training run along the lines of the Peking prison.

'Our aim is to give the prostitute a feeling of security, but because of her lazy nature it is often difficult to persuade her of the necessity for labour training, and in such cases training is necessarily prolonged. Most of these women come from the labouring or peasant classes, with the result that their ideological consciousness is of a very low level. Thus, we first have to make them realise the low nature of their position and the degradation of their work. Naturally, when they first arrive at Reception, they are frightened, for they believe they are going to be punished. These doubts and suspicions have to be dispelled before we can go on to their ideological education, but once we have done this we can then proceed to teach them social discipline, the need for patriotism, an understanding of Current Events and production achievements, and so forth. Alongside this, we also give them literacy classes. Many have learnt to read up to two and three thousand characters, and most of them can now read the newspapers without difficulty.' (One frequently had the impression that the whole of education was directed to achieving the latter end.)

'Labour-training, of course, varies according to health conditions. Some work on textiles in the weaving-sheds, but many are fit only to do light handiwork. After they have been trained in this, they are given payment—in the form of a prize of three to five *yuan* at first—but later they may be paid from twenty to forty *yuan* a month, according to the work they have done. When they have completed the reform period they are given jobs according to their techniques or, if their homes are in the country, they are sent back to take part in the agricultural programme. If, on the other hand, they have neither homes nor techniques, they are sent to work on farms run by Reception.'

This then was the secret of the greatest social clean-up in history. No fancy psychiatric nonsense about early environment, parental influences, latent emotional disorders; no invoking of the oversized libido; no passing the buck on to the male customer. Mobilise the people first, lay on the Reception, get cracking with the Current Events and the three Rs, and finish the treatment with a stiff dose of techniques and agri-culture. Not a programme to everyone's taste, you might say, but then neither was the spectacle of wholesale prostitution.

'In general these women are grateful to the government for changing their way of life, but we cannot claim to have abol-ished prostitution altogether,' said Chun, with exaggerated modesty. 'There are still cases of women who practise pri-ately, but these are very rare and, owing to our policy of mobilising the masses, they are invariably reported to us. The Street Committees work in close co-operation with Social Security and it would be difficult for any woman to practise for very long without the Street Committee hearing of it.'

That was the straightest piece of talking from any official I had heard to date. It was followed by an equally candid exposition from Ho Chi-wu, the grim-jawed chief of Social Security.

'In method and content we have used the same basic ap-proach in the treatment of opium addicts, petty thieves, beg-gars, gamblers and vagrants. Their labour-training consists of road-work, railway building, and machinery construction, and in the course of this programme many acquire high-level tech-niques and finish their period of reform as skilled workers. But,' he confessed, 'we have still not conquered this problem completely, although statistics for these crimes are five per cent down on last year's.'

I put it to him that juvenile delinquency was generally a more serious social problem than gambling and vagrancy: how had Shanghai fared in this respect since the Liberation?

He maintained that most cases of this kind could be at-tributed to early upbringing under the Kuomintang but, when pressed, admitted that children 'deficient in ideological under-standing' still tended to gang together in the streets or cause trouble in the tea houses. Within the past two months there had been an outbreak of this kind, but the police had swooped promptly and the offenders had been dispatched forthwith for a two-year spell of 're-education through labour-training'. He emphasised that this was an occurrence so rare as to be scarcely worth mentioning, but checking on it later, I discov-ered that it was not quite so rare as he suggested. As with the *stilyagi* in Moscow, Shanghai had recently produced its own version of the Teddy boy, teenagers in search of excitement, for whom 'productive work in the cause of national construc-tion' was a far less attractive prospect than making a nuisance of themselves in the streets. It was true that as soon as they revealed their intentions they were hustled off at the double without reference to their upbringing before or after the Liberation, but the significant thing was that they had appeared at all.

On the other hand, it was not surprising. For the greater part of the day the majority of children were necessarily left to their own devices. Their parents were out at work and they themselves attended school in shifts. 'In addition,' admitted Ho, 'in many families the economic needs have not yet been fully met in the production programme. So that many pedlars and street vendors work late to make more money, with the result that they rarely see their children at all. Add to this the fact that many of our six million population still live in pre-Liberation slums, where conditions encourage them to spend most of their time in the streets—and you will see that this problem has no easy solution.'

I appreciated more clearly the depth of this understatement a day or two later. Leaving the delegation to tour a new housing estate I made my way with a local interpreter to Fan Kua-lun, in the northern part of the city, one of the five remaining slum areas. As slums go, it ranked high on the list of appalling human habitations, making the Gorbals seem like a garden city; it could be compared favourably, perhaps, with the native shanties of Johannesburg or the compounds of Portuguese East Africa, but the demarcation line would have been hard to find. It consisted simply of an area of small, densely-packed mud and straw hovels, patched-up, damp, rotting, where swarming families of human beings somehow contrived to exist in conditions that would have disheartened many self-respecting animals.

Before the war, they said, this had been the site of a textile factory, but it had been destroyed by Japanese bombs. The houses had been put up by 'Kuomintang landlords' in 1940, but they had not troubled to fill in the bomb craters, which rapidly became stagnant pools, infested with flies and mosquitoes. Cholera, smallpox and tuberculosis had been rife. 'In those days', they said, 'we had a local saying: "Every day we see somebody die; every day we pass another coffin". But there were never enough coffins and often the dead bodies had to be left lying in the alleys until the undertaker could find time to collect them.'

Now the pools have been cleared, the alleys cobble-stoned, a sewerage system installed. The Street Committees have carried through an intensive campaign of instruction in sanitation and hygiene; the inhabitants work on a rota basis in keeping the alleys clean, and every week living-quarters are inspected by members of the Committee. 'So far no tenants have refused to co-operate,' they said. 'But some do better, some worse.

Many homes are still very dirty, and though we have won the main battle we still have serious problems of ill-health—generally with families who have failed to carry out our hygiene instructions.'

In places the ground was still soft and muddy and the stench lingered, dank and fœtid, in the air. Since I had lightheartedly left England without the usual inoculations I had no wish to hang around. But there was one thing more to do. Having seen the outside of the houses, I also wanted to look inside.

A gaunt hag of a woman sat washing her feet in a wooden bowl outside her doorway and I asked if I could go in. She paddled out of the bowl and beckoned me after her, her face dented and crumpled like a cracked walnut. She said nothing, but stooped against the mud wall waiting for me to speak.

The house was not more than eight feet square and ten feet high. The concrete floor was cracked and covered with a great patch of damp. On the wooden bed which stood about a foot from the ground and served also as a dining-table, a young baby was fast asleep (it seemed impossible to enter any house in China without finding a scene of similar domestic felicity). Beside it, indicated the old woman, she herself slept, and on a wooden plank three feet above slept the baby's father and mother.

The roof of the house had been blown off during a typhoon earlier in the year and had been replaced, but rain still came through and the walls were yellow with damp. There were no windows, so that you could only make out darkly the shapes of cupboard, oil-stove, lamp, cans, utensils and sanitary bucket stacked together in one corner. This was the home of four people; there were no goldfish bowls, no chrysanthemums, no pictures of Chinese opera, no photographs of Chairman Mao, no slogans about 'techniques'.

'I hope soon,' said the old woman, 'to have a brick home on one of the new estates. I hope you will come to visit me then.'

Back at the Cathay Hotel the interpreter asked me why I had gone into that particular home.

'Because the woman looked such a skeleton,' I said. 'I felt I would see conditions at their worst.'

'I can assure you that you have. But please remember if you write about this meeting that we are working to wipe out the slums completely. It will take another seven years because we have a million people to re-house. And if you will permit me to say so'—he pointed to the luxurious carpets and plush furniture inherited, like the hotel itself, from the Sassoon era —'the men who occupied these rooms before the Liberation did very little to help.'

[BOYD ORR, 113–114]

The obvious things to do in Shanghai are to look at the shops, visit the docks, go round the park which has superseded the racecourse, and walk through the factories. Instead, we limited ourselves to visiting the slums and seeing what was being done to remedy the appalling living conditions there, and to talking with some of the remnants of the foreign community. So first we drove slowly through the streets to one of the "new towns" where slum dwellers are rehoused, emptying their shacks for clearance.

A recent project has been the temporary patching up of a third of all the old houses, the worst of the lot, to make them more habitable, and we passed through newly-surfaced streets where householders were for the first time in their lives saved from the filth of wet, dirt roads, and able to enjoy electricity instead of vegetable-oil lamps with their flickering flame. The ultimate solution, however, is the establishment of dormitory towns on the outskirts.

The one we visited had rehoused 30,000 people in two-storey houses, each accommodating four or five families, and separated from each other by little lawns and gardens. The whole residential quarter is grouped round a shopping district and a medical station, and provided with schools and entertainment centres. The general layout appeared good, and the place was neat and well kept. "Can we inspect one of the houses?" we asked our faithful Mr. Li. "Anyone you like," he offered. "Choose!" We chose the nearest, and went in, and the householders opened their doors to welcome us.

There was nothing luxurious about these buildings. They were simply-constructed, concrete-block dwellings, with apartments of different sizes allocated according to the number of people in a family. Most had two or three rooms, with a private toilet and a charcoal cooking-stove (no electricity or gas was used for cooking), and for each apartment house there was a common workroom fitted out on one side for the women to do their laundry and on the other with a big stove where housewives could prepare meals too elaborate for their little charcoal stoves to accommodate.

First we inspected a single room occupied by an old-age pensioner and his wife, who insisted on making tea for us while they talked about their pension and what it meant to them, and their old life in the slums. They seemed very pleased with their surroundings, but what struck us particularly were the old man's teeth. Whenever he laughed—which he did uproariously at the poorest joke—he threw back his head and opened his mouth wide, and as far as we could see he had every tooth in his head. We had noticed before ho-a man of seventy showing off an admirable set of uppers-and-lowers, apparently without one false tooth among them.

Across the passage-way was a three-roomed apartment occupied by a young couple with a family, and above their flat other similarly-sized apartments, all of whose owners commented on the advantages of their present accommodation as compared to their previous dwellings. Since we had seen some of the remaining slums in the city this was easy to understand. As yet, of course, the problem of proper housing is hardly touched. Shanghai is being improved, but even here a great deal remains to be done, and the really formidable task lies in the hinterland, in the cities of the interior, and the rural areas, where construction materials and equipment are not so readily come by.

CANTON

[CROFT, 218–236]

The brown farmlands turned to green and gold, the soil of the distant foothills to deep scarlet. We chugged slowly on through fields of rice and sugar-cane, past lotus-blooming ponds and level swamps where water-buffaloes dragged ancient ploughs and peasants threshed their rice by hand as they had done since time immemorial. The abundant sun flooded the countryside. The fertile Kwantung plain stretched away into the blue haze of the western mountains like a triumphal harvest procession.

On the approach to the city the railway line swung in to run parallel to the River Pearl, sluggish and grey with mud. Propped above its banks, rickety and precarious like a street built on stilts, but firm against flood and deluge, stood the wooden huts of the peasants. On the water below floated the sampans and barges, the suburbs of the river-side people.

They had said Canton was 'different': they did not exaggerate. The difference dazzled the eyes as soon as we stepped off the train.

The reception party had dressed up to kill. There was not a boiler-suit to be seen, not a single padded jacket or high-necked tunic. They rushed down the platform in a blaze of colour like a holiday-camp crowd gone berserk. The young men looked startling enough in their vivid shirts and gay silk ties—but the girls were truly sensational.

It was not merely what they had done to their bodies, although their frocks were a riot of colour that would have stopped the show on the busiest Bank Holiday in Blackpool, but they had smeared and daubed their faces with enough make-up to supply an American musical for a month or an English touring company for a year. Their lips were aflame with carmine, their cheeks with crimson—as if, after years of prohibition, they had suddenly broken into a cosmetics factory and gone mad with the spoils. Their gaudy, grinning faces reminded you, at best, of the grotesque heroines of Peking Opera, at worst, of a group of newly recruited harlots out on the spree. For the first time on these occasions nobody broke into 'Unity is Strength', and you felt it would have been perfectly in order to have offered to any one of the welcoming young women a friendly, appreciative kiss.

We arrived too late for lunch, too early for dinner, so we were taken for a 'snack' at a widely-famed tea-house.

I had by this time discovered that Chinese food as cooked in delegation hotels bore little comparison to similar food cooked in the restaurants and tea-houses. The former was the work of men who cooked for a living, the latter of those who lived to cook. The *spécialité* of this *maison* was shrimp and we ate it in fourteen different ways: in rice rissoles, in lotus cakes, in cauliflower dumplings: fried with shreds of chicken, roasted in morsels of duck, and wound round in nameless leaves and weeds and bits and pieces of aqueous vegetation. Only Abou, whose stomach was allergic to fish of any kind, failed to appreciate the occasion.

There were the usual sights to be seen: a vast new park outside the city; an artificial lake; two enormous swimming-pools, and a network of smaller pools for the children; a football ground scooped out of a hill with seating for fifty thousand; and the Sun Yat-sen Memorial Hall, a magnificent circular building, meticulously fashioned in traditional style, capable of seating five thousand, and erected without a single supporting pillar between floor and roof.

Canton is proud of its revolutionary traditions. It was here that the famous seventy-two martyrs were executed, where Sun Yat-sen launched his first northern campaign and Mao set up the headquarters of the peasant movement. A new museum preserves the relics of those years of upheaval like a history of modern China in microcosm: the student risings, the secret meetings, the early achievements of the Kuomintang, the double dealings and subterfuges, the mistaken alliances, the tragic missions.

In the National Institute of the Peasant Movement the furniture used by Mao and the early peasant leaders in 1924 had been kept intact. Here Vladimir gazed in astonishment at a notice indicating the chairs on which the Christian members of the movement had sat. 'It is fantastical!' he exclaimed. 'Why, in my country at this time we were crashing down churches and wiping out Christians. There was a popular song of time'—he sang it first in Russian—it sounded like a merry little jig:

'We shall kick out all priests and kick down all churches,
  Then we shall climb high in sky and kick out God!

Of course,' he hastened to add, 'that was thirty years ago, not now.'

Canton had also its House of Sino-Soviet Friendship, a vast establishment recently completed at colossal cost but of immeasurable solidarity value. Similar Houses, on an equally grandiose scale, dominate the skyline in most of the other large cities and can be expected to do so, sooner or later, in all of them. They fulfil emphatically the function implied by their name, for they provide a mammoth showroom for displays of Soviet and satellite achievement which most of the populace seem willing and even anxious to queue for hours to see.

That week the Sino-Soviet House was holding something new in the way of exhibitions. China had put her own goods in the window: ostensibly of export commodities, the exhibition contained samples of practically everything produced in the country in the last seven years.

There were the latest show-pieces, of course—diesel locomotives from Darien, jet planes from Harbin, centrifugal pumps, X-ray equipment, Liberation lorries from Changchun —strictly not for sale—and the standard exports: tung oil and tea, bristles and porcelain, textiles and tallows, silks and laces —but there were more than forty thousand other products as well, which represented a performance of some magnitude.

The Foodstuffs department was more in my line than the machines; here the names alone constituted an epicurean lyric: Canton lichees, Tientsin pears, Tsingtao cherries, Fukien loquats, Lian Hsiang chestnuts and Hsingkiang Hami melons; Yunnan ham, braised bamboo shoots and long-tailed anchovies. Some of the meat exhibits evoked less pleasurable sensations: pig's sinews, duck's gizzards and—a great delicacy, they say— bear's paws; but these were cancelled out in the 'Bristles Room' of the Animal By-Products Section next door, where the labels read like a page from a Shakespearean glossary:

cock saddles and great bustard tails, mallard scapulas and teal plumages, red heron feathers, short white ospreys, Lady Amhurst headskins and black-eared kites.

There was no doubt the Chinese meant business. Everything had been laid on with a high degree of efficiency and considerable artistic sense. Two whole wings had been set aside for enquiries and orders, with well-appointed post and telegraph offices, elaborate facilities for banking and insurance, and a bureau of advice on customs, inspection and testing. The thought came again: if they can do all this *now* what will they be turning out in twenty and thirty years' time?

'Originally,' said the Director, 'over a hundred British business men had accepted invitations' (it was agreeably surprising to notice that all goods were labelled in Chinese, Russian *and* English), 'but,' he explained delicately, 'there were some difficulties of transport and communications as a result of events in Egypt.'

I did, however, find one Englishman, a Manchester cotton merchant who had just ordered £100,000 worth of textiles, and he confessed himself staggered by the whole turn-out.

'Goodness knows I'm no communist, but I've been overwhelmed—not just by a few home-made trucks and trains, but by the terrific range of goods. It's an astonishing achievement. I came here with the idea that everything was the same as a hundred years ago, but what they've done is beyond belief! And in the Cultural Palaces—I've never seen anything like it! Thousands of young people enjoying themselves in games and dancing—don't tell me that our Teddy boys are an improvement on that! The only odd thing was to see men dancing with men—I can't think that's good for anybody.'

'And what do you think,' I asked, 'about the Peace and Friendship? Do you think they really mean it?'

'Ah,' he said, 'there I am afraid. Now they are told to believe in peace but they could just as easily be made to believe in war—for the sake of peace—and if that should happen it could be the end of the western world. I believe the time will come—within our lifetime—when China could swallow the whole of the British Empire and America too—and do it without indigestion.'

It seemed a remote possibility; but seven years ago that exhibition must have seemed equally remote.

The main stream of the industrial revolution has passed Canton by. Although it can boast a thriving textile industry and a large paper factory, in essence it remains what it has been since the British opened it up last century, 'a land of fruits', an international market-place for oranges, bananas, pineapples and melons—the 'money crops' of the south.

Perhaps because it was the first Chinese city to trade with the west (it still maintains, they say, amicable smuggling relations with Hong Kong), its people have a peculiar sophistication of their own. They do not smile at strangers as readily as most of their countrymen do—are just as likely in fact to pass them with sullen glares; they do not make friends so easily, although when they do, they say, it is for life; they shout and bang and clatter more noisily about their business than most other Chinese, but they seem to chatter less. Perhaps because they have been bred eternally on the river or have had to eke their living from flood-washed land they seem dour even to the point of moroseness.

Facially in fact they do not look Chinese: they tend to have wide jawbones, exceptionally flat noses, eyes set deeply apart and curling negroid lips. They are famous throughout China for their habit of wearing clogs; it is thought to be very funny indeed that they should wear them 'even for receptions'. They are also addicted to their tea-houses, which even the poorer classes are said to patronise at least three times a day. They are colourful, individualistic and utterly enigmatic; even the Chinese of other cities confess to being baffled by them.

The lifeline of the city is the sampan-studded river, and it was the sampans I wanted to visit most.

The officials seemed surprised by my request; apparently it was not usual for visitors to express such a wish. When I went down to the river I quickly saw why.

The sampan is not, as the romantically-minded might imagine, a kind of exotic houseboat or cosy holiday launch. It is a habitation, a place of business and a public conveyance, and its resources are pitifully inadequate to most of the demands made upon them.

Over sixty thousand people, called for some obscure reason 'The Family of the Egg', live in these boats, for the most part in conditions as appalling as any in the Shanghai slums. The average sampan is about as spacious as a small motor-launch, which is to say that it has less overall space than a London council-house kitchen. It has to accommodate families of rarely less than four and often as many as ten people: strapping young boys and gnarled old women, new-born babies and crippled old men—they sleep on the deck and on wooden planks laid across the deck. If lucky, they have a timbered roof above them, but in most cases merely a canvas awning supported on bamboo rods. For most of the year they are dry, but when the rains fall they may remain wet for days on end.

In the stern of the boat they carry their goods and chattels: sticks of furniture, kitchen utensils, bags of wheat and rice, sacks of coal and crates of ducks and chickens. Many of the sampans reek abominably of livestock and excrement, but in some incense burnt at little Buddhist shrines in the bows provides an unusual deodorant. The sampan is not merely the river dweller's home—it may also be his temple.

For these people times have always been hard, and in some ways they have improved little since the Liberation. Most of their old work of haulage and transport is now done by steamboats. A few months before my visit a pool of co-operatives had been formed for ferrying and fishing, but it was too early to say what difference it would make. Some said they were making less money than before, some slightly more, but even at the best it amounted to a mere pittance.

The old people and the infirm were feeling the pinch most. They benefited from the new health service, of course, and inoculations kept them free from cholera and tuberculosis, but what was the point of being healthy if you had nothing to look forward to?

For the young folk it was different. It was a good time for them to be growing up; they had a fine future ahead of them. In the old days there had been no schools to attend. Nearly everyone was illiterate—and rather proud of the fact. They had despised schooling and had nothing in common with the folk of the city. Now they were glad to see their children going to primary schools and literacy classes, and some even to secondary schools and colleges. Of course, all this schooling meant that the young men were drifting away from the river to work in the factories and handicraft co-operatives, but it was good to see them doing well for themselves—some were even earning enough to buy luxuries like watches and gold rings, and they could all afford quilts for their beds. In the last year fifteen young people from the river had actually been elected to the local congress.

Oh yes, it was a great time for the young, and there was no doubt it was going to be better. There was even a wonderful scheme for building enough new houses within the next seven years to clear the sampans off the river completely . . . that would be fine for their children and their children's children—nobody lived on the river from choice—but seven years might be too long for some of the older folk to wait. . . . Meantime they would go on picking up what trade they could . . . waiting to hear more about the new houses . . . and watching the big steamboats go by. . . .

Cultural Palaces, spacious parks, schools, department stores, new housing estates; sampans and slums. The forces of the old order and the new rubbed shoulders here in starker propinquity than in any other city I visited.

There was, immediately behind the skyscraper hotel where we were staying, a wonderful market: bustling, colourful, gay, ripe with the smells of southern fruit. It was separated from the main street by a network of narrow alleys and passageways. They looked dark, sinister and dangerous, like the setting of a Fu Manchu story.

If it was really true that a foreigner could pass unmolested through any street in China even at night, these alleys, I thought, would be a good testing ground. They demanded to be explored.

Being of a cautious disposition I did not go alone but asked my Sinhalese friend to accompany me, on the protective principle that, should trouble threaten, his Asiatic instincts might anticipate it in time to take appropriate defensive action. On a more concrete principle, I also took an old Burmese dagger—acquired obscurely one night in Chittagong towards the end of the war—and a spiked ring removed from the finger of a French matelot in Beirut in December 1943, on the night the French killed one of our own sailors on the steps of the Savoy Canteen.

The Sinhalese did not stay with me for long.

As we turned off the main road the good ripe smell of the fruit from the market was swallowed up in a stench of such foulness that we both stopped dead in our tracks. It made the odour of the sampans seem like lavender, the smell of the Fan Kua-lun slums like sweet perfume. It almost dispelled my interest in the expedition—but it finished off the Sinhalese altogether. Declaring he would be sick if he went any farther, he put his handkerchief to his nose and quickly made his way back to the street.

Some stubborn streak of curiosity stopped me from following him. I took several deep breaths to get quickly acclimatised, tightened the ring on my finger and pressed cautiously on.

But there was nothing whatever to fear: no footpads, no bandits, no lurking watchers or loiterers of the night. There was instead a community of people quietly gathered in their homes for their evening rest. But the difference between these people and most others was that their homes were ramshackle sheds and stables, and they themselves were living little better than animals.

I had seen the slums by day, but never by night, and seen them generally from the outside, but here I was looking in—not through windows, for there were none—but through great slits in the walls where windows should have been. The sheds were lit by oil lamps, burning low, and perhaps their pallid glow made the interiors seem worse than they were: rotting timber walls and patched-up roofs; families of six and seven, sitting cross-legged, knotted tightly together, eating their meals on the floor; babies fast asleep on wooden planks in dark corners; children bent double against the walls trying to catch enough light to read by; two naked figures in cramped copulation on a carpet of ragged sacks, writhing under the lurid glow of the lamp like doomed souls in the shadows of the Inferno, while their three children slept on the floor at their feet; an aged scarecrow of a man, completely naked, standing to wash himself in a black iron bowl; ducks in wicker cages and hens roosting along the walls; every inch of space occupied either by human bodies or their basic impedimenta— the means of existence only, the bare, primitive equipment of survival.

From within the hovels rose the buzz and murmur of family gossip—the world in the evening, settled to its leisure—while outside, the alley-ways were hushed and deserted; but I had not yet seen the worst.

I turned into a passage so dark and narrow that it was difficult to move down it without bumping into the walls on either side. I sensed rather than saw faces watching me from the narrow openings and once I felt somebody's breath on mine. At that point I was afraid and would have gone faster if I could have seen the way. Eventually I came to a turning and saw with infinite relief the glow of a street lamp at the far end of the alley ahead. As I walked towards it the shapes of the alley-way became clearer; on one side the thin, ochre light of the lamp revealed some half a dozen habitations that could scarcely even be dignified by the name of hovels: they were, to be precise, human kennels. There seemed to be one man in each—there was no room for more—and these men, I repeat, *men*, were standing, partly because there was no room to sit, partly because they had no lamp to see by; standing, with their heads peering out of the black shadows of their kennels—as though their legs had been chained to the walls inside; standing to eat their evening meal by whatever light they could catch thrown from the lamp in the street.

It was too dark to make out their faces and I did not try too hard. I had a macabre impression of black eyes staring from sunken sockets in gaunt, bearded heads and—imagination, perhaps—when they were aware of my scrutiny a sense of glowering hostility and hate. I moved hurriedly on and was glad to get back to the street.

Why these men still lived like this nobody knew, or if they

knew they would not tell. 'Many things are still very backward,' was all the Cantonese would say. 'We cannot put everything right at once.' Even Shen, who always spoke to the point and had himself grown up in Canton, could not, or would not, explain it. 'At least you came back alive,' was his only comment. 'That might not have been possible before.'

The next afternoon, Shen took me on a tour of the oldest part of the city.

He was an excellent guide, unobtrusive, making no attempt to force things upon me, supplying information when he saw something of special interest, and willing to branch off from his appointed route down any alley-way I suggested.

We walked through a maze of centuries-old passage-ways and streets, round ancient bazaars and markets, past stalls still selling fine silks and scroll paintings, humming birds, intricate wood carvings and curios in ivory and jade. We looked in at workshops open to the street where men and women were busy weaving and spinning, shaping bowls and jugs and moulds for the oven, blending mysterious herbs, stitching pigskin bags, and mending copper implements on antique lathes.

It was a journey back through time into the orient of one's old imagining: people teemed and bustled through the doorways; vendors urgently shouted their wares; children clip-clopped about in their clogs with bundles of even smaller children slung across their shoulders—there was all the colour and confusion, the sweat and fervour of the ancient eastern market-places: a way of life as remote from the ideological background as the pedicab from the Rolls-Royce—or so you would have liked to think.

Then I stopped outside a carpenter's workshop. Within there was a scene of remarkable activity. Back to back, elevated on wooden benches, some four or five feet from the ground, two rows of boys and girls, about thirty in number, pedalled furiously away at old-fashioned drilling machines—drilling holes in wooden abacus beads. Some worked in their shirt-sleeves, some in grubby vests, some stripped to the waist. Two boys were taking time off to sleep on a makeshift platform opposite the primitive lavatory in the far corner of the building. Sawdust and shavings were piled on the floor; washing hung from the grimy walls. As they pedalled away to the grinding whirr of the machines, sweat glistening on their backs in the light of the single electric lamp, they looked for all the world like a squad of Dickensian waifs, born out of time and place, orphans of the totalitarian storm. But the illusion was short-lived: when they saw me walking in, without waiting for the supervisor's permission, they switched off their ma-

chines, scrambled down from their benches and practically
fell over themselves in the rush to be sociable. They were
children of Dekker rather than Dickens, of Eyre's shop rather
than Fagin's kitchen; if it had been a holiday they could not
have looked more carefree.

Their ages varied between fifteen and nineteen and they
were serving an eleven months' apprenticeship. They worked
an eight-hour shift and were paid between fifteen and thirty
yuan a month, of which they paid back twelve *yuan* for food.
When they qualified they would hope to join a co-operative
where they would start on fifty *yuan* a month and eventually
go on to piece rates. Were they happy about their prospects?
They could not have been happier. Drilling abacus beads was
nothing to rave about, but when they had learnt the 'advanced
techniques' there would always be interesting work for them
to do—with the satisfaction of knowing that they were directly
serving the people.

They were different from the usual Chinese youths I had
met in that they did most of the talking—and were uninhibited
in more ways than one: as they crowded round me at the
supervisor's bench I had the distinct impression that the boys
and girls in the rear rank were seizing the opportunity to
practise some Chinese variation of old-fashioned slap and
tickle. The occasion was altogether charming, friendly and
gay—then suddenly it burst into melodrama.

There were on the wall opposite me two drawings in black
and white. They were similar to posters I had already seen
on a larger scale, in flaming colours and giant lettering, on
the public hoardings, but they had an intimacy which the
posters had lacked. The first one showed a fat, bull-faced
Englishman and a leering Frenchman machine-gunning a field
of women and children beneath the bleeding shadow of the
Sphinx; the second depicted a magnificent young Russian giant
—a kind of Soviet Superman—wielding an enormous broom
to sweep the floor of a cluster of rat-faced counter-revolutionaries—while an evil-looking American hurried after them
dangling a bagful of £20,000,000.

Sensing my interest, the apprentices pushed forward the
artist responsible, a shock-haired, cheerful-looking lad of about
seventeen. I turned to Shen and asked him to translate the
inscription on the Egyptian cartoon. He looked extremely
perturbed and said he would rather not.

'Don't bother about my feelings,' I insisted. 'The words
can't be any more vicious than the drawing itself.'

'All right,' he said. 'But I've warned you that you won't
like it.'

'We condemn the filthy aggression of the imperialists,' he

read. '*Britain and France have invoked the wrath of the Chinese youth. We demand a peaceful solution to the Egyptian problem. We are against the use of force, but we will support to the death the righteous struggle of the Egyptian people.*'

I turned to ask the artist where he had found his inspiration —but suddenly, inexplicably, he had gone, vanished into the streets. Somebody explained that he had had to go home for an early dinner, but I found that hard to believe, since nobody else seemed to be under the same domestic pressure. It may have been, of course, that he was exceptionally shy and embarrassed by the occasion—or perhaps, even, felt that he had embarrassed the English visitor and ought to get out of the way.

Be that as it may, I thought it highly improbable that 'the Chinese youth' could be invoked to wrath over something they knew so little about or over the affairs of a country so far removed from their own: but I was mistaken.

'How many of you have learnt to read?' I asked.

'Ninety per cent of all the apprentices,' they said.

'Which newspapers?'

'*China Youth* and the Canton edition of *The People's Daily*.'

'And how many,' I put the question with caution, 'feel that Britain and France are in the wrong about Egypt?'

The atmosphere of relaxed good humour and youthful friendliness vanished in a flash.

'Everyone in this workshop does!' they cried heatedly. 'And everyone in this street! And everyone in Canton!'

'So if I go into every workshop I shall find the same feelings—and the same kind of drawings?'

'Everywhere you go. Not only here but with all the young people of China—they all think the same!'

One lad of about sixteen with a broken nose and hard-bitten face pushed his way violently to the front and launched into a fiery tirade against the British aggressors. He had, I felt, been eyeing me suspiciously all along. He snarled and shouted and stamped his feet and did everything except shake his fist in my face, while the rest of his friends angrily urged him on; and in the background Shen and the supervisor looked equally disconsolate about the whole thing.

'All right,' I said, when he appeared to have finished. 'Supposing that the British have done wrong. Don't you think that what the Russians are doing in Hungary is just as bad?'

This time he did shake his fist and all the other young people, so delightful and gay five minutes before, closed in towards me shouting in indignation. For a moment I had

a detached impression of the water-front gang moving in
upon their victim in the famous Kazan film. There were
thirty of them, and even with the faithful Shen at hand I
did not feel particularly comfortable. He had by now given
up trying to interpret and was anxiously urging the supervisor into action. The broken-nosed boy, quivering with rage,
thrust his face closer into mine while the others formed
a menacing circle behind him. I braced myself against the
wall, ready for action.

But there was no violence—somehow there never was. The
supervisor suddenly shot to life, pushed his way to the front,
spoke sharply to the ringleader, and ordered everyone to calm
down. The tension relaxed. They lowered their fists and in a
minute or two were all grinning at me rather sheepishly—
except, that is, for the broken-nosed lad, who turned his
back on the supervisor and went on muttering angrily to
himself.

'It's getting late,' said Shen. 'I think we'd better go.'

It seemed a trifle inappropriate on this occasion to leave
behind the usual message of peace and goodwill on behalf of
the young people of England, so I simply shook hands with
the supervisor and thanked him for having me.

'I would like to make it clear,' he said, 'that they do not
regard you as being personally responsible for the aggression
in Egypt. They know that you are one of the People and
are not to blame for what your government has done.'

'Tell them to remember that every government can make
mistakes,' I said. 'Even the Chinese and the Russian.'

I walked back with Shen for some time in silence. 'I hope
you were not too upset by what happened,' he said eventually.
'Canton people are sometimes quickly excited. You must
remember it is a different city.'

It was different again in the evening.

There was another Social, this time with over a thousand
in attendance.

My enjoyment of these over-gregarious occasions had by
now diminished in inverse proportion to the number of
people present; the more there were, the fewer with whom
you could achieve a state of mutual coherence. The young
people had looked forward to the event for weeks and had
queued and drawn lots for tickets; for many it was their
first opportunity to meet anyone from abroad, especially
from England, and it was unthinkable to disappoint them.
But the business of sitting surrounded by dozens of beaming
and largely incomprehensible admirers, feeding them with
endlessly repetitive titbits about the English way of life

through the medium of a third person—a schoolboy or student whose command of English was, in the nature of things, tentative rather than practical—and then being dragged round the floor by one vivacious girl after another because she felt that that was what you most desired, made them into an exercise which you started with mild exasperation and finished in a state of exhaustion. I even began to feel a sneaking sympathy for Bernini: several years of this would make any man look like a dried-up codfish.

But, again, Canton was a different city. . . . If you showed no desire to dance, the girls did not suggest you should; if you seemed reluctant to talk they did not force themselves upon you. As social evenings went it was admirably relaxed: gay but not boisterous, friendly but not frenzied. I wandered about casually, talking to nobody in particular, or sat back quietly listening to Pablo entertaining the crowd with his Cuban melodies; and then, unexpectedly the evening blossomed out into something strangely moving.

Out of the crowd there emerged an unusually animated young man who introduced himself in a kind of twitching ecstasy. He pumped my hand vigorously, bounced rapturously up and down and jumped about as excitedly as if Uncle Mao himself had popped in on the off chance of seeing his children at play.

He was, he said, 'mad for Shakespeare'. He had heard his tutor speaking Shakespeare in class, but he had never heard Shakespeare spoken 'properly'. Now his heart was full of joy because his great dream was about to come true: I could speak the great poetry of Shakespeare to him—any verses would do—in the glorious native tongue of the poet.

The circumstances were not exactly ideal. The orchestra had broken into an ear-splitting version of the polka; the dancers stamped and thumped their feet on the floor; young people milled around us, collecting their partners; but I did my best to oblige.

If he had been excited at the start he seemed on the point of delirium when I had finished, and when he had recovered rushed me off to meet a friend of his, a poet named Lan Li-Sing.

Lan was a student at Sun Yat-sen University, but with his loose-fitting red sweater and fawn-coloured slacks you felt he would have been more at home on some athletic campus in California. It took a little time to convince him that I really wanted to hear some of *his* poetry, but eventually, in a voice scarcely audible above the wailing of the *er hu* and the clashing of the gongs, he recited the piece he had just completed, '*So many days have passed*'. It ran into twelve stanzas and was translated line by line by his friend on some linguistical hit-and-miss principle worked out as he went along; but even this could not obscure the depth and sensibility of the writer's feelings.

The theme of his poem was the separation of a mother from her son, the son being obviously Lan himself. The boy has just left home for the first time to attend university and he asks his mother not to grieve at his going.

He imagines her counting the days to his return, smoothing down his pillow at night, cherishing fond images of his boyhood—their daily life together, his struggles at school, his father's death, the day his sister went away to be married, the mixed feelings of pride and sadness with which she heard that he had been accepted by the university. . . . *'So many days have passed . . . but every night I know that you remember . . .'* and finally, he imagines her thinking of his new life among the students, and, realising that now he is a man, he will give his affection to his comrades as well as to her. . . . *'So many days have passed . . . but do not believe I have forgotten you.'*

Although once or twice I thought I caught a dutiful echo of Youth League patriotism, it did not mar the poem's emotional impact. The young man's feelings broke through the crudities of the translation; he had written from the heart—so much so that when he had finished I felt I had intruded upon a private sorrow. Even his effervescent friend was affected and for a time could think of nothing at all to say.

Lan was unwilling to recite anything more and we fell to talking about the usual things, his work, his plans, the student's life, while the dancers swirled and stamped around us and the musicians hammered the helpless air. Before I left he promised to send me a copy of the poem, properly translated, but I have not received it; and all that is left of my one encounter with a genuine young romantic is this wholly inadequate paraphrase.

After the Social we went for a last look at Canton—Vladimir, Carl, Tamas and myself.

A few grain and ferry-boats were still passing down the river; the sampans, tied together in rows of seven and eight alongside the jetty, swayed and gurgled on the tide; bodies lay crammed and stretched across the decks; chickens huddled together in panniers in the stern, all the household paraphernalia stacked around them; but there was no movement, only a low murmur of conversation and the occasional sound of snoring 'How do such people *live?*' said Vladimir. 'It is impossible!'

In the harbour shadows pedlars hurried by with their bamboo loads of fruit and sesame cakes and hardware. In the streets beyond, children still roamed about, singly or in twos and threes. They clip-clopped past without curiosity, quietly enjoying the fading light of the lamps as long as they could. Here and there a few fruit-stalls were still open— what for, at this time of night, it was impossible to say— perhaps they hardly knew themselves; old women shifted loads and bundles for the night; families squatted round little stools on the pavement or stood at oil-stoves cooking themselves soup or fish or beans; all along the pavement people lay sleeping on straw mattresses, their heads against the shop walls, feet pointing downward to the street—on one mattress three babies, on another an old crone, between them a coolie fast asleep on a tiny stool, his bed for the night; the pavement-sweepers brushed carefully past, trying not to disturb them. 'It is a city of very *pure* people,' said Carl. 'Very different to Copenhagen.'

On the building sites work was still going on. Coolies glided by carrying buckets of bricks and cement under the bamboo yoke, their bodies swaying rhythmically from side to side to help balance the load. Four men dragged a great pine-trunk, about fifty feet long, into the road and hauled it painfully on to their shoulders, then set off, for some unknown destination; '*Wei ho . . . wei ho . . .*' gasped the two men at the front. '*Wei . . . ho . . . wei ho . . .*' came the groaning response from the back. Their faces as they passed us were taut with pain, their backs dripped sweat, and their eyes, tight-drawn, were fixed glassily on the road ahead.

'*Wei ho . . . wei ho . . .*' floated the cry from the river . . . from the barges unloading in the harbour . . . from the ferry-boats hauling to the shore. . . . '*Wei ho . . . wei ho . . .*' came the murmur from the markets . . . from the coolie gangs on the railway . . . from the labourers digging roads. . . . Canton was a different city, and the old order was taking longer to die here than anywhere else.

'I saw a very strange thing this morning,' said Carl. 'Two old bodies of men—how you say?—two skeletons—on sale in market. People say they have been found in ground under street, but nobody want to buy them.'

'That is very good story for bourgeois journalist,' said Vladimir sardonically. 'Make much money in American magazine: "In Red China people die in streets and dead bodies are sold in market!"'

'Ah, yes,' said Carl, with a nice statistical irony, 'but two bodies together—not one. "Before Liberation, only *one* man die, but after Liberation there is *two*!"'

Even Tamas, who did not normally banter about these things, permitted himself to enjoy the somewhat macabre joke.

The families squatting on the pavement began to pack their stoves and dishes away and lay down their mattresses for the night; in the houses behind, the bodies huddled tighter together on the floors and wooden ledges jutting out of the walls; an old woman shuffled out of an alley to empty a lavatory bucket down the street drain; and gradually the lights down the street and along the harbour side began to go out.

2. The Communes

[CLARK, 79–80]

Wang Feng-shu, a seventeen-year-old girl, is battalion commander at a "people's commune." She directs the work, efforts, and lives of 1,595 men, women, and children. Wang Feng-shu is young for the job; but then, as we have seen, this is a young person's country. The only thing that is old is a commune's meaning: ownership of everything by all the people. The idea is as venerable as Karl Marx, and yet the most revolutionary process that has ever embraced any country, including Russia, the mother of communism. Soviet leaders, in the early days of their revolution, did set up a few trial communes; quickly they abandoned them, because the semi-Westernized Russian people would not tolerate communal living. A commune represents the end of individuality, and at the very least a curtailment of traditional family life. Wang Feng-shu is a minuscule link in a vast, awesome network in which children are herded into nurseries and everyone becomes three beings rolled into one: a farmer, a factory worker, a militiaman. In other words, when the harvest has to be gathered, you go into the fields; when there is a demand for iron ingots, you work at the blast furnaces; and, in between, you learn how to handle a rifle. A whole new society is thereby bred, for in return you are on an equal level with the next man. Each man receives only a little pocket money (eventually he will receive none); the commune provides free food, shelter, clothing, medical care, and education. This is more than simply a theory. The first communes were set up only in July, 1958. The incredible part, in line with China's frantic haste to develop, is that within three months 98 per cent of the entire rural population was organized into communes, even if only on paper, Today 500,000,000 Chinese live in a total of 27,000 communes.

I met Wang Feng-shu at Hsushui in Hopei Province. Each commune, for production purposes, is organized on military lines and is divided into several work brigades and battalions. Wang Feng-shu, one of many officers, was overseeing the gathering of corn. The harvest, she said, with considerable pride, was "seven times" greater than in the previous year—thanks to better irrigation, increased use of fertilizers, "and above all the enthusiasm of the people." Whether or not there is universal enthusiasm is, of course, impossible to know. But from what I could ascertain, people appeared to be working hard and generally accepting life in a commune as a material benefit. Whatever it robs in individuality (a Western prize hardly valid in the East, where hunger is the watchword), it makes up for in security. To succeed, Chinese communism must feed the biggest population in the world. It must also satisfy the peasant that it is primarily in his own interest that the most radical social experiment in human history is now under way. The future of communism in China is locked in the land. It was there that it had its beginning.

[CLARK, 83–92]

The commune is the final stage in land reform and goes much beyond the co-operative. While the co-operative interested itself only in agriculture, the commune extends itself and integrates rural industry, fisheries, transport, and everything else that makes for a self-contained economic unit—in fact, 27,000 self-contained units. Physically, the commune is not very startling, not much more than a collection of villages scattered through open countryside about the size of a *hsiang*, or township. Shangchuang Commune, Hsushui County, Hopei, where Wang Feng-shu works, embraces forty villages and has a population of 56,000. For purposes of major projects, such as dam construction, Shangchuang is linked with other communes in the county, so that 320,000 people may be considered to function in concert. But it is not the physical make-up that stands out in my mind. It is what the commune represents *spiritually* that establishes it as a fascinating and, from a Westerner's viewpoint, a disturbing mechanism. In theory, the ultimate stage in the transition from socialism to communism has almost been reached. The principle of "from each according to his ability and to each according to his work" is being supplanted by the principle of "from each according to his ability and to each according to his needs." In the process, an anonymous, personalityless society is under cultivation, with the peasant expected to produce children for a mass experiment in obedience and Marxist inoculation that makes even the Soviet case history insignificant by comparison. How much of a loss of family identity the peasant is willing to trade for new security is as yet an unknown factor, and already the regime has seen fit to announce some words of reassurance that the family unit is not really threatened. Still, Wang Feng-shu, with a fervor notable in all young Communists, told me, "The family does not count any more. We provide all the needs."

I asked Wang Feng-shu whether there was any resentment among older people that a youth her age should be taking such a direct part in their destiny. Wang Feng-shu, a rather pretty girl, opened her eyes wide and expressed surprise at the question. "I was chosen by the people," she said simply. Wang Feng-shu, as I later confirmed, had indeed been elected to the commune committee by a show of hands at a mass meeting. She was, of course, one of the comparatively minor officials, but nonethless representative of other committee members, who must satisfy the wants of the "constituents." The cynical observer of China may claim that committee rule, even at the low level of the commune, is a sham, a synthetic device perpetrated by the regime to lull the masses into a false belief that they possess self-government. But qualified historians argue that the survival of regimes and dynasties in the past depended on winning, and holding, the approval of the governed, the vast majority of whom were peasants. Mao Tse-tung, it may be presumed, understands this need, and, whether for false or sincere motives, has ensured that grass-roots direction, which had its start in the co-operative, is continued in the commune. For their part, the peasants gratefully acknowledge a measure of self-government in the hope that they will have a real influence on policies close to their hearts, particularly in agriculture. The validity of this degree of self-rule may not be so difficult for the foreign observer to accept once the underlying feature is remembered. Simultaneously with committee rule, the machinery of persuasion and indoctrination ticks along smoothly. Every peasant attends, for at least two hours each day, a class or a rally or political meeting in which he hears over and over again the theme that the party knows what is best for all. The older people may easily weary of constant exhortation, and, rather than invite even more of it, slump into a state of confused or indifferent acceptance. The younger people, filled with ardor, willingly try anything the party suggests.

In Peking, when I spoke to senior officials about the rapidity with which communes had been set up, I was told that the movement was "spontaneous," that even the grand planners had not expected 98 per cent of the peasantry to be organized along communal lines in the improbable space of three months. I was skeptical of this official version of the way things happen in a Communist state. At that early stage in my visit, I still visualized an omnipotent Mao Tse-tung, in the hallowed confines of an office in the Forbidden City, pressing a button and intoning, "Let there be communes." But, as I later learned and saw for myself, this is not the obvious or simple manner of the regime of China. There is, of course, admitted "direction" from above, but the emphasis is on subtlety rather than the crude and barefaced dictation that animates the Soviet Union. In the case of the communes, an experimental one was formed as early as April, 1958, but little more was heard of the switch from co-operatives until July, when Honan Province announced the "success" of its own "Sputnik People's Commune." Mao Tse-tung went down to Honan on an inspection tour, was duly impressed, and, according to Hsinhua news agency, "indicated the correct direction to take in organizing people's communes." Mao's words were lavishly reported in press and radio, and after this the movement gathered incredible momentum. Like everything else that happens in China today, once an idea catches the public imagination every loyal party worker wants to do the same thing at the same time. Implementation of any of Mao's philosophy, in other words, is carried out by young enthusiasts who simply read the *People's Daily* and then go out and beat drums and proclaim, "Chairman Mao came, and happiness came with him." Within the few months, China's 700,000 co-operatives were converted into communes. Most of these were nowhere near the skillfully organized state of the communes of Hsushui County, which was one of the pioneer areas and a showplace, but at least they represented a final step toward the ideological goal: "Ownership of means of production into ownership by the people as a whole."

Chatting with Wang Feng-shu and some of her senior comrades, I could easily sense the vigor with which they approach their own people, in rallies and in village-to-village marches, inciting them into acceptance of the commune as the end result of all their labors and the beginning of the happiness promised by Mao. "Many of the villagers," said Wang Feng-shu, "were so inspired that they renounced the few pigs that they kept as their own stock. The pigs now belong to the commune." There was slight exaggeration in Wang Feng-shu's report to me, as we shall see in later developments, but nevertheless she had pinpointed the ultimate objective: the elimination of any kind of private possession. Even now, all land and industry are the property of the commune and are administered by the commune committee which also runs the home militia. China's new-style mandarins are not, as might be expected, academic experts sent out from the cities and universities. Nor are they, in the Soviet style, alien party bosses suddenly thrust into command of a people who would resent strangers. The ones I met, all under the age of thirty, came from the district, were the sons and daughters of local farmers, and, in fact, had gained Communist party membership only in the past few years. This employment of native cadres served, of course, to heighten the impression of genuine self-government. It also was meant to ensure that any local party men, who might take on slothful or officious habits, would be under the watchful eye of kinfolk who would remind them of their duties to the commune, as well as to the party. At Hsushui, I was told with great emphasis that only the committee chairman and vice chairman spent their full time at paper work; all the other members, including Wang Feng-shu, had to work at least half time in the fields or factories. Wang Feng-shu's commune of Shangchuang comprises twelve work brigades, each in turn made up of two or three battalions. Wang Feng-shu commands her unit of 1,595 souls with great devotion and fidelity to the orders of the brigadier above, a man aged around twenty-eight. "Having these battalions," she explained, "gives us great flexibility. When there is need for people in a factory, or to work on the irrigation ditches, it is simple to move a whole unit, rather than to pick up a few men and women from here and there, as you must do in a capitalist society. Right now, with the harvest to be collected, most of the units are in the fields." Wang Feng-shu was plainly proud of the great field of corn, waving gently in the sunshine as far as the eye could see. Women and men husked the corn, methodically and diligently. When I asked to speak to some of them, Wang Feng-shu produced first a man named Wu Lo-ming, a lean peasant of about forty-five. Now through an official interpreter, obviously, I was unlikely to discover for certain what Wu felt or thought. But the story he told coincided in fundamentals with the stories others told both here and in other communes. Ten years ago Wu worked for a landlord; then the Communists consolidated their power and divided the land into tiny plots. Wu received his share and worked it himself until co-operative farming was introduced. Even with joint effort shared by his neighbors, said Wu, production was on a small scale, because irrigation depended largely on outlying districts with which there was little liaison, and crop yields were very uncertain. Moreover, said Wu, when farming was inactive during the winter, he had no other resource or industry to fall back on. But now, in the commune, he insisted, life was orderly, and he was kept busy, if not tilling the soil at least stoking the blast furnaces.

Does he work as hard now as he used to? "I work harder," said Wu, "I have more motive." But how does he feel about once having had land and now owning nothing, not even a farm cart or a pig? "I am happy because now I have nothing to worry about," said Fu, echoing the words of other commune members. This—the security it offers—so far is the main essence of the commune's appeal. Wu's wife does not have to fret about where food for the next meal will come from. Instead, the two of them march off to a communal mess hall, where they share meals with five hundred others. They receive, free, all the sweet potatoes and vegetables they can eat, and pork twice a month. This may not sound like much to us, but in this particular part of China the peasants used to eat meat only twice a year, at festivals. Wu's wife, who puts in a day's work digging irrigation ditches, no longer stitches together shoes or clothes. Wu is now entitled to pick up two garments a year from the commune's own clothing workshop, and he knows that when he is old there is the "happy home for aged people." It is all rather drab and depressing by Western standards. The "happy home" I saw was no more than a stone hut with bare earthen floors. A dozen men and women, in their eighties, lived in three rooms; but in former days old people who had no children to look after them did not even enjoy mud floors. They were reduced to begging for survival. At the moment, the "happy home" at Shangchuang is occupied by men and women who have no sons or grandchildren to support them; and even though it is a showplace, a pioneer model, the ultimate intention is that similar institutions will be provided for all elderly folk, so that they can pass their last years without burdening their families. The state guarantees dignity not only in old age but ensures its own stake in young age. When a couple is married, the commune pays for a reception for twenty guests. And when a baby is born, the commune hands out a gift of a chicken and other extras. There is something naïvely touching about all this, but when people tell you about it they have tears of gratitude in their eyes.

They also speak with thankfulness about their own small industrial revolution. Ten years ago there was no industry of any description in Shangchuang. Now the farmers have set up tiny plants that produce alcohol and sulphuric acid, and they make simple farm implements with the iron they themselves smelt from the ore that comes from nearby mountains. There are still very few machines, but nevertheless a few do exist; and the people escort you down the village roads, past the model pigsties and the freshly whitewashed huts, proud to show off in a vast field a lone tractor, almost ludicrously lost amidst the horde of manual laborers. The muscles are still available, even if the machines are slow in coming in, but the point the men all make is that the machines are coming. A small steam donkey-engine wheezily and erratically grinds corn; when it isn't required for grinding, it is dismantled and carried by hand to the pig-iron furnaces to turn the blast fans.

A few years ago even a primitive steam engine was unknown in Shangchuang. The start in mechanization is in keeping with the policy of encouraging the growth of cottage industry alongside agriculture. If it appears a laborious process, say the Chinese, it is because they have learned from Russian mistakes. Unlike the Soviet Revolution, which created chaos and dislocation by attempting a single massive leap from the hand plow to the combine harvester, the Chinese transformation encourages local communes to develop as much as possible their own technology rather than rely on machines coming off assembly lines in the cities. Local peasant initiative is plainly evident in Shangchuang and in other parts of Hsushui County. Wang Feng-shu is one of the few educated persons in her village. Yet she and two other committee members were able to draw the plan for a small dam, which was nearing completion while I was there. Actually, the credit for the diagram goes to the local schoolteacher, who had a cousin in Shanghai send her an old technical book; the teacher simply copied the diagram, and Wang Feng-shu and her comrades adapted it so that packed earth could be used instead of cement, which was needed for building sites. One of the rising buildings, a single-story affair, was to be used for the manufacture of farm tools.

In the meanwhile, a score of smithies toiled in a makeshift shed, converting old plows into what Wang Feng-shu called "modern" equipment. The plowshares were being extended about a foot for the deep plowing that government agronomists claimed would increase the crop yield. Nearby, a half-dozen women were engaged in the processing of ball bearings. The government had proclaimed that ball bearings made even the wheels of crude farm carts turn more efficiently, and so, characteristically, virtually the whole country took up the challenge of carving ball bearings by hand. Some of the women were slicing an iron rod, which they had produced in their own little back-yard blast furnace; others were grinding the pieces with stones; while still others rounded and polished the end product. It was, of course, a tremendous expenditure of

human energy, but then this is China we are describing; man-
power is cheap, and machines are not. I asked Wang Feng-
shu how quickly she thought her commune's farm fields might
be fully mechanized. "Maybe in a year or two," she said, a
trifle optimistically in view of their present primitive state. But
her next statement was the telling one: "Anyway, we cannot
wait for the big equipment. We will make do in the meanwhile with the little machines." And, she might have added,
with the abundance of muscle power. In Hsushui, five thousand men and women worked at a complex of blast furnaces,
hacking iron ore out of a nearby hillside with crowbars and
picks, then heaving it into the furnaces made of stone and
mud.

The resourcefulness of the people of Shangchuang, and all
the communes of Hsushui, may be partly attributed to the
particular history of their region. During the war with Japan,
the neighboring hills were occupied by Communist guerrillas,
who swept down to rout the Japanese from the villages. The
Japanese kept returning, and the area became a kind of no-
man's land, trading hands no fewer than twelve times. Local
government was soon disrupted and eventually vanished entirely. Left to their own devices, the peasants learned to harry
the enemy and to help the guerrillas who, in line with official
Communist policy, found time to teach them something of
self-management. During this unsettled period, the peasants
seized the land and ran their own community. Later, under
an established Communist government, they were the first in
China to form cooperative farms, and among the first to set
themselves up in communes. Hsushui's background undoubtedly made transition comparatively easy, and the county is intended as a model for other areas undergoing the change
from commune in theory to commune in practice. In some
places, only the rice is prepared communally; each family
brings to the mess hall its own meat and vegetables. In other
communes, every bit of food is cooked by squads of women
who are assigned to this task and none other; the families eat
all they want, provided each member has done his or her
stint of daily toil. In a few communes, no one receives any
money reward; in others, payment varies from one yuan (40
cents) to eight yuan ($3.20) a month.

But basic features are common to all communes. All property is nationalized, all people are expected to adjust to the
immediate demands of their local economy, even if this means
firing bricks one day and picking sweet potatoes the next.

Chinese energy and ingenuity are other universal features.
In one commune, where the peasants had heard that artificial
light can speed the growth of crops, electric bulbs hang over

an experimental rice paddy; the farmers now say the rice grows at night as well as in the daytime. The residents of one inland county wanted a spurline on the railway; there was no local steel for rails, so they made cast-iron ones and, to prevent splitting, used thousands of wooden ties, spacing them a few inches apart. In another commune, where neither steel nor iron was available, and transport was needed to move the locally made fertilizer, the inhabitants used wooden rails, replacing them every few weeks as they wore out. The over-all result is the "great leap forward" in agriculture as in industry, with local effort taking credit for record, bumper harvests in rice, wheat, cotton, and other crops. The Chinese claim that in 1958 they doubled their grain output (to 375 million tons), and became second only to the Americans as wheat growers. China, they also say, now takes first place as the biggest cotton producer in the world. Perhaps the statistics are inaccurate; no one knows whether the Chinese are deliberately exaggerating or whether, in their enthusiasm, local cadres add up too quickly. But there is little doubt that the over-all output, as viewed by foreigners, bespeaks of a considerable gain.

In every commune, the visitor is saturated with facts and figures about this season's harvest and assured that next season's will be even greater, thanks to closer planting, deeper plowing, wider use of fertilizer, and rapidly expanding irrigation systems. Devotees of the commune, like Wang Feng-shu, insist that all this has come about because peasants no longer need to feed, clothe, or house themselves, and are thus free to concentrate on working for the community, "under proper and organized direction, instead of the selfish and unproductive ways inflicted on them in the past." This Marxist dialogue aside, the peasants appeared warmly clothed and well fed, and among the children I saw no signs of distended bellies or distorted limbs usually associated with malnutrition. Westerners who knew China before 1949 say that the material standard of living of the ordinary Chinese has risen appreciably. But what is happening to the other, the spiritual, side of their lives? Enough uneasiness has been felt to cause the regime to take a second look at the communal society it has spawned.

[SCHMID, 134–146]

There is in China one big collective village—a real Potemkin village—for display to thousands of visitors, journalists, delegations, etc. It is magnificently organized, as is only proper in a Communist State. Paths and houses are kept meticulously clean. The inhabitants have been trained as actors, and each of them knows his cues and his lines: about the wicked landowners who used to squeeze the last drop of blood from their tenants, seduce their daughters, and barter away or kill their sons. And how everything had suddenly changed. . . . There is no reason to doubt these stories; such things did undoubtedly happen. And it would, of course, be too much to expect the Information Service to drag foreign visitors to unknown places where the peasants might not be disposed to tell their stories, or which were not so conveniently situated near the capital. Anybody applying in Peking to see a village was immediately booked for this particular spectacle, and so I declined the offer from the outset. Instead I made my application in Canton, which most correspondents 'cover' hurriedly on their way out to Hongkong, and where I had some hope of penetrating journalistically virgin territory.

One evening Chin informed me that we were going to Hsiao Chou on the following day—a remote little village reached only after two hours' sailing down the Pearl River. Splendid, I said. And, indeed, the next morning an enormous motor-launch arrived chugging outside our hotel; we were the only passengers to board it. We passed two ocean steamers undergoing repairs and several junks in full sail, their canvas majestically unfurled; we slipped past a labyrinth of islands and islets, and eventually turned into an arm of the river to our left, which brought us to a landing-stage shaded by bushy trees. As usual, I found myself welcomed by an entire reception committee, whose hospitality I instantly offended: since it was impossible to take photographs if one was surrounded by a crowd I asked that only two of them should accompany me.

We entered the village by a gate in a stone wall which separated it from the river, as if by way of protection, and I found myself channelled along hot, narrow stone streets. The stones are the foremost and fundamental feature that has remained engraved on my memory in connexion with the village. The paths were paved with flagstones; the bridges were made of stone slabs piled one upon another and linked with wooden beams; the garden fences, the walls of the houses— everything was made of the same rough-hewn grey stones. The gables rose up like rounded hummocks, so that the rows of houses along each street looked like the waves on the sea.

As a matter of fact, Hsiao Chou did not in the least conform with my idea of a collective village. The word kolkhoz automatically conjures up visions of hard-driven, tired peasant faces, haunted by the fear that they might not reach their output target, and might therefore be criticized or even liquidated. But this village looked every bit like any other village in Eastern Asia. Under a stone gateway opening on to a street half a dozen young people were sitting on the ground, right in the middle of the morning, playing cards, while a little way behind them an itinerant tinker heated his holed cooking-pots and cans over a flame. It was the familiar picture of people who had all the time in the world and who enjoyed their time in a contemplative manner. As a stranger I was instantly surrounded by a thick throng of people—adults and children. Like a moving wall the crowd followed me about, pop-eyed: a European, a real European!

Presently we found ourselves sitting in the co-operative centre, which was housed in an old temple. In front of me sat Lu Si, the head of the collective farm. For Hsiao Chou, as he proudly explained, was one of the most advanced villages in China, which had long passed beyond the stage of semi-Socialist co-operative farming, in which most other villages still remained. The meaning of this transformation emerged most clearly from the story of the young man himself, as told through our interpreter.

Lu Si was also totally unlike one's idea of a collective-farm boss. He was not a tub-thumper or an ambitious slogan-parrot, but a quiet young man with almost timid fawn's eyes, which made one feel that the slightest sudden movement would immediately cause him to scamper into the bushes. He looked as if he would not hurt a fly. His shyness was best illustrated by the fact that, at the age of twenty-seven and in spite of his position in the village, he had not yet found a wife, but was living with his aged mother in the same dilapidated little house on the edge of the village that had been allotted to him before "Liberation" by his landlord. For at that time Lu Si had only been a simple farm-hand without land of his own, and his annual income, in terms of present-day value, would have been no more than 80 yuan, although, of course—rather like a farm-hand in Europe—he had received free board and lodging from his master.

His fate had been shared by many others. Among the seven hundred families in the village of Hsiao Chou only thirty-six had been big landowners, owning between them more than two-thirds of all the land. Even so, their holdings needed a magnifying-glass to be regarded as 'big estates.' There were no big landowners in China, certainly not in the South American style, and many of the 'feudal' landlords would have been regarded even in Europe as, at the most, medium peasants. Nevertheless, the fact remained that half the peasants at

Hsiao Chou had owned no land at all, or only a little scrap that was not big enough to live or to die on. Needless to say, these have-nots were delighted at the arrival of the Red Army and, with it, the prospect that they too might join the ranks of the possessing.

In 1950 came the Land Reform, under which Lu Si received as his property not only the little house he occupied, but also 9 mau of land, an acreage calculated according to a man's family—in Lu Si's case his mother and younger brother. One mau equals about 645 square yards, or three-twentieths of an acre. For two years Lu Si enjoyed the independence of free landownership; at last, in 1952, the peasants were persuaded to give up their 'lone-furrow ploughing' and to work in co-operation. There was not much compulsion about it, nor did it mean surrender of one's property: the Government was moving very warily in first bending and then breaking the individualism of the peasants. The 'mutual-aid teams' flourished. Nobody could deny the advantages of joint, concerted effort, and even those who had at first kept aloof were forced to admit that co-operation had its points.

In 1954 came the next step towards the mousetrap of the *kolkhoz:* the semi-Socialist co-operative. Why keep the land parcelled up in individual plots, asked the 'cadres' who had been posted to the villages as advisers and administrators. We can work more profitably, they argued, if we put our fields together and cultivate them as larger units. It will then be worth while to lay out irrigation schemes on a bigger scale, and one day our manual and draught-animal labour will be replaced by tractors. The persuasion campaign lasted three months; by the end of it 96 families had organized themselves into three co-operatives. Lu Si's annual income rose to 600 yuan, including the interest which the co-operative paid to him on the value of his piece of land.

By 1955, 407 families had joined the co-operatives, and in January 1956, when the Peking Government accelerated its drive towards collectivized agriculture from a moderate trot into a mighty gallop, Hsiao Chou was ready to take the final step, the step into the *kolkhoz,* which turned the entire population into the wage-earning labourers of a single super-enterprise. Now the villagers were divided into six separate teams. Everybody worked eight hours a day. To check any idleness that might result from a flagging of private interest, payment was governed by a system of points. Every job done represented a definite number of points; even Lu Si was allowed to book points for his committee meetings and chairmanship duties, which accounted for about 15 per cent of those he earned by the work of his hands. Now even the last claim to ownership of the land had expired—a claim which before had existed at least in theory—and each individual had become a complete slave of the organization. Only 65 square yards per head remained in private cultivation as a personal vegetable plot.

I tried in vain to get an answer from Lu Si as to the advantage of collective farming over co-operative farming. He replied with a vague assertion that a further degree of centralization must result in even more economical management and hence in higher yields. 'Higher productivity,' it appeared to me, was to him as magical and unquestioned a concept as rain-making and the exorcism of spirits had been to his superstitious ancestors. And would he really maintain that the whole village had voluntarily and enthusiastically taken this step? This time it had not taken three months but a mere five days to condition the peasants. He merely nodded his head with the timid fawn's eyes.

Perhaps, I thought, I would get more information out of his former master, the landowner. I asked if I could see him. Kang Wang-po occupied two ramshackle houses behind a fine temple, now serving as a collective-farm storehouse. The houses did not look exactly lordly. He had given up the better of the two to his daughter and sons, and he and his wife lived in a room where the rain came through the ceiling. One of his daughters was cooking in a primitive, cave-like hole. The two superior houses which he had owned in the past had been taken away from him during the Revolution, together with three-quarters of his land. Kang had been a very shrewd and active landowner, and had owed his wealth chiefly to his own initiative. He had increased his patrimony of 30 mau to 62 mau—which is about 8 acres—of which 16 mau had been left to him after the Land Reform for his family of nine. He had, in fact, come off lightly compared with some of his class companions who had been tried as reactionary villains by People's Tribunals and liquidated.

And now Kang had become a small peasant like everybody else—or, rather, with one difference. Hitherto, because of his suspect past, he had not been *permitted* to belong to the co-operative in case his former authority should enable him to regain his old influence. But now he had been *allowed* to join the *kolkhoz*—on a provisional basis, on probation. Voluntarily and enthusiastically, needless to say. Why? I asked him, though I thought I knew the stereotyped answer in advance: for the sake of higher productivity. But Kang's reply contained an element which went beyond the usual pattern. In

spite of his fifty-eight years and his reduced circumstances
one could still feel the master in him, and by his side Lu Si,
the new boss, still looked as if he was about to ask how much
sugar-cane he should bring in from the field to-day. "I've got
a family to feed!" he protested almost indignantly. "And independently I couldn't do it any longer—not on what land
I've left, or with my outdated methods. The collective farm
fields are producing better crops: they get fertilizers, better
seed stock, young plants. . . . I am simply better off by joining. . . ."

Kang, moreover, kept silent about an aspect which the businessman King in Shanghai had at least hinted at: he had
been not only lured into the *kolkhoz* by the bait of better
seed stock, fertilizers, and other advantages, but had also been
whipped into it by taxes and all kinds of chicanery which the
authorities of Communist countries contrive to inflict on any
freedom-loving individual until his independent existence is
made such a hell to him that he prefers the sweet servitude of
kolkhoz membership. On the other hand, the tendency in some
Western countries to regard the *kolkhoz* as such as an inven-
tion of the devil and its members as pitiful victims of some
irresistible terror seems to me to go too far. Undoubtedly a
collective farm that is not functioning must be hell itself, if
only because it keeps a merciless hold on any individual who
might wish to escape from its state of decay. But since my return from China I have been to Poland, newly freed from
Stalinist compulsion, and have spoken to collective farmers
who were not muzzled. And even in that country, where individualism has always been almost an endemic disease and
experiments in collectivization would seem to be foredoomed,
there were co-operatives which were functioning well and
which continued their collective existence of their own free
will. As in so many other things, *C'est le ton qui fait la
musique*—in other words, it depends on the spirit in a *kolkhoz*
whether it will be a going concern or get stuck in the mud.

Naturally this is not an easy thing to discover on a two
days' visit. Lu Si conducted me over the fields of his farm,
where, instead of entire families toiling each on their own
little patch of land from early morning till late at night, properly organized labour teams were harvesting sugar-cane or
digging irrigation trenches across newly laid-out sugar-cane
plantations. Apart from sugar-cane the village lived mainly
by its orchards, the produce of which was sold in Canton. I
was struck by the fact that wherever I saw people working
there was a distinctly cheerful and relaxed atmosphere. I
thought with a smile of the strict discipline in the sugar-cane

plantations of Central America, where, against the Biblical injunction that the ox who treadeth out the corn should not be muzzled, the workers were strictly forbidden to chew any sugar-cane. Here, in a terrorized China, the workers calmly went on chewing even when the *kolkhoz* boss approached them, and only one team of men in a new field decided, when they caught sight of him, to cut short their prolonged siesta and with a few groans throw up some more spadefuls of soil.

This suspicion that collectivization was perhaps not, after all, an inhuman and despotic manœuvre was further confirmed when I watched at his work one of the three 'cadres,' who had been sent to the village by the Government to explain its intentions to the peasants. He was engaged, together with the peasants, in constructing a platform for the impending New Year celebrations, in front of the school, which was also housed in a former temple. He was easily identifiable because he wore, not the black pyjama-type garment of the peasants, but the blue overall which had become a political uniform. He was not a native of the village, but came from a neighbouring province; he had got his post here not so much because of his Communist beliefs—for he was clearly not a man of theories—as for his practical ability and drive. Wherever a job needed doing he was the first to tackle it, encouraging the young men who were hanging around to lend a hand. And not for a moment did his example seem to meet with sullen opposition; on the contrary, there was a distinct measure of cordiality in the way he was obeyed.

I had my evening meal with Chin at the local inn, whose landlord must have been, politically speaking, living on the moon, or else endowed with second sight: from his wall an over-lifesize portrait of Malenkov gazed down upon his guests. On leaving the room we saw the landlord's wife light a stick of incense on the altar of a house god; Chin smiled contemptuously at this piece of superstition. We spent the evening at a meeting of the collective-farm council, composed exclusively of former farm labourers. The meeting went on for hours without any spirited speeches or argument. Even the two women members of the council denied their sex's virtue and vice by wrapping themselves in silence like the rest of the taciturn peasants. Lu Si, who was in the chair, did most of the talking. As the peak of hospitality one of the 'cadres' had put his house at our disposal for the night; he himself was being put up by friends. The house was one of the best-built in the village and had obviously seen better days—*i.e.*, a rich owner. Evidently not all the upstarts were as unselfish as

Lu Si. The altar of the house gods still dominated the room where I slept, but their benign features had been supplanted by Mao's.

Before going to bed I had an argument with Chin when I criticized the peasants' lack of freedom.

"Nonsense," he said; "nothing is done here unless it has been decided by the collective-farm council."

"But what happens," I rejoined, "if the council happens to differ from the Government?"

"That never happens," declared Chin. "The Government does not demand anything without first explaining it to the peasants."

"But suppose the people stick to their views in spite of all explanations?" I persisted.

"In that case," Chin said disarmingly, "they continue to be invited to explanatory lectures until they agree."

In case the reader doubts whether observations made in one village carefully picked by the Government can have any general validity, I was lucky enough to conclude my stay with an adventure that was clearly possible only in the relaxed atmosphere of Canton—an improvised, unexpected visit to another village.

For February 14, New Year's Day proper, a "race of dragon ships" had been announced on the Pearl River. I imagined some wildly romantic and colourful race, something in the nature of the water festival in Cambodia. But when I inspected the so-called dragon ships during a kind of preview I was disillusioned. They were quite simply ordinary river steamers, dressed in coloured pennants and huge portraits of Mao, which were to parade along the river. They could keep it! But at that moment I noticed on the quay a lorry into which blue-clad figures were being loaded as tightly as sardines. "Long live the Alliance of Workers and Peasants!" a banner proclaimed in huge letters. Chin explained that the workers of Canton were driving out into the countryside to bring the peasants gifts and good wishes on the occasion of the New Year.

"Splendid," I said. "Let's join them."

But naturally the scheme proved more difficult than I expected. The leader of the workers' delegation wrung his hands and assured me that, though he would be delighted to take me along, he could not possibly do so without an official permit, and such a permit was unobtainable because the local office of the Foreign Ministry was closed on holidays. Here it was again—that constant, irritating attachment to the umbilical cord of the bureaucracy which had obstructed my every movement throughout my visit. In Peking I had been held a prisoner in the Principal's office of a Russian-language school for several hours because I had entered the building without an official letter of introduction. Even when I tried to watch the pickling of cabbages in a vegetable garden outside the gates of Peking I was chased away, because that too, presumably, required a Ministerial letter of introduction to the cabbages. I now really lost my temper and vented my anger on poor Chin.

"There, you see," I fumed, alluding to our discussion at Hsiao Chou, "what a slave existence you Chinese are leading. I'm not even allowed to drive out into the country with these workers, although they would like to take me along, simply because you've got to ask permission first for every damned thing."

Chin, obviously at a loss for a counter-argument, bade me wait, and disappeared into the office of the China Travel Service. A little while later he emerged triumphant.

"You're wrong," he crowed. "I've got the necessary document—not from the Ministry but from our Service. It ought to be sufficient."

So I climbed cheerfully into the lorry, and we left the city in a northerly direction. Soon, however, I discovered that something was wrong. Somewhere along the road there ought to have been decorations and a cheering reception committee to welcome the workers and lead them in triumph into the village. But there was not a soul along the road anywhere, and the townsmen did not know the way to their destination. The lorry pulled up, we climbed out, made some inquiries in near-by houses, and eventually cut across some fields. The first person we met at the entrance to the village was an old man: his eyes opened as wide as saucers. The whole village, he told us, had turned out the previous day in their Sunday best and waited for us; to-day most of them had gone to Canton, including the headman. Nevertheless, they would see what could be done. The old man hurried off to alert the villagers; the workers returned to their lorry in order to approach the place by another route so that they could, after all, arrive in triumph and among cheers.

I for my part went off to explore the village. To my amazement, I suddenly found Chin a changed person. At first he rehearsed the full range of his persuasive skill to keep me pinned down over a glass of tea at the co-operative centre. When he did not succeed he next tried planting himself in front of me, and, like a traffic policeman, diverting me into side-streets. Stubbornly and with growing astonishment I pursued my own course. Suddenly, after turning a corner, we saw an unusual sight before us: at our feet, right across the

village square, crouched a whole army of male figures in
khaki uniforms, eating their midday meal. Questioningly I
turned to Chin, whose mysterious attitude had now given
way to undisguised anxiety. "Come away from here," he
whispered. "This is a punitive column of the Army. We are
on military territory." Now I saw the sentries guarding the
prisoners with sub-machine guns at the ready; one of them
abruptly pointed his weapon in our direction and with an
imperious gesture waved us away.

I did not for a moment hesitate to obey. The military in
China are not a joking matter. But I could not deny myself
a little reconnaissance of my position. The village where we
found ourselves was situated right in the middle of a military
zone: barracks, ammunition dumps, and living quarters were
scattered over the surrounding hillsides. The only strange
thing was that the prisoners I had stumbled upon had not
been engaged on military work. They had been busy in a
pineapple plantation belonging to the Army! Presently, when
I had climbed up to the village burial-ground on a small hill,
I could see hundreds of acres all around me planted with this
sweet fruit. The prisoners, many of them, no doubt, political
offenders, were engaged in gathering it. Each group was
guarded—and, as I judged from their extreme haste, also
spurred on—by at least two soldiers with sub-machine guns.
They did not, by the way, look underfed. A glance into their
billycans had revealed ample helpings—certainly more plentiful than ever dreamt of by their comrades-in-misfortune at
Auschwitz or Vorkuta.

Meanwhile a 'cheering crowd' of about a dozen people had
assembled at the entrance to the village, and the lorry with
its load of joyfully beaming workers could at last arrive. The
men dismounted, unloaded the presents, and bore them in triumph on their shoulders to the co-operative centre. There
they were exhibited to the admiring glances of the villagers.
They included the latest novelty in Chinese agriculture—a
twin-furrow plough. For to this day throughout the length
and breadth of the country a simple ox-drawn plough is still
in use, which scratches rather than turns the soil. The gifts
further comprised ten pounds—literally only ten pounds—of
rice seed, of a new, especially heavy-cropping strain, and
about forty pounds of Communist propaganda literature.

Nothing could illustrate better than these presents the
primitive condition of Chinese agriculture to-day. One twin-
furrow plough for a whole village is regarded as a tremendous
innovation at a time when visions of tractors are already being
dangled in front of the peasantry, and when these tractors
are used as a justification for the amalgamation of privately

owned plots of land and the compulsory establishment of collective farms! And ten pounds of seed! The seed, I was told, would presently be planted, and only the harvest from it would provide the seed stock proper.

From all this one may not only draw the conclusion that the collectivization of Chinese agriculture has been a quixotic experiment for the sake of Marxist-Leninist theory, but may also ask, what is the use of tractors in a country as overpopulated as China? Why save human labour at the cost of expensive diesel oil, which still has to be imported from abroad, when providing work for this surplus of human beings is a difficult enough problem anyway?

[GREENE, 247–255]

In many cities communes adapted to urban conditions have made their appearance. In the beginning this was by no means a mass movement, as it has been in the countryside, but an experiment, rather cautiously undertaken.

The Communist Party Resolution adopted on December 10, 1958, approaches the matter in the following terms:

"There are . . . certain differences between city and countryside. Firstly, city conditions are more complex. . . . Secondly, socialist ownership by the whole people is already the main form of ownership in the cities . . . therefore the switchover of cities to people's communes inevitably raises some requirements different from those in the rural areas. Thirdly, bourgeois ideology is still fairly prevalent among many of the capitalists and intellectuals in the cities; they still have misgivings about the establishment of communes, so we should wait a bit for them. Consequently, we should continue to make experiments and, generally speaking, should not be in a hurry to set up people's communes on a large scale in the cities. Particularly in the big cities this work should be postponed except for the necessary preparatory measures. People's communes should be established on a large scale in the cities only after a rich experience has been gained and when skeptics and doubters have been convinced."

By June 1960, when I arrived in Peking, there were already more than a thousand urban communes in operation, with a membership of fifty-two million. There seems little doubt that such communes are here to stay.

I visited a number of them in different cities of China and

I have selected the Red Flag People's Commune of Shenyang as being fairly typical, in its organization and activities, of the whole group. In size this happens to be relatively small —84,000 members. (I visited a commune in Harbin with 182,000 members.)

I met the director, Mr. Kao Peng-fei in a clean, whitewashed upstairs room. Because of the heat, some bright toweling had been thrown over the leather chairs. There were no pictures of Mao, no slogans, no banners on the walls, which added to its unstandardized, and therefore welcoming, appearance. But it was a poor room nonetheless. The rough boards had just been sprinkled to keep down the dust. One geranium grew in a pot. The lampshade was of brilliant Mexican pink.

Mr. Kao struck me as one of the many eager, professional Communists who form the backbone of the Chinese revolution. He spoke deliberately, thoughtfully, taking his time to think out his answers. There were, as usual, two other persons in the room, who said nothing at all, but they took no notes.

The Red Flag Commune, Mr. Kao told me, was established in September 1958. It had passed through various stages of development and experimentation but everyone believed it to be now on the road to a healthy growth. There were 17,383 member families, 84,375 people. (It is significant that I always have to ask for the total population. This has been true in every commune, they always think in terms of families, not total numbers.)

Mr. Kao proceeded, interrupted by occasional questions from myself, "Many of our families live in very old houses, forty years old or more. These are very poor and they will have to be pulled down as soon as we can arrange for new buildings.

"Altogether, seventeen workshops belong to the commune, employing 6500 workers, of whom 85 per cent are women. The men work in the larger state-owned factories also situated within the commune area. In our commune workshops, we make 259 different kinds of products. One hundred and fifty are for local, home use (consumer goods, I presume he meant), eighty are parts for the factories, and the rest are for several rural communes outside the city.

"Total value of our production has risen very fast," said Mr. Kao, "as more and more women joined and as our skills increased. In 1959 total production was 18,660,000 yuan ($7½ million). This year our target is 150 million yuan, more than eight times our last year's product. From the figures so far, we believe we will reach this target. The value of our production is determined by standards set by the government, based on national average production costs.

"The Red Flag Commune operates nine primary schools (ages seven to twelve), four middle schools (thirteen to eighteen), and twenty-one spare-time schools for adults. We run thirty-two nurseries and kindergartens of medium size and 130 small nurseries. In all we look after nearly 17,000 children. Of course, we also have our own hospital and many clinics and health stations. Also we have three markets, and 137 dining halls which provide meals for some 49,000 people a day. The rest eat at home, or in state-owned factories where they work."

I asked how he thought the communes had started.

"It seems to us the people's commune system didn't come into being all of a sudden," said Mr. Kao, "but that it came out of the political awareness of the people, out of the kind of economy we have in China." And he quoted from the General Line: *"dwo kwai hao sheng*—more, quicker, better, more economical." The higher level of political understanding, particularly among women during the great leap forward, the excitement and enthusiasm all made it difficult for housewives to sit quietly at home—they all wanted to come out into life and take part. No matter how little they knew or how unskilled they were, they wanted to contribute what they did have.

"So they began to set up little workshops together, in the streets, in people's houses, anywhere there was a spare room. And they began, as we say, 'with empty hands,' that is, without any financial help from the government. Then, of course, because the workers were housewives, something had to be done about the children. They started kindergartens and the nurseries, and then the canteens so the women wouldn't have to cook after they went home.

"At first," Mr. Kao continued, "all this was handled by street committees in the various neighborhoods. But there were many difficulties and it became very complicated, there were so many things going on at once and overlapping one thing over another. At this time we began to hear about the rural communes and some of us went to see them, to see if we could use some of their ideas for our situation in the city. Many of us thought an equivalent movement could be started and we heard this was actually being done in some places. So we went ahead and that's the way it got started here."

I asked, "How much resistance did you encounter?"

He thought for some time before he answered, "I'm not

sure one can say there was resistance, although many people doubted whether we could make a success of the idea. What you must realize is that 85 per cent of our members are house-wives, women who were very isolated, and rather fed up with household chores. They were eager to start something new which would bring them out into the world more. But there was a lot of fear, too, and people looked down on women's capacities just because they were women, even the women themselves. 'No good can come out of a group of women, they can't do anything!' And we certainly ran into problems because the women had so little experience and didn't know what they could do—or what they couldn't, either. We made many mistakes sometimes because we tried too much, and other times because we didn't try enough.

"You must remember, too, that membership in the com-munes is *entirely voluntary*." He spoke with great emphasis. "No one was forcing these women to join. So those who weren't sure waited to see what the others would do and how successful it would be. When they were reassured, they ap-plied for membership."

"*Applied?*" I repeated.

"Oh yes; membership is by application. Each new member is discussed beforehand and must be approved by the man-agement committee. You see," Mr. Kao concluded, "if those of us who were starting out had forced or overpersuaded the others to join and then had made a mess of it, what a ter-rible discouragement that would have been! The last thing we wanted was a group of disgruntled women, they could have ruined the whole project."

I asked, then, if we could set out on a tour of the com-mune.

Our first stop was at what they call a "service station." No, they were not selling oil and gasoline. The Chinese service station is the Chinese commune equivalent to an American shopping center. There was a row of small booths, each offer-ing some particular service. Here was a tinker repairing pots and pans. Next door was an artist hand-lettering notices and posters. Then watch repairs, keys made, the cobbler's; there was a service station (staffed by women who enjoy sewing) for altering or repairing clothing. There was an electric-fan repairer, a laundry, a place where movie tickets could be bought, a bank, a post office. There was also a rental shop where bicycles, tools, electric motors, etc., could be rented by the hour, day, or week. All these services are run on a no-cost, no-profit basis. The women attending them are paid the same wage as those in the workshops. Prices were very low. I asked how much it would cost to patch a small boy's trousers; about ten fen, they said (four cents); to launder a shirt, four fen (one and a half cents); to rent a saw, fifteen fen (six cents) a day.

Farther down the street we came to a machine shop. This was a very simple structure, built, Mr. Kao told me, by the women themselves. None had ever laid brick before, but two old craftsmen from the old people's home had showed them how. (The men were too old to walk around, so sat in chairs directing operations.) Walls seemed a bit out of plumb, doors not very square; but here it was, housing over 150 housewives all hard at work with power machinery, hack saws, drill presses, stamping machines, armature winders. I also noticed two first-rate precision lathes.

Over the clatter of the machines, I shouted, "Who started this?"

Mr. Kao pointed to a red-cheeked woman of about thirty-five, adjusting a drill press. I went over and yelled, "May I ask you some questions?"

She nodded vehemently, wiped her hands on her trousers, and led the way to a window where the din was slightly less.

"What gave you the idea of a machine shop?" I asked.

"Oh, I didn't do it all by myself. There were twelve of us." She waved over to another woman to join us, and the two of them talked, sometimes one, sometimes the other. "It was in 1958 when there was all the talk about everybody pitching in, the great leap forward year. And we wanted to do *something*. So we went to a small bicycle factory nearby and asked if we could make parts for them and they said yes."

"Did any of you have any experience, or money?"

"No. But the factory lent us two hundred yuan, and another factory that makes generators did the same. We needed a stamping machine, and we found where there was one, but not working; it was all broken down. Then the bicycle factory helped us repair it and gave us a few lessons on how to use it. So we started. We worked at first in a shed at the back of my house."

I asked, "What did the neighbors think?"

"Oh, they were very sarcastic. *'Now let's see how these women will do!'* " Both women burst out laughing and one added, "Till the Party heard about us and sent some technical people to help us. From then on it went pretty well. We filled the orders for the bicycle and generator factories and others came in and more and more women wanted to join."

"How many women do you have working now?"

"Four hundred and fifty."

"Four hundred and fifty! Here?"

"Oh no, they don't all work here. We have another workshop we built a little distance away. And, of course, we work two shifts in each place. We only work four or five hours a day, the women have housework to do at home or children to see to. Oh, we feel very confident now. We feel we could do almost anything."

"How much did you turn out last year?"

"Well, it was only in September 1958 we began. And in 1959 we really were just getting under way. We had to take time off to build the workshops, and find the brick and all that."

I tried again. "But how much did you actually produce?"

"Our income?—what we got paid for our products? In 1959 one million, thirty thousand yuan" ($257,000).

"And what do you expect it to be this year?"

"If the whole year keeps on like the first half, ten million yuan" ($4 million).

"Who paid for the machinery?"

"We paid for it, out of our profits." One of the women pointed to a new drill press. "That's paid off completely. The others we're still paying for little by little."

"Did you borrow any money from the government?"

They shook their heads. "We only had the loans from the bicycle and generator factories, four hundred yuan in all" ($160).

"What's the average wage you pay these women?"

"We don't pay them. This is a co-operative. We all get the same wage. Usually, a little over thirty yuan a month" ($12).

"Do you use piece rates or an hourly wage?"

"At first we tried piece rates. It didn't work. Caused lots of trouble and argument. Now it's all hourly."

"How old is your oldest worker?" I asked. "And how old is the youngest?"

"Forty-five. And nineteen."

I thanked them and after a quick handshake they went back to their machines.

Urban communes are now an established and growing feature of Chinese life and one can legitimately ask what effect they are having on the national economy. By altering the status of millions of women, both national productivity and national income have been increased. The output of the urban communes in 1959 was reported as 2 billion yuan ($800 million) and they expected to at least double it in 1960. This is not a large sum in relation to a national productivity of over 241 billion yuan. But this addition to national production, it must be remembered, has been achieved with virtually no capital investment by the state.

3. The Schools

[SCHMID, 155–156]

The kindergarten of Tio Er Hutung was housed in one of those magnificent Peking buildings which undoubtedly belonged to some grand reactionary gentlemen in the old days and which are now, upon the former owners' disappearance, used as institutions, schools, or nurseries. Among all the innovations in China these occupy the first place numerically: kindergartens and workers' palaces are the sights to which every visitor, unless he has a very definite programme of his own, is treated by his guide in interminable succession. Besides, kindergartens really are among the most attractive things to be seen in the new China. Chinese children are, without exaggeration, the most charming children in the world, gifted with an innocent *buffo* nature which continually gives and exacts smiles. The hardening to which the souls of the adults are subject from Communist indoctrination and intimidation has not yet touched them. There is about them a delightful self-assurance and familiarity. I shall never forget one of the most pleasant incidents of my trip: a bunch of little children were following me about the darkening streets of Hankow. *"Sulyen"*—i.e., "Soviet citizen"—they called after me lovingly, and each in turn would push his way to the front, to walk alongside me, proudly and delightedly holding hands with a "big brother." Their charm had turned into a warm reality the propaganda phrase drilled into them.

Propaganda starts early in their lives. Yang To, in charge of the Tio Er Hutung kindergarten, told me that their political training began at the age of three. When I asked her the purpose of such training she defined her educational aim as triple love: love of the motherland, love of work, and love of Chairman Mao. In her kindergarten there were seventy children, their ages ranging from four months to four years, looked after by no fewer than twenty-six adults, counting everybody from Yang To down to office staff, teachers, and cooks. It was quite obviously a kind of luxury establishment, and I was presently informed that her charges were the offspring of senior officials of the Party and Governmental hierarchy. Unlike most other small children, they were not delivered in the morning and collected in the evening by those

amusing bicycles which enliven the street scene in Peking
with their special enclosed baby trailers. So that their parents
should be free to devote their energies fully to their higher
tasks these children stayed at the kindergarten throughout the
week, and were taken to their homes only at week-ends, that
they might at least get an occasional glimpse of those strange
ladies and gentlemen who were regarded as their physical
progenitors. Yang To was surprisingly young for her appointment: she was only twenty-two. When I asked her why the
post had not been entrusted, as would be the practice in the
West, to some older and more experienced teacher she replied that for this kind of work a person's political qualifications were more important than her pedagogical ones.

These political theories, however, did not seem to make
much difference to the kindergarten routine. The children of
the élite 'cadres' were mainly busy with rubber balls, cham-
ber-pots, and picture-books whose pages were peopled with
Disney-inspired fairy-tale beasts rather than with Commis-
sars.

[CROFT, 58–63]

The Secondary School was another crack job. It had been
built nearly a hundred years before, but since 1949 had been
enlarged and modernised. It catered for fourteen hundred
pupils and had a staff of seventy-three, of whom one-third
were engaged in 'administration'—a comprehensive definition
which covered every conceivable activity from duplicating
lesson sheets to sweeping the kitchen floors.

To say that schooling is compulsory in China would be un-
true but not altogether misleading: it would be compulsory if
there were sufficient schools for the purpose. Education was
formerly the preserve of those who could afford it or who
could obtain it as charity from the churches and missions.
Now, given the bricks and mortar, it will become a universal
reality within a very few years. I was given so many statistics
on the advance in education since the defeat of the Kuomintang that it would be difficult to quote any of them intelligibly
without reference to the rest. Suffice it to say that four times
more children go to school than did in 1949, but in the primary schools there are still only sixty million places for
eighty-five million pupils (although many schools work a
two-shift system)—and the biggest advance has been in secondary education.

Secondary schools are divided into junior and senior departments, with pupils from twelve to sixteen at the former and from sixteen at the latter, although technically they are eligible to join the senior at any later age. (I came across several young men in their early twenties who had recently gained admission after working their own way through the entrance tests.)

The average size of a junior class is fifty pupils, that of a senior forty, but where accommodation permits these numbers are often exceeded. As far as I could gather, all secondary schools are residential and house not only pupils from outlying towns but many who live locally in conditions prejudicial to study. Those who can afford pay tuition fees of five *yuan* a semester while meals cost about five *yuan* a month, but are provided free in cases of hardship. The schools are mixed, but the boys and girls work in separate classes, meeting together in the evening 'for songs and dances, poetry-readings and the celebration of cultural occasions.'

'The daily life of the pupils,' said the Headmaster, 'is regulated by their own Students' Association. They have their own Youth League and arrange their own after-school activities. In this way they are encouraged both to express themselves individually and to accept responsibility as members of society.' (For a moment my mind wandered dreamily back to my own teaching days; the last person I had heard expressing precisely those sentiments was the headmaster of an English public school. Take out the Youth League and you had an identical point of view—on second thoughts, perhaps, leave the Youth League in and read prefectorial system instead.)

The Headmaster was, of all the officials I met in China, the one with whom I felt the most immediate affinity, which is the more strange, since my own skirmishes with the teaching profession have left me allergic to most of its higher representatives. He had an eminently civilised respect for the mentality of his visitors and showed no inclination to dodge awkward questions. His statements were mercifully free from both classroom and political jargon, although if he had any ideological reservations he did not reveal them. As a practitioner in the most complex, exasperating, heart-warming and nerve-wearing craft of humanity, he seemed generously endowed with the qualities of inner conviction and practical good sense which distinguish the good teacher in any school the world over. Through his gentle, unruffled manner there glowed a spirit of missionary dedication and behind the easy good humour you sensed the formidable self-assurance of a man completely on top of his job.

I guessed he would be about forty-five, although in China it is impossible to estimate the age of any adult male with accuracy, especially when he had reached middle age. (Even at seventy some of them go on looking at least twenty years younger, for the wrinkles have come imperceptibly and the hair has a perennially youthful texture.) His dark-blue tunic with trousers to match—the popular uniform of the professional classes—seemed ill-suited to his benignly sensitive face; and the stone floor and stark white walls of the study, unadorned except for the ubiquitous portrait of Mao, suggested a severely monastic retreat rather than a control centre of knowledge and ideological enlightenment.

In his opinion, the function of the teacher was to exhort and encourage, not to coerce or compel. Pupils were entitled to criticise the teacher if they felt they were not being properly treated—although that was a rare occurrence, he emphasised, and could only happen after the Students' Association had given careful thought to the complaint. The students were certainly not *encouraged* to criticise the staff—that was far from the official intention—but in cases of serious injustice 'or some such matter as excessive laziness on the part of the teacher' the students would wish to express their grievance. 'In this way,' he added, 'the students can do a great service to the teacher by enabling him to realise his failings, and their criticism will help him to become a better teacher.' While I was still musing upon the impact this admirably unorthodox scheme would make if introduced into schools in the purlieus of Camden Town or Hackney Wick, the Head went on to speak of corrective principles:

'Pupils are punished only in order to help them improve their work. A lazy or negligent pupil is given a bad mark, and this will make him ashamed of his shortcomings. The other pupils also will try to help him through the process of criticism and self-criticism. If he still persists in his fault—which is unlikely—his parents will be told and they will urge him to improve himself, for they value the opportunities he has been given. No,' he smiled rather wearily, as though at a threadbare joke, 'we have no corporal punishment. That is forbidden in the Constitution. In any case,' he added, 'the teachers themselves are opposed to it.'

From what I could see, the curriculum was much the same as that of an English grammar school, except that there was no specialisation, and Music, Arts and Crafts, Botany and Hygiene were compulsory subjects. There were, however, certain differences in nuance and approach; and there were also the two periods per week of Political Instruction.

'What is the philosophical basis in your teaching of History?' asked the indefatigable Crabb.

'Since the Liberation,' explained the Head patiently, 'we have, of course, introduced new text-books in this subject, as in all the natural and social sciences. The basic facts remain the same, but we no longer regard History as a colourful list of generals and emperors—it is interpreted as the evolutionary struggle of the peoples of the world.'

'In other words,' said Crabb, 'the subject is merely an historical extension of the Marxist doctrine?'

'Let us say,' said the Head, 'there is a difference in viewpoint and analysis of the facts.'

'In your Political Instruction do you teach any other philosophies besides Marxism?'

'I freely admit that our ideological basis is Marx–Leninism, but we also consider the western philosophies. The aim is to encourage students to develop their powers of independent thinking, and this will only be achieved if they are introduced to different systems from their own.'

'Suppose they discover that they prefer those systems to their own?'

'We should not prevent them from expressing their ideas.'

'Or acting upon them?'

'If they acted against the interest of the people that would be a different thing. We should never tolerate that. In any case, we believe that ultimately, through the process of discussion, they would form correct opinions.'

'What is your attitude,' asked Littmarck the Swedish Y.M.C.A. man, 'to pupils from homes where there is a strong religious background?'

'Every pupil has the right to his individual religious beliefs. He is not compelled to accept Marx–Leninism.'

'But the atheistic teaching at school must conflict with the religious teaching of his parents. Surely it is undesirable to subject him to a strain of this kind?'

'The School has never had complaints from parents about this. I think that they regard the problem the same as we do —the solution is to let the pupil choose for himself. You see,' he observed with winsome impartiality, 'today our country respects religious belief. We believe in tolerance and compromise, and there is freedom for religious propaganda as there is for Marx–Leninism. It is true to say,' he added, with what could hardly have been intentional irony, 'that the State *protects* religious beliefs.'

Outside on the bone-hard turf of the recreation ground the

School was at play. A dozen different activities were going on at once. In one corner, boys were playing on the swings; in another, practising the high jump or vaulting the gymnasium horse. Down the centre of the field two separate games of football were in progress, and all along the perimeter, regardless of the hurly-burly around, pupils of all ages bunched together in little groups to practise basket-ball. Suddenly the sombre considerations of Marx–Leninism, the necessity for forming 'correct opinions', the philosophical basis in the teaching of History or anything else, seemed irrelevant: here was a scene of enjoyment unqualified; gay, noisy, robust, invigorating—just what a school should be, and not laid on for anyone's benefit, but demonstrably the way it normally behaved when it was let out to play. The pupils paid little attention to us until Galal borrowed a football and we began kicking in at the goal. I soon understood how Galal had won his international cap; from twenty or thirty yards out he fired the ball time and again into the net with professional nonchalance. The word quickly spread and pupils crowded round to watch. I left Galal to it, delighted that he had found at last something positive in the way of Physical Education.

From one of the classrooms came the excited din of high pitched young voices and, wandering away by myself, I looked in through a broken window: two young boys were playing table-tennis while a hundred or more, jumping, leaping, shouting, screaming, urged them on from the sidelines with a competitive enthusiasm which you would have expected to put the players off their game altogether. Instead it seemed to have the reverse effect, for the protagonists maintained a concentrated calm which many older players would have envied. On each side of the room, oblivious, it seemed, to the fiendish clamour around, equally young children sat in almost motionless pairs, solemnly playing chess.

None of the children noticed me until the table-tennis battle was over, and then they rushed out to drag me inside. While they chattered and babbled and I spluttered to say something by way of reply one silent, serious-looking boy ripped a metal badge from his tunic and thrust it in my hand. It was a gift not to be refused, but it merited, I felt, something in return. I fumbled through my pockets, but could find nothing there. All I could do was to squeeze his hand, pat him on the head, and mutter something which was neither English nor Chinese, but which would convey, I hoped, that I was both touched and grateful. It was not a badge I would have chosen for myself, being a likeness of Chairman Mao, but it was given with a good heart and I wore it in my duffle coat during the rest of the trip.

[GREENE, 56–62]

I went out the other day to visit a kindergarten near Peihai Park. There was, of course, the usual briefing on general background, over cups of tea; the same emphasis on growth ("We started our kindergarten in 1949 with thirty children; today we have four hundred"). And here too, 1958, the "Year of the Great Leap Forward," had been decisive, because that was the year in which perhaps tens of thousands of mothers went out to work for the first time in industry. There was also the same sense of boundless optimism, the same conviction that human happiness would be achieved through solution of immediate tasks. It would have been senseless, here, to have raised a question as to the *purpose* of education. The purpose was to produce citizens each of whom would carry his fair share of the burden of socialist society—just as the purpose of the steel mill was to produce those structural members which would support the roofs and bridges of socialism.

My hostess, Miss Chiang, was the director. She sat very trim and neat in a blue skirt and rose-colored blouse. Rather "correct"—like schoolteachers all over the world. Her voice was gentle, but I suspected this concealed a very determined and efficient nature. The room we sat in was full of sunlight and we could hear the children at play outside. "Our children," Miss Chiang said, "when they grow up, will take their place in the country's work—they will be children trained in Communist ideals. They will love labor. They will respect people."

"How can you teach them proletarian politics at four?" I inquired.

"The principles," of the education of children," said Miss Chiang, "are expressed in the *Five Loves:*

"1. Love of Motherland,
"2. Love for People,
"3. Love of Work,
"4. Love for Knowledge,
"5. Respect for Public Property."

"How . . ." I began.

"These principles," Miss Chiang continued, "are taught according to age levels, in conversation, songs, nursery rhymes, art, and games."

I went with her into several of the classrooms. In some the children ran up to me, catching me by the hands and tugging me this way and that to see the things in their room. (How much, I wondered, was all this really spontaneous?) They seemed not at all disturbed by the arrival of a stranger, and a foreigner at that. In one room I found the class gathered in a circle around the teacher, all singing together while the children took turns acting the parts of the song. They performed their parts with much gusto. One little boy, when his turn came, leaped to his feet and shouted his lines at the top of his lungs. I asked what the song was and learned it was about the pig-breeding campaign on the farms and a man who raised a pig that weighed five hundred kilos.

Here are the words of other songs they were singing, as they were translated to me word for word:

> I have a good mother,
> She works in the fields;
> She works so hard that the commune
> Has presented her with a red flower.
> Our mothers are all good.
> All are working
> For the benefit of our new country.

> We clap our hands we are so happy!
> The communes are so powerful!
> My father works in a factory!
> Our country is led by the Communist Party!
> My brother drives the tractor,
> My sister works the loom,
> The electric light lights every household.

As I walked back to the reception room with Miss Chiang, I learned more about the kindergarten.

Many of the children go home every evening, some stay from Monday through Saturday. The school keeps close contact with parents, and parents may visit whenever they wish. Some children, having lived happy-go-lucky lives at home, find it difficult to adjust, at first, to the ordered routine, and particularly in the all-week group, children get homesick when they first arrive. For this, there is a period of "full-time looking after"—which means that a single nurse or one of the younger teachers is in constant contact with the child, and becomes (though this was not the term Miss Chiang used) a mother-substitute. The child looks to this person for comfort and help, and the teacher or nurse, by watching the child closely, learns what his problems are: eating and sleeping habits, likes and dislikes. In this way the child learns quite quickly to adjust to the community life of the school.

Personal possessions are not allowed. Everything is *ours*, nothing is *mine*. Toys brought by the children are put into the common pool.

I asked about the signs one looks for in emotionally disturbed children. About bed wetting. Very infrequent. Nurses on duty at night know the ones who need to be wakened during the night. Thumb sucking? Only a few suck their thumbs when they first come—but it doesn't last long. Night terrors? Never more than a few weeks.

"None of the teachers are permitted to tell gruesome or frightening stories," Miss Chiang told me quite severely. "If you walk around the bedrooms at night, you might hear children laughing in their sleep. Fears are very rare."

"Temper tantrums?" I had to describe the symptoms.

"No, we never see children in that condition," Miss Chiang said. "We have naughty children, of course. But we always believe that these naughty children are the clever, specially-gifted ones—we just have to direct their energies. So we let a naughty child be captain of a ship, or locomotive driver. We let him use his talents and he ceases to be the naughty one."

"Do you teach them," I asked, "about American imperialism?"

"Yes, we do, as far as they can understand it. We tell them that American imperialism is the greatest enemy of the world. But the ordinary people of the world, even the ordinary workers and farmers of America, are their friends. The teachers here, for example, took part in the great anti-American rally a few weeks ago and they told the children about it."

Miss Chiang filled the teacups. We were now back in the reception room bright with chintz slip covers and sunlight. There was a fragrance of incense in the room, and from outside, the sound of the children calling to each other on the playground. Flowering quince brushed the open window and beyond I could see the shadow of a willow tree against a wall. A Chinese miniature.

"Do you not think," I asked Miss Chiang, "that these international enmities will have been resolved by the time these little children grow up? And what can a child of four or five understand about these affairs so far removed from their young lives? What can they possibly *mean* to them?"

Miss Chiang replied, "We are socialists and proletarians. Imperialism exists. It is a fact. And we believe it to be the greatest single danger to our world. Even children must know these realities. We tell them about China's past, too. These children were born after liberation, but they must know something of conditions before that. They ask, 'Did you have kindergarten then?' No, we were so poor we could hardly keep ourselves alive, we tell them; and many of us died of hunger. You from the West can have no concept of our poverty and hopelessness in those days. But our children must understand this. They must know of our past, our present, and our future—and the dangers that lie ahead from imperialism.

"We have a Chinese proverb: 'Think of its source when you drink water.' We want our children to think of the source of their improved lives when they enjoy planning and eating and singing at a nursery school like this. The source is the socialist state which we are building. . . ."

And with steady hand Miss Chiang refilled our cups.

*

A Letter to a Friend, a child
psychologist in California   June 18

Dear Isabel

Hardly a day goes by without my wishing you were here so we could talk. There's so much going on—this country is in full creative ferment, but much of it remains a puzzle to me. The *outside* stuff is reasonably easy to follow—the material progress since I was here before: the schools, the new hospitals (hundreds of them), factories, kindergartens. Vitality and confidence in the future are apparent everywhere—you should just see the young gals stepping down the street with pigtails swinging, as if the wide world belonged to them. And the kindness they show to each other and to strangers! That's fine; one can make some sense of all this. But what goes on *inside*—especially what goes on inside children? It's just here I am most baffled. . . .

I have spent a lot of time watching children playing in the streets—little tots all on their own. They are endlessly inventive in their games—a piece of wood or a bit of string will keep them happy for hours. *They never fight. Why* don't they? They never snatch—never "that's *mine!*" They seem to have almost no *personal* achievement motive, no combativeness; another child coming along will immediately be included in the group (no exclusive "gang" feeling); and no apparent anxiety about absence of adults. They not only never fight but they *never cry*. The only child I have heard crying was one who was physically hurt. *What's* going on?

Some of this can be explained by the almost total permissiveness in the handling of children. I saw a small boy piddle in the middle of a big department store. *He* didn't mind, his *mother* didn't mind, other people didn't mind; the department-store man who came to mop up smiled as if it were his special pleasure to mop up little boys' messes. I have seen a child squat outside a store-front, and the storekeeper came out with brush and pan and stood courteously waiting till the boy had finished. A small child can do no wrong, and is surrounded by people who look after him. If he is traveling alone in a bus, an adult gives him a seat. To him *all* adults are "uncles" and "aunts" and so the need for the presence of his *own* parents seems less important. His assurance comes from the adult world in general, not his own parents in particular. All this must have a very profound effect on a child and his feelings about himself.

But that's too simple and too pat. Because from our point of view these Chinese children are all *too good*. It seems as if total permissiveness leads to total docility—and a docility that continues into adulthood. I have never known a people who all think so much alike—and they *really* do, it isn't put on for reasons of political security. I am quite convinced that if there was an absolutely free vote in this country, an overwhelming majority—way up in the 90 per cent bracket—would vote the same way. It is a monolithic structure, *not* based on external coercions but on what is much more powerful—a psychological unity. This in the end may have its profound weaknesses, too.

I have tried to make some cross-checks about children in the kindergartens and hospitals—places where young children would be away from home. Bed wetting? Very rare. Only in three- and four-year-olds. At the big kindergarten I visited today, the director could recall only one instance of persistent bed wetting at the six-year level—and this turned out to be a girl with a physical bladder ailment. Homesickness? A little at first. Easily handled. Crying at night? No known cases. Temper tantrums? Lying on the back, kicking the heels, screaming? They look at one another in amazement. No they have not had any problems like *that!* Fights? Very rare. Their idea of genuinely *naughty* behavior seemed to be for one child to push another. At the kindergarten I visited, and in several nursery schools, I have asked, "Do they own anything of their *own*? A doll? A toy?" And the answer is *no*. If the child brings something from home, it is put in with all the other toys.

Here they have a great many toys that belong to all of them, was what the teacher at the kindergarten told me. *They don't want anything of their own.*

But *don't* they? If they do, and are angry about having to give up their own particular thing, where does the anger go? Where is the aggression going? What's happening to the normal childhood hatreds? I haven't the faintest idea, and I can find no clue. The collective, *national* aggression finds outlet through hatred of an externalized enemy, *America;* but this cannot be an adequate channel for individual frustration among the young.

Here are some other facts to throw into the melting pot: Young children take on responsibility very early. You see a child of four caring for a baby of one—feeding it, playing with it, keeping it warm, carrying the baby for blocks, staggering under the weight. Also helping with family chores, cutting up vegetables—really tiny children.

Adult docility. I went to Peking's only prison a few days ago, having been interested in penal reform in England, and here I found the Chinese doing what we had been trying to get the English authorities to do for years without success. Mainly, of course, to get the stigma, the moral stigma, out of imprisonment. Peking has a total prison population of 1800 —an incredibly low figure in a municipal area of seven and a half million. Forty per cent of these are political cases, but all mixed up, no segregation. The "security" is minimal. There is one guard at the gate with a rifle (the gates are open) and there is one guard in a tower. No one else is armed. The walls are low. No locks anywhere. The window bars have been replaced by large casement windows. In one workshop of about fifty prisoners I asked where the guard was and was introduced to a smiling youngster in a T shirt who was showing a prisoner how to fix a machine—he was the only warder in this room. If these were American prisoners they would all be out of that place inside three minutes. Why don't they escape? (Very occasionally a prisoner walks out—one every two years or so; they are ready to take that risk, for the benefits that an "open" prison confers.) Here is docility taken to an extreme. They have great re-education sessions—"reform through education" is the slogan.

Now to my point . . . Can it be that the Chinese child, having had a total sense of *belonging* when young, has a permanent, built-in dread of being "outside," of *not* belonging? A Chinese child, unlike ours, has never had to learn to be on his own bucking opinion around him, has never learned to stand on his own rock. So that the worst possible psychological pain to a Chinese adult might be to be socially outcast. Is this at the back of their "re-education" process? Is it the permissiveness, the total security for the Chinese child, that makes possible the monolithic quality of their social structure? In other words, that dissent becomes a psychological impossibility?

Or is the structure of the unconscious itself different? After all, the Chinese developed their society for four thousand years uninfluenced by Western concepts and behavior patterns. Is it possible that the highly separate, individuated consciousnes which some of our psychological historians believe develope in Western man only at the time of the Renaissance, has neve had to evolve here? In other words, that the consciousness of being separate from *you* is not so sharp here as it is with us? *Me* and *not-me* tend to merge in the collective *we?*

If we are to understand the Chinese (who are rapidly moving to a position of world influence) we simply cannot go on taking for granted some of our own psychological assumptions. We must escape our own cultural conditioning sufficiently to see them in terms of *their* assumptions. I stand here baffled at behavior which seems to turn some of our neat conclusions upside down—behavior which cannot adequately be explained by any of our accepted theories but which to them, of course, appears commonplace. . . .

4. Universities and Institutes

[ESKELUND, 39–49]

When I woke up, I lay wondering for a moment. What was I was looking forward to? Then I remembered where we were going today. I shook my wife, but she merely grunted and turned her back to me.

"Chi-yun," I said, "we're going to Yenching!"

That worked. A moment later she was out of bed, sweet and smiling, and I even got a good morning kiss. Yenching is our old university. It was here we first met, and just the name brought back memories of the time when we were eighteen and in love.

"Don't forget to put on your woollen underpants, Chi-yun," came Mrs. Fei's voice from the next room. She still treated her daughter as if she were a child. I was not excluded from her motherly solicitude, either. When we were about to leave, she came running with a woollen scarf. I had better tie it over my head, she said—the wind was very cold and I had no hat.

I assured her that it was quite unnecessary. I would turn up my collar, I never caught colds . . . I did not quite succeed in convincing her, but at least I escaped from being dressed up like an old farm woman.

Half an hour later Chi-yun and I drove out through the Western City Gate. For a moment I thought that we were on the wrong bus. I knew the road so well from the old days— this was where the city stopped and one was suddenly in the country. But all the little farmhouses with paper windows had disappeared, and where there once were fields was now one great building complex after the other.

They must be factories, I thought. The air was full of smoke and the place had the impersonal atmosphere of an industrial district. But for the characters above the gateways, one would not have thought that this was China. Chi-yun translated them for me.

Geological Institute, School of Metallurgy, School of Mining, Department of Chemistry . . .

And so it went on. A whole town had mushroomed since the Communists came into power in 1949, and it was still growing. Scaffolds reached towards the sky, horsecarts came rumbling, loaded with bricks.

It was refreshing finally to see old Yenching which is one of the most beautiful universities in the world. Chinese-style buildings are scattered over a large campus among artificial lakes and hills and a lovely pagoda. The sunlight sparkled on the glazed tiles of the slanting roofs as if to bid us welcome home.

We got out of the bus and walked towards the entrance. I took Chi-yun's hand. Do you remember . . . Over there was the library where I had sat at the same table evening after evening, well groomed and in my best suit. I don't think I ever finished a page—I was too busy gazing at a Chinese girl who blushed and pretended not to see me. And beyond, underneath a big tree by the tennis court, was the bench where I had kissed her the first time . . .

"Hey—where are you going?" A uniformed man beckoned us back to the gate. In the old days we had entered and left as we pleased, but now we first had to telephone Mr. Liang with whom we had an appointment. We did not know him; the meeting had been arranged by the foreign office. We filled a printed form with our names and address and the gateman stamped it.

"Remember to have Comrade Liang sign it," he called after us. "Otherwise you cannot get out."

Mr. Liang, a plump youngish man who was secretary to the president of the university, received us in a small meeting hall. In Red China, all contact between people seems to take place in meeting halls. As soon as I saw Mr. Liang, I began a guessing game which I have become addicted to since our arrival in this country. I try to figure out whether or not people belong to the Communist party.

Liang seemed to possess all the characteristics of a Chinese Communist. He was kind, understanding, straightforward, but his smiles and movements seemed deliberate. There was a slight touch of condescension in his manner, and he seemed to lack the usual sense of humour of the Chinese. He was very sure of himself, one felt that no sudden impulses were ever permitted to disturb his composure. It was the head that ruled, not the heart.

"Are you a member of the Communist party?"

He looked at me and nodded. Opposite us sat a bespectacled young man with notebook and pencil held in readiness. That was Mr. Liang's secretary who was going to take down our conversation. The mere sight of him took away my desire to make the interview. Now I understood why some people suddenly become dumbstruck when I take out my notebook.

"How many students are there at the university?"

Mr. Liang handed each of us a mimeographed sheet, filled

with statistics about new China's progress in the field of higher education. It was impressive. Since the liberation—that is to say: since the Communists came to power—Yenching had been merged with two other universities. The number of students had increased from barely 800 to 8011. 21.5 per cent of them were girls, 22 per cent came from worker or peasant families. There were also 310 students from the Soviet Union and the other Peoples' Democracies. In Peking alone there were twenty-one new colleges and universities, and in all China, 217,000 youths had graduated from higher institutions of learning since 1949. That was 7,000 more than during the previous fifty years . . .

I got up and thanked Mr. Liang. Here was all the factual information I needed. Now we would like to talk to some students, but we could manage that ourselves—we knew the place so well.

Oh, no, Mr. Liang would not hear of that. It was his duty to help foreign guests, he said. He told his secretary to make some telephone calls. A while later six students came, two of them girls.

It was as if twenty years suddenly vanished. These students could easily have been my old schoolmates. They had the same intense earnestness that made them seem older than European students of the same age. Then suddenly they would start laughing and giggling over nothing. How childish, one thought, until one realized that it was shyness. They felt unsure of themselves, especially in the company of foreigners. Perhaps it was partly because they had been brought up under the Chinese family system. They had been taught to obey, not to think and act independently.

But when Chi-yun and I had talked for a while with the six students, we discovered that there was a difference after all. The first thing they asked me was what I thought of new China. I replied that there were many improvements since I had been here last. The distribution of wealth was more equal than before. Those who belonged to the former lower classes were no longer cringing and humble. They had acquired self-confidence. The amount of building done since 1949 was fantastic . . .

I kept waiting for them to contradict me. Common courtesy almost required them to do so—when you praise the food in China, the host must answer that it is poor fare, not fit to be served to guests. But these young people nodded and smiled—and then they even began to outdo me in praising their own country!

Chi-yun and I soon discovered that they kept repeating certain words and phrases. Now Chinese students have always had a tendency to learn by heart. I suppose it is because they have to start memorizing the many Chinese characters from early childhood. Their memory is highly developed, but not their ability to judge. When during my student days I had discussions with my Chinese schoolmates, I would often catch them reeling off something which they did not understand. They had just learned it by heart from some book.

But in those days they had at least memorized whatever they pleased. Now they could hardly say anything without quoting Marx or Lenin or Chairman Mao, as he is called in China. If one student got stuck, another one would quickly complete the quotation for him. And when one of them said something, the others would nod approvingly. That was almost the worst part of it—they did not seem to disagree about anything.

I could tell that Chi-yun was also disappointed to find the students so one-track minded. We had no feeling of contact with them. I soon got a suspicion, though, that the Marxistic phrases which they kept reciting did not mean very much to them. Sometimes they did not even seem to understand them. But they could clearly see the progress which China had made under the Communists. *That* meant a great deal to them.

"I'm going to be an engineer," said Wu, a stocky fellow who bit his lips when he became excited. "What opportunity would I have had if I had lived under the reactionary Kuomintang régime? I could have taught other Chinese students who, like me, would never get a chance to practise what they learned. Or I could have got a minor position in a foreign engineering firm. At that time, the foreigners were in charge of all important engineering projects in China. Chinese were never given important posts. The foreigners looked down on us.

"It isn't like that in new China. We're respected now. We build our own bridges and dams and power plants. We're even beginning to make motor cars and airplanes . . ."

One of the girls broke in. She had a habit of emphasizing her words with sudden nods that sent her plaits flying. When the Communists entered the large cities along the coast, there were many girls in the Red Army. They all wore their hair in two long plaits, like farm girls, and since then it has been the fashion.

"I'm going to be a journalist," she said. "What chance would I have had when the reactionary Chiang Kai-shek clique was in power? A journalist couldn't get anywhere except by writing lying, reactionary propaganda . . ."

"Don't Chinese journalists write propaganda today?"

"Yes, but that's *true* propaganda." The plaits flew. "It is

our duty to make the people join the struggle against reactionary enemies inside the country and imperialistic enemies outside. We must make the people realize how grateful we all
should be because Chairman Mao and the Communist party
have united our country and made it strong and respected . . ."

The others nodded eagerly. I thought of the anti-Japanese
demonstrations that had often taken place when I was a student here. Then the students' feelings had also run high, but in
general they had been disillusioned and apprehensive about
the future. In those days China was corrupt and torn by civil
war. The students had no respect for the government. They
longed to do something for their country, but how could they?
As the girl had said: in those days you got nowhere except by
licking the boots of those in power.

"In new China there is no corruption," she concluded. "All
the people work together towards a common goal."

"Yes, there certainly is a new spirit," I said. "In many ways
the Communists are idealists . . ."

"No–" they all protested. Chi-yun and I looked at them in
surprise.

"Idealism is a form of bourgeoisie romanticism," one of the
students explained. "In new China we strive for realism. Idealism is the opposite of realism and is therefore contrary to the
principles of Marxism-Leninism."

I mentioned Hungary where the peoples' rebellion had just
been crushed by the Russian army. The students protested
vigorously against what I said. They had read in the papers
that fast fascist elements had tried to seize power and deprive
the Hungarian people of its freedom. This they believed.

"But let us assume that the Hungarians really were dissatisfied with the Communist government . . ."

"But how can one assume that?" interrupted the girl who
was studying journalism. "The Communists are the only ones
who really do something for the people. We have seen it so
clearly in China—all our former governments only plundered
the people. And Chairman Mao has said that the people can
always distinguish between its friends and its enemies—so of
course the Hungarians would never rebel against a Communist government . . ."

I changed the subject. I had heard that the students were
now organized in small groups of six or seven each. Was that
for political purposes?

They looked questioningly at Liang who was listening with
a fatherly smile. No, one could hardly say so, replied Wu, the
engineering student. There was practically no political activity
at the university.

"It's to help each other," the girl studying journalism broke in. The members of a group studied together and discussed whatever problems that came up. They looked after each other —if something was wrong with one of them . . .

Something wrong—what did she mean by that.

Well, a student might have a "dark spot" in his past— maybe something he had not confessed. Or maybe deep inside he disagreed with some of the changes brought about by the Communists. Such things were bound to come out sooner or later—when he was in a bad mood, or when he lost his temper. Bad moods and fits of temper were the very symptoms one could expect from people who still held reactionary views —people who put their personal interests ahead of the group and the country . . .

"And what if you find such a dark spot in someone?"

Then they would talk to him and make him see that he was in the wrong. If he disliked something which the government had done, they would explain why it had acted as it did.

"And in the end, the student always realizes that he is in the wrong?"

"Yes, of course. After all, nobody else in the group agrees with him—the majority is against him. You can't go on thinking incorrectly."

At the end of the semester, each student has to write a report appraising himself and the members of his group. These reports are compared, and in this way it can also show if a student thinks "differently."

If he does, it will be noted down in his political dossier. This dossier tells everything that is known about the students' background and his attitude towards the new society. When he graduates from the university the dossier is sent to his employers together with his diploma. From then on it is the duty of the employer to keep the dossier up-to-date . . .

But all this I learned later on from a private source. Foreigners are not given such information. Nor do they learn how the professors at China's universities were "re-educated" after the Communists came to power.

In each case, the "re-education" began with a mass meeting. The professor in question was surrounded by the students, who made accusations against him. I learned that the former president of Yenching had to answer five hundred questions prepared by his most "progressive" students. Was it not true that he had had many American friends? That he despised Marxism and believed in liberalism? That shortly before the liberation he had said to some foreign friends: "When the Communists take over I may be forced to say things which I don't mean?"

Sometimes the interrogations would continue over several

weeks. The professor knew that if he did not follow the "new course"—or pretend to do so—he would lose his job and would not be able to get another one. In practically every case he ended by writing a public "confession"—he had been led astray by capitalistic and imperialistic ideas, but now he realized that Marxism was the only way for China . . .

One reads these humiliating confessions with perplexity. Some of them were written by the most brilliant men of China. Did they really mean it? One cannot ask them, but the confessions are suspiciously alike.

The universities also keep political dossiers for the professors. Once a year they have to send in reports on their political progress and to appraise the attitudes of their colleagues. If a professor is the head of a department he has a political "adviser". Purely academic problems are left to the professor, but in all other cases he has to consult his adviser, who is a member of the Communist party or a "progressive".

Later on I talked to a teacher whom I knew from the old days. I promised not to use his name. That is why he dared to talk freely.

"Even when we are teaching botany or physics, we have to inject politics into it," he said. "Let's say that I tell the students that milk bottles should be sterilized. I have to add that thus one can save lives for Chairman Mao and democratic new China."

The teachers meet daily to discuss their work. They often attend each others' lectures. In this way the more progressive teachers can make sure that their colleagues have a "correct" influence on the students.

"I must admit that in some ways, education has improved," the teacher said. "We have to prepare our lectures much more thoroughly than before—if one doesn't, one will soon be found out."

The students meet regularly to discuss their teachers. If they are dissatisfied with a professor, he is asked to come and hear their complaints. Maybe he speaks indistinctly, or does not write clearly on the blackboard. Of course it is much worse if he is accused of having a "reactionary ideological attitude".

When the Communists came to power, practically all lessons in English, French and German stopped. They were not prohibited, but everyone knew the attitude of the Communists towards the capitalist countries. Those who wanted to study their languages might easily be suspected of having reactionary views.

All over the country, people began studying Russian. Those in public positions—teachers, engineers, journalists, doctors scientists and officials—took concentrated courses of eight hours—yes, *eight*—a day for one or two months. After a couple of years this method was dropped, however. It turned out that people forgot their Russian even faster than they had learned it.

Most of the old textbooks were replaced by Russian ones which were translated into Chinese. Once a university needed a textbook about typhoons—the violent tropical storms that rage along the China coast. The word is of Chinese origin and means "big wind".

There were excellent works on typhoons in both Japanese and English, but they could not be used, as they had not been written by people with the "right attitude". There are no Russian textbooks about typhoons—they do not occur in the Soviet Union—so the students had to manage without.

About a year ago the Communist leaders must have realized that education was becoming dangerously one-tracked in China. The country was isolating itself from the rest of the world by using only Soviet textbooks and by making Russian virtually the only foreign language. Chairman Mao made a speech, stating that China had much to learn from the capitalist nations. He encouraged the students to study western languages.

So now English had suddenly become popular again at the university. "But we have to start from scratch," said one of the students—in his class they had not progressed much beyond the ABC.

As a result of this new "liberalism", Marxism had lost its all-overshadowing positions at the universities. Students of philosophy have recently resumed the study of Confucius, who had been put in a corner ever since liberation. Shortly after our arrival in Peking, workmen even began repairing the old Temple of Confucius, which had become sadly dilapidated.

But the professors have been instructed to emphasize that all the non-Marxist philosophies—the products of civilization during thousands of years—are unrealistic and false . . .

It was noon when Chi-yun and I left Yenching. As we stood near the gate, waiting for a bus, we were joined by a foreign student who was also going to town. It turned out that he was a Yugoslav. He had studied at the university for a year and spoke Chinese well.

Did he like being here? He shrugged. It was interesting, but in a way he was disappointed. Why? He looked around. There were only the three of us, so he began telling us about his experiences at the university.

Every foreign student has a Chinese "friend" who helps him with the language and gives him advice. Three months ago the students from the Eastern European countries had called a meeting with their Chinese "friends". The Soviet students were not included—they always keep to themselves.

The foreign students were indignant. Under cover of friendship, the Chinese students had spied on them—they had written "reports" about the European students for the authorities.

The Chinese were more astonished than anything else. Why all this fuss? They wrote reports about each other all the time —why shouldn't they do so about their foreign friends?

At this point the Yugoslav was interrupted by the arrival of the bus. It was crowded as usual, so on the way back to Peking we talked about other things. One never knows who is listening—one might just as well be careful . . .

[WILSON, 175–180]

After breakfast we drove to the Northwest University on the opposite side of Sian and were met by the vice-president, Professor Cheng Po-sheng (a distinguished and charming scholar); Professor Wang Yung-yu, who had accompanied us the previous morning; two grey-headed, stalwart geologists, Professors Chang Pei-shen and Mo Shi-chen; and the head of the physics department, the intelligent, nervous and bespectacled Kiang Jen-shu.

After polite introductions, we were ushered upstairs in the main building of the university to a plain room that might have been a meeting-hall or a faculty dining-room, for it held a U-shaped table covered with a white cloth at which sixty-five people could sit. In the corners were pots of flowering plants, and on the walls an electric clock and pictures of Mao and of famous local buildings.

When we were seated with our tea and cigarettes, the vice-president explained to me the history and work of Northwest University. (He was kind enough to allow me to take these notes while he was speaking.)

"At the beginning of the Sino-Japanese war, three universities that had been located at Peking were moved to Chengtu and became united into Northwest University. At the end of the war the university was divided into medical, teaching, engineering colleges and so on, some of which came to Sian. Some of the university professors left Shansi for Peking. Thus before the liberation the staff was weak and the building poor. Since the liberation, new buildings have been started facilities and instruments have been provided. The teaching staff has been increased, so that now there are fifty professors and another two hundred and fifty junior instructors, but because the university is so newly established, the proportion of new and inexperienced teachers is high. The number of students has increased from seven hundred to three thousand.

"After a period of reorganization, there are now ten departments: mathematics, physics, chemistry, biology, geology, geography, law, economics, history, and Chinese literature.

"In general, class-room education is combined with practice. For example, at the present time many geologists are making maps in the country; students of geography and biology are in the mountains exploring; students of economics are working in the factories, and only the freshmen are to be found in Sian when the term is about to begin. This year there will be nine hundred new students, but only three hundred are coming from Shansi, the rest from all over China, mainly from Honan and the Yangtse valley. Although the number of high schools in Sian has been increased from four to twelve, and six more are being built as part of the Great Leap Forward, there are not enough high-school graduates to fill the four universities now located at Sian—this one, Northwest Industrial University, the College of Commerce and the College of Architecture. We have therefore brought students from elsewhere.

"Students get free tuition, dormitories and medical treatment, and at least 70 per cent of the students get subsidies or scholarships to pay for food and clothes."

"As at the University of Peking?" I interjected.

"Yes," he said, "but of the senior middle-school students, only a quarter qualify for college; the rest have too poor marks. Any that qualify can go to college.

"The students have some choice of courses. The decision is based partly upon preferences and partly upon the results of entrance examinations taken upon arriving at the university. Thus if the physics department plans to take one hundred and twenty students and three hundred students wish to enter, the one hundred and twenty students with the highest grades are accepted and the other hundred and eighty have to be content with their second or third choices. The university course is four years and, in the College of Commerce, five. As yet we have no graduate work.

"After graduation, the method of placing students is democracy mingled with centralism. There is a general shortage of university graduates, and of course every ministry and academy wants them and sends lists of requirements. Each graduate writes a report about his wishes and then in turn takes part in a public debate. After discussion, it is decided to what place each student is to go. The university does its best to meet the desires of the students. For example, if a man has to look after his family, he may be certain he will be sent to a position near his home; but if he has no family he may be called upon to go farther away. Ultimately, the school authorities will persuade students to go to the best places."

A bell at 9:30 brought some of the students to the courtyard to exercise. They did not appear to be very enthusiastic about it, but after five minutes quite a number were doing calisthenics. This reminded the vice-director to point out that care was taken of the students' health and that less work was given to weaker brethren.

"Every year the university has a new building program which is regulated according to the growth of the student enrollment; this year, for example, buildings to accommodate five hundred more students are being added."

The physics professor then asked me to explain what we were doing in physics at the University of Toronto. After I had replied, he told me that the physics department wished to exchange literature, particularly in the fields of low-temperature physics and the viscosity of metals. He said, "Although we have no graduate students, we professors do research."

We then toured the campus, starting at a meteorological and seismological observatory that was contained in three rooms. There was a receiver for radio time signals, a clock made in China and a room devoted to interpreting earthquake records. I went down some stairs into an underground vault and saw two sets of horizontal seismographs—mechanical recorders of the 1951 Type 1 and Type 3 models—for recording the large earthquakes that occur in the Yellow River valley. In a third, unlighted, room were three Chinese Kirnos instruments. On the roof were ordinary meteorological instruments.

Outside, a new library building, five stories high and perhaps two hundred feet long, was nearing completion. It was completely surrounded by the traditional type of bamboo scaffolding, tied with ropes, but I noticed that an electric hoist instead of man-power was being used to pull up materials.

Another new U-shaped building, which we did not visit, was said to house biology, geography and literary studies.

Physics and geology were housed in a typical well-built,

three-story grey-brick building. Most of the few students in it were busy putting up wall posters, written in Chinese characters on old newspapers and on green and purple paper.

On the ground floor were physics laboratories, many of them equipped for advanced, if old-fashioned, experiments in optics. The vice-president, himself a geologist, remarked that optics was the president's specialty. The instruments had been made in many countries. There were optical instruments from Zeiss in East Germany, electronic equipment from Hungary, chemical balances from the United States, spectrographs from Japan; but most of the common meters, resistances, batteries, cathode-ray oscilloscopes, and common electrical parts were made in China; so was one big arc generator. I asked whether they had much Russian equipment, but they replied that the Russians were busy. On the walls I noticed tables of the technical elements and other charts printed in Chinese. The laboratory had many pictures of Russian scientists and of Mao Tse-tung on the walls. The only books that were actually in use by the few students there were in Chinese or English. The library had about 150 periodicals divided into Chinese, Russian and Western language sections; the last were mostly in English, but there were also some Italian, French and German periodicals, and I noticed the *Handbuch der Physik*. While showing them an article in it, I discovered that it was a multilithed copy; so were the copies of *Nature*. When I remarked on this, they became confused.

There were a few men and women working in every laboratory, and there was a meeting in the physics library. When we entered, all the participants politely stood up. Somehow it gave me the impression of being a political meeting rather than a technical one.

On the next floor I visited two large rooms devoted to a geology museum, and containing a more academic selection of specimens than I had seen in the Institute of Geological Prospecting. On the walls there were charts in Chinese illustrating evolution, Peking man and progress under the new régime.

They had a good geological library in which I found long series of such standard journals as *Economic Geology, Bulletin of the Association of American Petroleum Geologists*, and the *Journal of Geophysical Research*. I noticed that *Economic Geology* was in its original form up to 1956 but that subsequent issues were multilithed. When I again asked about the change in style, they remarked that it was hard to get Western periodicals. They had masses of Russian journals, including multilithed back numbers of *Transactions of the Academy of*

Sciences of the U.S.S.R. All the professors understood a little English, but clearly they were for the most part unpractised in speaking it; they mentioned that although there were no departments of foreign languages, all graduate students in physics were expected to read English, Russian and German literature as well as Chinese.

[CROFT, 64–68]

The novels of Maria Edgeworth lay dusty and abandoned in the cramped recesses of the room; unwanted, unmourned, the epics of Bulwer Lytton and the homilies of Hannah More, with half the silt from the turgid stream of nineteenth-century English fiction, had been washed up on the shelves around them.

I was in a remote wing of the library at Peking University with Wu-ping, a student of English. "Why don't they burn them?" I asked. "Or simply give them away?"

"They may be useful for future research," she said. "They will help us to understand your literary development, although of course we are not yet advanced enough to study it in detail."

The prospect of some advanced Chinese student in years to come refreshing herself on the tracts of Miss More and the dainty delights of Miss Edgeworth seemed so preposterous that I thought for a moment she was joking, for she was an exceedingly jolly girl; but she was stating an accepted academic fact.

She had been studying English as her main subject for three years. Most of the time was devoted to linguistics, but each pupil made a special literary study of various novels on the approved list. They were expected to take a year over each one, during which time they discussed the subject for one period a week with a tutor.

"Is he the expert on that particular book?" I asked.

"Not always," she said with unexpected irreverence. "Although he always thinks he is."

Her own special choice this year was *Wuthering Heights*, but the favourite with most of the students was *Vanity Fair*. The novel they apparently liked least was *Tom Jones*—'It is too difficult and old-fashioned for us'—a judgment which I should have thought much more applicable to the moralisings of Thackeray.

Wu-ping was a delightful girl: vivacious, attractive in a

buxom way, and with a mind of her own. But her light-hearted approach to things seemed somewhat out of place on the campus, where the prevailing atmosphere was one of diligent studiousness and academic care. Nowhere have I seen book-learning more assiduously pursued. In the reading-rooms and libraries every chair was occupied, and every occupant wore a look of furrowed concentration—a collective awareness of youthful responsibility—which set me thinking back humbly, but not regretfully, to wasted afternoons in White's and evenings frittered away in the Randolph in the Oxford of ten years ago.

Foolishly, perhaps, thinking I might catch her out, I decided to question her on the compulsory course in Political Economics.

'What does the teaching consist of?' I asked.

'We are taught what is correct,' she said, as though nothing could be more obvious.

'But do you learn anything about systems besides your own?'

'We believe that the capitalist system will fail and socialism will follow.'

'What kind of socialism do you mean?'

'Marxism, of course. But you cannot export socialism. We know that every country will follow its own path and evolve its own kind of socialism.'

'But'—I hesitated to embarrass her—'don't you know that we already have our own kind of socialism in the west? In Scandinavia, for instance—and we have it in Britain.'

The question did not so much embarrass as strike her completely dumb. Perhaps it was something she had never been told before. Perhaps she knew the answer but couldn't quite remember it. Perhaps she was simply afraid of being tricked into unwitting heresy—she should have been more on her guard from the beginning. At any rate, she said absolutely nothing until we changed the subject.

We made our way into one of the women's dormitories and eventually met a group of geology students. None of them could speak English, but they were delighted to welcome me and to talk about their work and plans for the future.

When they had completed their course, they said, they would be employed in work of national development, probably in the oil and mining camps of the north-western provinces. Yes, they would expect to be away from home for long periods—for three or four years at a stretch, perhaps—living in tents and huts in the wilderness of Kansu, Tsinghai or Sinkiang, prospecting for coal, oil and iron ore. Yes, they knew it would be a hard life, that the work was rigorous, conditions primitive, and the winters especially severe, but what of that? 'It is our great adventure,' they declared. 'We are working for the future. We shall be pioneers in building the new China.' (Did their eager enthusiasm strike a slightly chilling note? A shade too naïve perhaps, a little too ardent? Only, I reflected, to the westerner, brought up in a world too smart and complacent to be enthusiastic about anything.)

Marriage? Yes, they hoped to get married sometime. But that was a thing for the future. Why hurry into marriage when they had not yet started to live? Yes, they had boy friends at the University, but nothing serious, of course. No, boys did not make love to them—that would have been too serious. When a boy got to that stage it was as good as a proposal of marriage—something they could not allow. Looking round the little room where six of them lived together (some rooms were shared by as many as ten students) in double-tiered bunks packed tight against bare concrete walls, where the only furniture was a plain table and two rough benches, and their clothes and belongings were crammed into trunks and boxes under the beds, it was difficult to see how the boys had any opportunity to become even mildly serious. 'Of course it is overcrowded,' said the students, 'but what do you expect? Before the Liberation we could not have been here at all!'

We walked down gaunt barrack-like corridors and concrete stairways where washing had been hung up to dry, into the grounds of the old University. It was like stepping suddenly from the back streets of Cowley to the lawns of Magdalen Park, except that the contrast was more immediate and more extreme. Students dawdled at leisure in beautiful groves, under the shade of willow trees, or loitered along cypress-studded paths which ran down to the boat-house at the edge of a sleepy lake. On the far side of the water, pink lotus glowed in the sun; wistaria cast its blossoms on the lake, and gilt- and purple-tiled roofs gleamed through the trees. . . . But we had to move on to keep up with the Programme . . . past the playing-fields, the vast gymnasium and the massive new Philosophy building; past the ramshackle shed where the students had their bikes and shoes and suitcases repaired, past the huge canteens where overcrowding was so acute that, even working on a shift basis, the students had to eat their meals standing up; over the graceful lawns and the shale footpaths; back to the large and splendid Reception Room in the old building where the delegates were impatiently waiting and Dean Yen Jeng-ko was about to start his peroration.

'Before the Liberation,' he began, not boastfully but in relation to his problems, 'we had eight hundred students. Now there are over eight thousand. It is what you might call a headache and we know there is no easy cure.

'The University has been completely re-organised on a comprehensive basis. We have altogether fourteen departments and employ more than one thousand teachers. Many of these are American-trained and have recently returned to the University as a result of our new policy of permitting "flowers of all kinds to blossom, schools of diverse thoughts to contend".'

That statement, as he probably anticipated, set up a babble of interrogation, so much so that he invited delegates to put their questions in writing. He might have spared us the effort, for when he attempted to deal with the written questions he was still interrupted by a barrage of supplementaries; and with French, Swede, Canadian, Spanish and English tongues carrying on a strident argy-bargy with each other while, in an inimitable cacophony of their own, the interpreters laboured to serve all parties at once, it was impossible to make out much of what he had to say. (This unspeakable confusion was, of course, an occupational liability wherever the delegation went, although on more tedious occasions it provided welcome moments of light relief.)

The Hundred Flowers, explained the Dean, had made a fundamental difference to the teaching of economics and political philosophy. Although Marx–Leninism was, of course, the basis of the teaching, it was no longer denied that there were many rational features in the non-Marxist philosophies. Hegel and Kant, for instance, were now accepted in the Philosophy schools, although 'critically', while Malthus had been admitted into the teaching of economics. Many of the lecturers were known to be anti-communist, which was perfectly permissible so long as they did not translate their ideas into action. 'The anti-communist,' said the Dean, 'must accept implicitly the democratic dictatorship of the People's Republic. Within that context he is entitled to express the theory of other philosophies. In this university, for instance, are several students of the American teacher, Hanson, and the Englishman Keynes. They are free to teach what they wish and their views will be openly debated in the seminars. So that you see we have complete academic freedom. Only in this way do we believe we can arrive at the truth'—and the truth, the depressing truth at which you eventually and unfailingly arrived, however bright the prospect had seemed on the way—was: 'to make clear by the process of discussion why Marx–Leninism is correct.'

[CROFT, 191–193]

I betook myself one afternoon outside the city, beyond the sprawling new estates and technical institutes, the cabbage-fields and collective farms, to Futan University.

This was originally a Catholic establishment supported both by the Chinese and French, but it was now run as a comprehensive university with English instead of French—or Russian—as the main foreign language. New dormitories and lecture blocks were going up all round, but the central building retained its original character; and on the lawns in front of it, where students loitered casually arm in arm, the only visible sign of the new order was an enormous red banner proclaiming: 'Solidarity with the Glorious Soviet Republic on the Thirty-Ninth Anniversary of the October Revolution'.

I had gone without an interpreter and wandered about at leisure with senior students of the English faculty. It was an afternoon when I felt utterly relaxed, cheered by their enthusiasm and warmed by their friendly curiosity. We talked about the books they were studying—*Oliver Twist, Jane Eyre, Wuthering Heights, The Vicar of Wakefield*—and others of more recent vintage which I thought they should study; discussed the B.B.C., which many of them listened to; the English theatre, English games, English customs; and it was they, not I, who suddenly digressed on to the subject of Marx-Leninism.

'Is there a compulsory political course in English universities?' one of them asked, and when I replied that there was not, they debated the matter among themselves and then expressed these views:

'*It is unpopular with the English faculty here. . . .*'

'*It is popular with a minority, but we are opposed to it.*'

'*You cannot force people into believing a thing simply by making them learn it.*'

'*We are not opposed to communism, but only to the compulsory teaching.*'

'*We believe communist control is good for the country, but bad for the university. But we have made great progress since the policy of The Hundred Flowers and are allowed to express our views openly. We have been able to criticise the political teaching in our debates and discussions.*'

'Criticism is not enough; we are opposed to the teaching itself.'

At this point, I suppose, I should have sought to elicit further disclosures. But whether for fear of embarrassing them or through sheer mental indolence on a restful afternoon, I listened to the only expression of political heresy I was to hear anywhere in the People's Republic and did nothing whatever about it. Whether their remarks had any real significance I could not tell, but in a few moments they changed the subject rapidly as we were joined by a group of eager-eyed students from the Department of Journalism.

There was no doubting their views on Political Education. They were, without exception, delightful young men, vivacious, enthusiastic, bubbling with good humour; and they were also embryonic editors who would never be able to express a single original thought, apprentices to the deadliest form of hackwork devised by man. Their knowledge of Marx–Leninism not only had to be 'correct'; it had to be capable of accepting without a murmur that what was 'correct' one day might be equally 'incorrect' the next.

The one English newspaper they read was the *Daily Worker;* it gave them a chance, they said, to know what the People of England were thinking. They were astounded when I told them what most English people thought about the *Daily Worker.* They also had access to the *Manchester Guardian* and *The Times,* but the available copies were out of date. Recent copies of the *Worker,* however, alongside its American counterpart, were handily placed in each of the reading-rooms.

The availability of these was depressing enough, but even more so was the vast physical evidence of Soviet penetration on the intellectual front. Libraries and lecture-rooms were tacked with recent Soviet literature; the bulk of the textbooks were of Soviet origin; Soviet magazines and technical journals were piled on the tables, and those not from the Soviet were almost without exception satellite hybrids.

In the evening the students took me to their English Social. It was a bi-weekly event, in which they gathered at their tutor's flat to hold idiomatic conversation and play what their tutor assured them were 'English party games'. The latter bore as much relationship to English life today as Dotheboys Hall to a modern grammar school—but that was not the point. It was an evening of unequivocal pleasure in which the delight of the students at having a live Englishman in their midst was inhibited only by their inability adequately to express it. One can too easily be cynical about such occasions, but to these young people at least it was abundantly obvious that Peace and Friendship meant rather more than a worn-out Party slogan.

[CHANDRASEKHAR, 94–104]

"How does one obtain admission to these technological universities?" I asked the Dean of Tsinghua University in Peking, himself an engineer of some distinction. "We have given much thought to this question of admission," said the Dean, "and we have found that we could admit only the very best of our young men and women to become engineers and technologists." "Have you laid down any criteria for admission?" I asked. "Yes, we have three important criteria, and we follow them strictly. The first is that the prospective student must be oriented in socialist thinking; that is, he must be familiar with the Marxist approach to all our problems. Secondly, he must be in excellent health. The courses are strenuous, and we don't want students dropping out of the college for health reasons. And third and last, a student must have the requisite intellectual ability to cope with his studies."

"I can understand the second and third criteria, but how do you judge a candidate regarding the first?" I asked. "We have our ways. We keep tabs on the students right from their high school days. We know who is enthusiastic about socialism and the present regime and who has merely accepted the present order as inevitable. The convinced and enthusiastic are likely to become active and prominent members of the Communist Youth League. We know who is a real Communist and who is not among the students."

That was it. It was not enough if the student had the necessary aptitude, ability, and inclination to become a good physicist or geologist. He had to be a good Marxist physicist or an ardent Communist geologist.

Once the students are admitted to the portals of the technological institutions, their organized indoctrination begins. One would think that this was unnecessary, since only the converted among the youth are admitted. But the authorities are taking no chances. The student is exposed to the labor theory of value and the materialistic conception of history with the same vigor as he is to higher algebra and thermodynamics.

All the normal needs of the students are taken care of, though there is nothing luxurious about the accommodation, clothing, or food provided in the hostels; on the contrary these appeared to be Spartan and uniform and without any diversity or variety.

In Canton, I visited the well-known southern university, Chungshan (one of the given names of Dr. Sun Yat-sen). The Assistant Dean told me that, since Liberation, the university had grown enormously in buildings, equipment, and, of course, in student enrollment and faculty strength. What the Dean did not tell me was that Chungshan University had taken over (like Peita in Peking) the buildings, the library, and the entire equipment of the old Ling Nam University, a well-endowed American institution. Ling Nam is no more, and its assets have been transferred to Chungshan University without even a word of thanks to the Americans who had built it up through the years.

A singularly unacademic feature of the colleges and universities that forcibly strikes a foreign observer is that the heads of all of them are invariably fervent and seasoned Party men. Normally one expects the head of an academic institution to be either a distinguished scholar or an eminent educator or at least an able administrator. But one discovers in Communist China that the heads of even technical schools and colleges are not necessarily scientists or engineers—they are always veteran revolutionaries or prominent non-academic Communists.

Wuhan University is a typical example of this. In People's China, the city of Wuhan has become famous for four attractions. The first is the huge iron and steel plant. The second sight is the impressive Soviet-constructed bridge over the great Yangtze river. The third important attraction is the Heavy Machine Tool Plant, and the fourth is the university.

The university was not a post-Liberation affair but was founded in 1913 as the Wuchang Sun Yat-sen University. The campus enjoys a picturesque location. The beautiful buildings, typically Chinese in architecture, rise on the undulating Lo-ka hills beside the rippling and shimmering East Lake. An ideal environment for study, work, and living.

The President of the University, a stocky man in his fifties in the inevitable blue uniform, looked more like a retired prize-fighter than a professor or college president. Over innumerable cups of green tea and homemade cigarettes in his well-appointed office room, he made me an impassioned little speech:

"Before Liberation, there were less than a thousand students in this university. In 1952, as part of the reorganization of the educational institutions throughout the country, the

university expanded to some twelve departments and thre
independent colleges of engineering, agriculture, and medicine

"There are now 3,700 students, of whom 45.4 per cen
come from worker or peasant families. Women students con
stitute 15 per cent. The faculty consists of 450 members.

"Since the rectification campaign and especially since th
Second Plenary Session of the Eighth Party Congress pro
posed the general line of socialist construction, great result
have been achieved in carrying out the educational policy—
namely, education must serve politics, and education must b
combined with productive labor. Much valuable experienc
has been gained in carrying out this educational reform c
integrating politics with studies, combining theory with prac
tice, education with production, mental work with manua
work.

"Up to the present, this institution has set up over a hun
dred small factories and farms to provide students with oppo
tunity for participation in labor. These enterprises includ
iron works, a building materials plant, a chemical plant, an
farms producing a variety of products. Because of the utmo
exertions of students and teachers, the emancipation of the
minds, and the throwing overboard of their superstition
some of their scientific researches as well as their experime
tal products have reached and even surpassed advanced wor
levels.

"At present, in this university, struggle on the education
front is being carried on, the struggle between the two road
the two lines, and the two different points of view of t
capitalist and the socialist. Educational reform is proceedi
in a deeper and a more thorough way. We are thus endeavo
ing to build a new Communist Wuhan University."

After this speech, he poured me some more tea and ask
me if I had any questions to ask or any "friendly criticis
to offer. I wanted to know where he had been trained a
what his field of specialization was.

"I am the new President of this university," he told m
"I have had no academic training, for I have been all my l
a revolutionary Communist soldier."

A new slogan has recently been introduced into the C
nese educational system; I saw on every campus banners a
posters proclaiming: "Education Must Be Combined w
Productive Labor." This departure was one of the two me
ures introduced into China's school system at the end of l
year. The principle was novel enough, for the Director
Assistant Director of every educational institution tha

visited, from Sun Yat-sen University in Canton to Heilung-kiang University in Harbin, harped on this theme.

The other measure introduced last year and which was in the process of implementation during my visit was the establishment of Agricultural Middle Schools. I visited a couple of these institutions. They are modeled after trade schools or technical or vocational high schools, and young working farmers of both sexes receive some practical training in the three R's of Chinese agricultural methods on a part-work and part-study basis. The practice of working while studying aims at combining ordinary schooling with productive labor. It breaks the age-old scholastic Chinese, or for that matter Asian, tradition of looking down on manual labor.

This new movement has led to the dissolution of schools and colleges as one ordinarily understands them. It is not that students do some part-time work of their own choice to earn a bit of money. This should not therefore be confused with what the Americans call "working one's way through college." Nor is it to be equated with Mahatma Gandhi's well-known Wardha scheme of a craft-biased education. This "study with productive labor" is based purely on the Marxist theory of education, a welcome theory for present-day China, which does not have the resources in buildings, books, and teachers to educate her entire population of school-going age.

Karl Marx, in the first volume of his *Das Kapital,* talks about "an education that will, in the case of every child over a given age, combine productive labor with instruction and gymnastics, not only as one of the methods of adding to the efficiency of production but as the only method of producing fully developed human beings." Writing on another subject, *The Directives to the Delegates of the Provisional Central Council on Some Questions,* Marx observes: "In a reasonable social order, every child must become a productive worker starting at the age of nine." He goes on to suggest that "children from the age of nine to twelve should do two hours' work every day in a workshop or at home, children from thirteen to fifteen years of age four hours, and from sixteen to seventeen years of age six hours." He believed that "the combination of remunerative productive labor, mental education, physical exercise, and polytechnical training elevates the working class considerably above the level of the higher and middle classes." Marx pleads for this repeatedly in his writings. In his *Critique of the Gotha Program,* he observes: "An early combination of productive labor is one of the most potent means for the transformation of present-day society."

Lenin faithfully echoes this Marxist belief in ideal education. He says: "It is impossible to visualize the ideal of fu-

ture society without combining the training and education o
the young generation with productive labor. Neither trainin
and education without productive labor, nor productive labc
without parallel training and education could have bee
raised to the height demanded by present-day techniques an
the state of scientific knowledge."

All this Marxist-Leninist thought on education is sum
marized by Chairman Mao when he says that the aim of Con
munist education in China is to produce "a cultured, socialis
minded worker." A Chinese official explained to me th
meaning of Mao's term thus: "A cultured, socialist-minde
worker is a man who is both politically conscious and edu
cated. He is able to undertake both mental and manual worl
He is what we regard as developed in an all-around way, bot
politically and professionally qualified. He is a worker-inte
lectual and an intellectual-worker." In other words, any edu
cational policy which divorces mental labor from manu
labor cannot meet the demands of a Communist society.

The Chinese interpretation of Engels' theory that labc
creates the world is something like this: "Physical labor ha
pened before mental labor. The latter is therefore based upc
the former and is of secondary importance. We must con
pletely weed out the bourgeois theory of the superiority
mental to physical labor and must realize that physical labc
is the most important thing under the sun."

The fidelity and vigor with which the Chinese leaders a
translating this Marxist view into action reveal that the fait
ful believe in the complete relevance of Marxist doctrine
education to present-day China's needs. It is no wonder th
China is waging a war against the intellectuals and again
anyone who maintains that "education should be led by tl
experts" or that "professors and educators must head ar
run the schools."

When this Marxist view of education is grasped, one easi
understands why the heads of even technological colleges ar
universities are seasoned Party men or revolutionary Comm
nist soldiers. I met many professors who seemed to apologi
for their past academic training, which was "mere acquisiti
of textbook knowledge" divorced from the realities of t
people's needs. These professors are now making amends
working on farms and in factories in the mornings or evenir
or during the weekends. They included teachers from almc
all disciplines. The new outlook is work—not the armch;
or ivory-tower variety—but work that produces somethi
tangible or directly serves the workers.

In Shanghai, I wanted to visit the old and formerly Ame

an-supported St. John's University. I had gone around this university once years earlier and had met some of its graduates in American universities. I was told that this university had been transformed into the new Shanghai Academy of Social Sciences. I expressed a desire to visit it since this was the only institution (apart from the Institute of Economic Research in Peking, which I had the pleasure of addressing) devoted to study and research in social sciences—subjects which receive such low priority in the new China.

We drove to the academy, and I was received by two Vice-Directors, former professors at the university who continued to teach in addition to their administrative duties. The first Vice-Director, Dr. Lin, is an economist, a graduate of London University, and was at the London School of Economics between 1935 and 1937. The second gentleman, Dr. Pan, received his doctorate in political science from the University of Vienna in 1935. They both apologized for having forgotten English and German respectively, and our conversation was carried on through my inseparable companion and official interpreter who was assigned to me the day I arrived in Peking and who traveled with me all over China.

As we went around the various buildings, I noticed that these were more or less deserted.

"Is today a working day?" I asked.

"Yes, indeed, today is a normal working day."

"How many students are enrolled here?" I queried.

"About 4,600 in all."

"Are they all on this campus?"

"Technically yes, because they are enrolled here, but about 2,000 are working in the factories in Shanghai."

"Is it part-time work?"

"No. They put in eight hours in the factories. But they take a course once a week."

"What about the other 2,600 students?" I wanted to know.

"Another 2,000 are working on the farms on the outskirts of Shanghai."

"Do they come for the weekly course?"

"No. They will come back to the campus in a year or two when the temporary food problem has been solved."

"This means you have some 600 regular students actually here?"

"Not quite," replied the Vice-Director, "because some 200 are on steel duty. That is, the campus has set up a cottage-style steel furnace, and they are making steel."

Later we visited this traditional-style steel plant. It was just a furnace that was melting all the scrap metal gathered up by the students.

"The rest are regular students, I suppose."

"No, another 200 are practicing in the Student Militia, for they are assigned to join the Fukien Front." Here the Vice-Director gave me a little lecture on American imperialism and the necessary chore of shelling Quemoy and Matsu in the imperative task of "regaining" Taiwan.

Finally we entered a building where some student activity was discernible.

"This is the economics lecture hall," volunteered the Vice-Director. There was no lecturer present, but some twenty students were poring over books. The Vice-Director told me that he taught the course on "History of Economic Thought." I informed him that I myself had taught the same course for some years, and we began discussing the scope of the course, the textbooks adopted, and the favorite writers and questions of the students. "In India, we begin with Adam Smith and end with Keynes, though, of course, a few lectures are devoted to such economic thought as there was among such early Hindu writers as Manu and Kautilya."

"That is the conventional course we have been taught in the West," he conceded. "But we have changed all that since Liberation. Our 'History of Economic Thought' begins with Marx and ends with Chairman Mao."

"What writers do you specifically study?" I inquired.

"Marx, Engels, Lenin, Stalin, and Chairman Mao," was the reply.

We visited the economics seminar room, where a discussion was in progress among a score of students. There was no professor present, but the student leader invited us to join them, and we did. I was told that these were advanced students.

"Do they write an examination or submit a thesis?" I asked.

"They do both; but these students are working on a thesis," I was told.

At random, I asked a student what the subject of his thesis was.

"We don't have different subjects, for all of us are working on a single thesis," was his answer.

The Vice-Director intervened and informed me that the whole class works on a single thesis—a kind of cooperative effort.

"What is the subject of this collective thesis?"

"The communes," was the reply.

"Is there any objective evaluation of this collective thesis?" I asked.

"Oh, yes. The whole class criticizes the thesis and points out the deviations."

"But you said the whole class writes the thesis."

"That's right."

There was nothing else to do but change the subject.

Though I was told at every campus that the students had regular terminal and annual examinations, I could never find a question paper. Some professor or other was always trying to find me a question paper, in the Chinese language, of course, but they never seemed to manage it. At the University of Wuhan, the President had informed me that the question papers were kept at the Ministry of Education in Peking! Even last year's question papers!

After much discussion at various campuses, I discovered that question papers and examinations have been abolished for the present. No degrees or diplomas were granted. After a prescribed course of study, the student was sent to some school or office, factory or farm to do the work for which he had been trained. If he didn't learn his job properly and fumbled at his new occupation, it was just too bad. And yet no professor would concede that this was the true state of affairs in present-day China.

[CROFT, 239–244]

Most of the delegates were anxious to get home as soon as they could, but there were still some things I wanted to do. First was a visit to the Foreign Languages Institute, or, to be exact, to the English Department of it. There being no need for an interpreter I went there one morning by myself.

It had been built well out of the city and, under the damp grey sky and falling snow, the square classroom blocks and asphalt surrounds looked unusually stark and forbidding. The whitewashed walls and concrete corridors within were scarcely more cheerful. It was like entering a particularly Spartan public school which had decided to concentrate its traditional resources on the character training of young technologists. Large spittoons stood at suitable vantage points along the corridors; on the staircase, oblivious to anything else, a number of students were privately engaged in oral language exercises; on the notice-board were posted various students' essays: 'A Day at the Agricultural Co-operative'; 'Tractor Driving in the Holidays'; 'A Young Girl Goes to Meet Chairman Mao'.

The English faculty, over four hundred strong, was the largest in the Institute. Within the last six months there had been a great increase in the number of students taking English as a first choice—both here and in the schools and universities. In the light of The Hundred Flowers policy and the need to learn 'advanced techniques' from the west, it was also in great demand in the engineering schools and science colleges. 'Our problem,' said the Director, 'is not one of a surplus of teachers but of a severe shortage.'

Most of the present pupils had started from scratch. Their four-year course would soon daunt and exhaust the spirit of the average English languages student in a comparable position. Learning English, after all, can be no whit less mentally numbing for a Chinese boy than for an English boy to grapple with Chinese; and, with the limited equipment at their disposal, it remained a mystery to me how these students ever succeeded at all.

They spent eighteen hours a week on 'intensive analysis' in the classroom and eighteen in 'preparation and study', although analysis, said the Director, 'was not the focal point. 'Our main aim is to achieve a practical understanding. Thus, all lessons are conducted in English from a very early stage. Fourth-year students, for instance, should be able to study in detail four novels in a period of six weeks. Of course, our main problem is still to bring the student from the ABC stage up to the top level. Until recently the material has not been very good, but with the new emphasis on The Hundred Flowers we are getting a better quality of student from the secondary schools.'

The range of literature seemed to have been dictated by the books available when the communists took over; it was catholic, if a little bizarre. *Pride and Prejudice*, *Vanity Fair* and Jack London's *Martin Eden* were the most popular novels and, for specialised tastes, there was *Silas Marner*, *Babbitt*, *Our Mutual Friend* and *The Cloister and the Hearth*, with a good ration of Dickens, George Eliot, Galsworthy and various Georgian anthologies. On the language side the course seemed designed to instil a judicious blend of linguistical appreciation and ideological enlightment. I picked up at random some third-year comprehension exercises: one was headed 'Bethune's Interview with Chairman Mao', another, 'How the Soviet People Beat Hitler', and a third, 'Byron and the Cause of National Freedom'. The latter was a model of Marxist interpretation.

On the other hand, the fifth-year research papers had an austere purity which one could but gaze upon with a kind of dumbstruck awe. In addition to translating from the Anglo-Saxon some of the beefier portions of *Beowulf* and several hefty slices of the Chronicle, the students were required to deal with 'The influence of Latin in the English language', 'The nature and extent of the Scandinavian influence in Middle English', and 'The situation of French and the English dialects in Middle English times and the rise of the modern English national language'.

From *Aelfred cyninge on fest Radestone* I went down to a fourth-year class and *The Grapes of Wrath,* with Tom Joad driving west through the Colorado desert. . . . This turned out to be the most remarkable lesson I have ever sat through.

In the bleak, bitterly cold room, a mixed class of fourteen students applied themselves with iron concentration to the idiomatic peculiarities of America's most indigenous epic. They sat hunched grimly over their narrow desks in blue winter kapoks and white plimsolls, with here and there a bright splash of yellow sock or red scarf. The text-books consisted of half a dozen extracts from English and American novels stencilled on to thin sheets of quarto-size paper—a practice adopted in schools and colleges throughout China in lieu of bulk purchasing of new foreign texts.

The teacher himself had been at an American university before the War. A slim, quietly-spoken man of about thirty-five, smartly dressed in a brown check suit and a rust-coloured tie, he was manifestly on top of his job. His manner was friendly but his reactions swift and emphatic and, before the lesson had gone very far, I realised that he knew a good deal more about the English language than I did.

The compilers of the present selection had chosen to inflict on these already heavily overburdened students what, to anyone outside the sociological field, must surely be the grittiest passage in the whole of Steinbeck:

Along 66 the hamburger stands—Al and Suzy's place—Carl's lunch—Joe's and Minnie's—Will's eats. Board and bat shacks. . . . Near the door three slot machines. . . . And beside them the nickel phonograph piled up with pies. . . .

For some time the students read round the class in flat, plodding monotones. The dialogue meant nothing to them—how could it? It broke every grammatical rule they had ever learnt; it spoke of objects they had never seen or heard of and could not possibly have imagined.

'Now,' said the teacher, with patient optimism, 'we will start our analysis. "They set their faces to the west and drove towards it, forcing the clashing engines over the roads." Now, Liu Chung, why did they *force* their engines?'

After a minute or so of painful concentration, Liu Chung

ventured: 'Because the engines were in a wretched condition.'

After further strenuous thought: 'Because the cars were old.'

'Right. Now, in this sentence, "Why, sure, be proud to have you. What state you from?" Tsao Liang, how do you interpret, "Sure, be proud to have you?" '

Tsao could not interpret it at all: and nobody else offered to. 'It is not possible to paraphrase such a sentence.'

'But how do we interpret, "be proud"? Does it mean "we *are* proud"? Or "*will be* proud"?'

A slow shaking of heads confessed that nobody knew.

'No! It means *would* be proud. Now I want you to learn the use of "would" which is alien to our language.'

While he clarified his point my eye wandered detachedly round the room. The whitewashed austerity of the walls was broken only by two red-and-gold banners immediately behind me: they were worth a second glance. In large block capitals the first proclaimed the unusual message: 'BE ACTIVE AND HAPPY!' and the second, like a text removed from a missionary hall, the pious and homely injunction, 'UNITE AND LOVE EACH OTHER!' No mention of productivity, national construction, advanced techniques.

' "And the great question. How's the water?"

' "She doesn't taste so good. . . ." Now why does the writer use *she?*'

Nobody could tell.

'Would *you* use "she", Chien Hsia-tung?'

A slow pause: 'I . . . don't . . . think so.'

'Or *you*, Wu Nu?'

'Does it perhaps mean . . . "it"?'

'Yes, but what is the rule from this?'

There was a moment of tortured silence.

'Well, the general rule, comrades, is what we call in phonetics the loss of plosions. Now, what do we mean by plosions?'

There I confess he had me as well as the students; I hoped he would not feel tempted to seek my opinion.

' "Why, sure, be good to have you." . . . Now what general rule can we deduce from that?'

A shy suggestion from the girl at the back: 'The loss of the auxiliary . . .'

'And, "She doesn't taste so good?" Don't you find something wrong with the use of "good"?'

She appeared not to.

'This reference to genders, now. Can we make a rule for their use with inanimate objects?'

The question was rhetorical. 'I don't think we can. But we

find it sometimes used as a term of endearment, peculiar to slang or pattern speech.'

' "Then down from the car the weary people climbed." Now what linguistic fact do we need to take care of there?'

At first, profound uncertainty; then, a hesitant murmur: 'Inversion.'

'Now we will go back and paraphrase the passage from the beginning. I want you to make a frontal attack on the text.'

He clenched his fists together to emphasise the fighting approach required. 'Employ your whole resources—and don't bypass any difficulties!'

The students went tenaciously into battle. I shook the teacher warmly by the hand and, feeling chastened and humbler than before, crept quietly out.

'Although it is a very concentrated course,' said the Director, 'the students have the satisfaction of knowing that there will be opportunities open to them when they are qualified. Teaching is only one of them. For years to come there will be a continuing demand for translators in political and scientific work, while in the literary field the possibilities are immense. There is a great renaissance of interest in foreign literature and many world classics are now being translated for the first time in China. We want many more—and many versions of them so that the best will stand out.'

Noticing with some surprise that there was an old Everyman copy of *Cakes and Ale* in his bookshelf, I asked if Maugham was ever likely to come up for translation.

He replied rather curtly that he was not. 'We don't particularly like Maugham'—somehow I had not supposed they would—'but many of his novels are still available because they were taken over from the old college libraries. We shall, however, be translating a number of Thackeray's works. His novels are very popular here, *Vanity Fair* especially.'

Ever since I arrived in China I had been puzzled by this extraordinary predilection for Thackeray. In Russia perhaps, where the nineteenth-century novel has some affinities with its English counterpart, the taste could be better understood, but in Red China it seemed unfathomably perverse. Here at last, I thought, is the man who will know. But it was not to be. The Director left the mystery veiled in a kind of neutral obscurity. 'We feel on safe ground, linguistically speaking,' he said, 'with the nineteenth century—and with Thackeray in particular because the style of his books is most interesting, as well as their content. You see, one of the good things about studying English in a foreign language is that you don't have to follow the fashion.'

I readily took his word for it; but for the life of me I could

still not understand why they should choose to follow Thackeray.

[SHENG, 89–92]

Because they do not dare tell the truth, even when it is
obvious, the Chinese today give some foreigners the impression of being stupid. I found them clever, sensitive people,
living under a continual cloud of fear which kept their lips
sealed. They are suspicious of one another; they are definitely
suspicious of foreigners. Everyone lives within and hides behind his own invisible wall.

Tension, born of suspicion and fear, dominates university
life. I spent three years at Peking University, the alma mater
of many leading Communists, long famous for its revolutionary tradition, and, incidentally, for the fact that Mao
Tse-tung once worked there as an unknown librarian. It is
still the most important institution of general higher education
in China, at the vanguard of the movement to establish Communist universities.

The university itself was established at the end of the last
century by imperial decree, but its ten thousand students and
teachers are housed today on the lovely campus which before
1949 belonged to Yenching University, founded by American
missionaries. Situated in the western suburb of Peking, not
far from the Summer Palace, these grounds seem to me one
of the most beautiful spots I saw in China. Entering the university from the richly decorated west gate, painted in Mandarin red, one feels he has walked into a garden. But it takes
only a few days in the garden to feel the strain of living constantly in a highly charged, tense atmosphere.

During my time, there were more than two hundred foreign students at the university. Most of them were from the
fraternal socialist countries; the rest came from friendly non-
socialist states. I never knew one who did not want to leave
China and go home. In one sense, this is surprising, for living
conditions were quite good, much better than those of the
Chinese students, and in some cases better than those of the
foreign students would have enjoyed in their own countries.
We were given either a single room or put two in a room;
the Chinese students lived six in a room, with double-decker
beds. There was a special dining room for the European
students, one for the Mohammedan students from the Middle
East and Indonesia, one for the Indians, and another for the
Koreans. In cases where the Chinese Government gave a

monthly stipend, it amounted to as high as 200 Chinese dollars (U.S. $82) for the Russians, against only 12 Chinese dollars (U.S. $5) for the Chinese.

Yet, all the foreign students, Communist or not, were unhappy. I heard Russians and Czechs and Poles complain of the trying conditions on the campus; many of them were amazingly frank about their opinions of Chinese Communism, so different, they thought, from Communism back home.

My first year at the university, 1956, was a comparatively liberal one for Chinese students. They had some time to themselves and the liberty to do what they liked with it. Lessons were similar to those in any of our schools, except that there were no prescribed textbooks, because ideas about what was good for the students had not yet been formalized. Cyclo-styled lesson sheets were distributed every morning; students attended a regular number of classes and did their homework in the dormitories or in the library, as they wished. Besides the political lessons which were an integral part of the curriculum, sometimes there were compulsory political lectures or meetings.

In general, 1956 was not a bad year. But from the time of the Blooming of the Hundred Flowers in the late spring of 1957 to about the end of 1958, I wondered whether I was in a university at all. Peking's original idea was to rectify or reform abuses and faults in the Party by allowing the people to air their grievances against it.

Certainly the Party never realized that so much criticism would pour out. Overnight the walls of Peking University, as of other schools, were plastered with critical letter news-papers. Some asked for Khrushchev's report on Stalin, which had never been published in the Chinese press. Some inquired why only Soviet science was taught, when it was well known that scientific knowledge in the United States and England was also very advanced. Some demanded that the Party withdraw from the university. Groups of students organized themselves into discussion groups and elected representatives, who, with representatives from other universities, were to form a joint front against the Party's interference in academic matters. For the first two or three days of Blooming, there was a spirit of democracy which had never been witnessed before.

Then the Party stepped in and meetings began. The first-year students studying the same subject met together. Everyone discussed the "errors" in the criticisms made against the Party. Each meeting was attended by a Party member or cadre, who sat in the last row and guided the performance. The sessions were usually very long, sometimes lasting a whole day, and went on day after day. All regular classes stopped;

the university became a vast camp where more than ten thousand students and teachers collected in classrooms, in dining halls, in the open air under the shade of the trees to discuss and rediscuss the true approach and the wrong approach. When students were not meeting in such discussion groups— for example, during meals—the university loudspeaker system would broadcast long talks by Party members and important officials. Often, listening to these talks was compulsory; after them, students gathered in small groups to discuss the contents of the speeches so that no detail, however small, was overlooked or ignored.

At last, everyone—all the thousands who had only a few months earlier been so violent in their various criticisms— "voluntarily" came to the conclusion that the leadership of the Communist Party was the only correct leadership and that only because of its correct guidance had China been able to throw off the shackles of imperialism and make such rapid progress on the path of true democracy. Everyone also "voluntarily" came to the conclusion that those who dared raise their voices against this leadership were the reactionary products of the old feudal and capitalist society.

In the early fall of 1957, a new campaign was started—the campaign against the rightists. The *People's Daily,* chief Communist Party paper, once said in an editorial that the Blooming of the Hundred Flowers had been a trap to catch the rightists. The catch was rich! Hundreds of young men in the university and many lecturers and aging professors were among those trapped. As one of my Chinese friends put it, the Party started with the intention of rectifying itself with the help of the people's criticism; it finished by rectifying the people with the Party's criticism.

The so-called rightists had to stand, facing hundreds of their onetime friends and colleagues, and hear that they were treacherous enemies of the people and reactionary agents of Chiang Kai-shek or imperialist America. Sometimes emotions ran so high that the frenzied crowds became mobs howling for blood. Students were even beaten up. These maniacal meetings, the shrieking voices of condemnation and the accusing fingers, the abuse, the venom—I find them hard to forget. The rightists were not allowed to escape these trials by simply confessing their guilt. And those rightists who stood by what they had said, who felt that they were not guilty of any crime, were not only condemned as traitors and enemies of the people but boycotted and ostracized.

One such student found that his roommates refused to talk to him, and the cook in the dining room refused to serve him. And he was not allowed to leave the university campus, he could not go outside to eat, so he decided to lie down quietly on his bed and wait till something happened. But a crowd stood outside his door shouting slogans and cursing him. His girl friend tried to provide him with some food on the sly. She was caught and tried separately as a rightist. On the third day, hungry and bitter, the boy committed suicide.

Many young people who could not stand the strain killed themselves during this period. One student jumped from the third floor of his hostel but did not die. While his mangled body was removed to the hospital, his roommates wrote a letter newspaper and pasted it on his door in the dormitory, saying: "What treacherous thoughts did you harbor against the state when you planned to take your life?" When I heard that he died, I actually felt relieved.

Many lecturers and professors also took their lives, or tried to, during this period. Others suffered their punishment. A professor who had taught English in the university for many years, now found to have rightist tendencies, was immediately ordered to work as a typist so that he could rectify his thinking through labor. Another teacher was reduced to the position of a janitor and made to sweep the floors so that he could learn the dignity of labor and re-establish his lost contact with reality.

The number of rightists discovered at our university ran into several hundred. Political commentators announced happily that China had been saved from becoming another Hungary, and the campaign was concluded early in 1958.

During these months of long meetings and conferences held to rectify the thinking processes of the people at large, two important political developments took place. One was the decision to use education to make the students "Red and expert." The other was the policy of encouraging students, teachers, and cadres to volunteer for manual labor in villages and factories. There was considerable discussion as to whether a student should be made Red (given political training) before he was made an expert (given academic scholarship) or the other way around.

Finally, it was decided that the two should go hand in hand. Actually, the accent was heavily on the political, or Red, side. Therefore, students, teachers, and cadres were to remold their political thinking by volunteering for work in factories and fields. Everyone in the university, students and teachers, most cheerfully demanded to go. When the selections were made, one noticed that only the suspects and near-suspects had been chosen. Many of these never came back.

Another type of voluntary labor required only a temporary stay of three months or more in some village or factory. Practically all the students and teachers of Peking University were sent for this short course in the study of Marxism through labor, from the spring to about September of 1958. When the 1957–1958 academic year ended in July, naturally many students who were in the final year of school were supposed to graduate. But, since they had hardly studied at all for one whole year, it was clearly not possible to make them take examinations. The university decided upon a novel expedient. A sample test was given to a few students from each class. On this basis, diplomas and degrees were awarded. Thus ended the academic year 1957–1958.

The foreign students usually left Peking during the summer vacation, which lasted about two months. I went to the beach at Tsing Tao, leaving behind the fever and fret of Peking. I came back in September to find a totally different environment. Life had become rigidly organized. The student's day was minutely arranged for him. He got up at six in the morning to the sound of military music and did compulsory exercises. He ate his breakfast and began work by 7:15. Classes finished by noon; then followed lunch and a rest until 2:30 when classes started again. School finished by about 4:30 followed by compulsory games. Dinner was at 6:00. After a short period of rest, the students collected in their dormitories or the library to do their homework or attended a compulsory meeting. Lights went off at 10:30.

The Chinese permitted no deviation. To ensure conformity excellent military discipline is necessary. And this is exactly what has been achieved. It takes less than twelve hours in China today to get the whole nation of 650 million to reach unanimous verdict on any matter of national or international importance. During the Lebanon crisis, one evening when the university lights were going out and students were going to bed, the loudspeakers suddenly began to broadcast very noisy, martial music. Every two minutes the announcement was made that all students and teachers were to gather at the football grounds within fifteen minutes. I went out to find the paths jammed with sleepy students hurriedly dressing their way to the field. It took about five minutes to get them together.

The secretary of the university Communist Party spoke to us about the danger to world peace arising out of the American imperialists' occupation of Lebanon. Within an hour "volunteers" had gathered in front of the dining room; within two hours, they were outside the British Embassy carrying banners and shouting slogans.

It seems to me that the Party is trying to convert China into a vast military camp in which everyone will be a soldier

*:*rforming every action with the efficiency of a machine. In *:*ct, after the exchange of fire between the mainland and *;*aiwan over Quemoy and Matsu, the Government declared *;*at everyone should have military training. All adults had to *:*ill for an hour or two every morning; peasants in the fields *:*arched to work with weapons in their hands, and even *;*hool children started drilling with toy guns.

The new school year in September, 1958, started in earnest, *;*t by the end of the year there was a general call for par*:*cipation in the steel campaign. Furnaces were set up at the *:*iversity and scrap collected to prove, in the words of the *:*esident of Peking's Tsinghua University, that "productive *;*bor is the best merging point of teaching, research, and *:*eological training." When I quit China at the beginning of *;*59, the students in the university were busy making steel.

It was a cold, gray day when I drove out of the Mandarin*:*d west gate for the last time. I was not sorry to leave, but *:*' the time I reached the railway station I was already feeling *;* little sad. Three years of interesting, tragic, and friendly *:*periences will bind me for a long time to the lovely campus *;*lled Peking University.

[GREENE, 226–229]

Professor Wang Shê-chen, vice-dean of Peking University, *:*d I were sitting in one of the smaller houses on the campus. *;*e room smelled faintly of incense and the light filtered *;*rough the green foliage of the bamboo outside the window. *;*Founded in 1898, the university was, for many years, a *;*tbed of radical activity. It was sparks from on campus that *;*ndled the May 4 literary renaissance just after the First *;*orld War. Mao Tse-tung was an assistant in the library. *;*ounders of the Chinese Communist Party studied and taught *;*re, and Lu Hsun, later known as the Chinese Gorki, was a *;*ofessor of literature during the early twenties.

Since 1952, Peking has been graduating more technical and *;*ientific personnel than any other university in China. There *;* a liberal-arts school, but more than 70 per cent of the *;*arly 11,000 students are in basic and theoretical science. *;*e college of medicine and department of agriculture were *;*nsferred to Peking Medical College and Peking Agricultural *;*ollege after the nationwide amalgamation in 1952.

The average age of entering students has gone down to *;*hteen, with the increase in secondary-school attendance. *;*idents of the arts get a five-year course, science students, six—those who show special ability can stay on for three year of research.

Women make up 20 per cent of the student body, a lowe percentage than in teacher-training and medical colleges There are three hundred foreign students from thirty coun tries.

Tuition, rooms, books, and medical care are free. Thos who are able to afford it pay 12 yuan ($4.80) a month fo food, those unable receive a subsidy. Sixty per cent of th students get grants for food and clothing. The library the showed me contained over two million books—it is too smal and a new library is about to be completed.

The top salary for teachers is more than that of the genera manager of a steel mill. Depending on seniority, salaries rang from 62 to more than 300 yuan a month; the average i about 200.

There is a two-month stint at "putting theory into practice for students. Chemistry majors, for example, spend their tim at a chemical plant; a physics student will work in metallurg or electronics. The second month can be spread out over th school year, a few days at a time depending on the student schedule. Professors go for one month, the ailing or age being excused.

I talked to a number of students as I wandered with Pro fessor Wang around campus, in the workshops, through th dormitories, and into the dining hall. We were joined by young student who was an English major—he had studie English since secondary school and now he had a chance t make use of it.

In the women's dormitory I found four girls having a lat lunch. Their room was extremely simple: four stacked bunk one chair, and one table by the window. It was neat and clear There were a few pictures, one of a film star, and on th table some bright artificial flowers. The girls were in thei second year, studying Chinese language and literature. In an other room a girl wearing glasses was reading at a table. Sh told me she usually got up at 5:30, had her first class a hour later, and went to bed by half-past ten. She put in eigh hours a day in class and study.

As we were on our way to one of the workshops, a volle ball bounced out across the walkway. My young frien knocked it over to me and I volleyed it back across the ne This seemed an enormous joke and they were still laughin about it when we walked on.

There were twenty large precision lathes all in operation i the workshop. One of the lathe operators, quite the prettie girl I had seen in China, told me she was nineteen and not a student. She was a factory worker who, as she put it, helped teach new students who never had done any mechanical work.

Strains of un-Chinese music grew louder as we went on. A band was tuning up in a wooden shack not far from the workshops. It sounded like a terrific row, everyone seemed to be playing something different. When I appeared in the doorway everything stopped except for the bugler who, with his back to me, played lustily on. They told me they were practicing a number called "The Young Commune Worker." An answer to my query about American jazz, they said emphatically, "Never!"

Loudspeakers blared a message over the campus. It was a report on the accomplishments of students who had gone to work on a commune. I noticed a few couples strolling along hand in hand. Only the other night I had read an account by a recent Canadian visitor who declared that young Chinese regard such displays as "decadent."

As we passed the water tower—like a phony pagoda temple—and circled the lake in the late afternoon sunlight, I brought up to Professor Wang the freedom issue. I told him that one of the things I was concerned about in China was the unanimity of thought, everyone thinking alike, talking alike. Any healthy society must make room for disagreement, and dissent should not be construed as disloyalty.

He hesitated before speaking. "Our society makes room for the man who disagrees as long as he doesn't attack socialism and the government."

"But that's just the point," I said. "There must be some people who disagree, why can't they express themselves?"

"Because this government is what the majority wants."

"Majorities can be wrong. All advance comes from a few who don't like things as they are. After all, *your* revolution was led by dissenters."

"You don't understand. You cannot realize what great changes and improvements have come to us. We know we are being led by those who have our interests at heart. Why would we want to attack them?"

"I don't say you should attack them. But you must acquire the habit of criticizing them. Your leaders today may be wise. But one day they will no longer be living. As you know, unwise people can attain leadership. What if you can't dissent then? This happened in Russia, no one was allowed to criticize Stalin, not even Khrushchev, until after Stalin was dead and many terrible mistakes had been made. Why were people not allowed to point them out?"

"What about *your* country?" he asked. "What about Senator McCarthy and loyalty oaths? Isn't there hypocrisy in all the talk about freedom in the United States?"

So it went, around and around, alongside the lovely lake in the quiet sunlight—not angry or defensive, but our minds never quite meeting because our terms of reference and our vocabulary and concepts were so different. And above all, I did not have behind me the specter of previous degradation, oppression, and hunger. Success brings its own persuasion, and against this enormous fact of China's emergence into self respect and health and vigor I could see how my talk about intellectual freedoms must appear to these young men as so much chatter, an idle and rather profitless verbal game.

"Come and see China again in a few years' time," Professor Wang told me as he said good-by, and added with a smile, "perhaps you will be convinced then that our system works."

My visit to the university and my discussions there left me with some mixed feelings. But what I did come away with was the picture of those students' faces. This remained more vivid in my mind than anything else. These were faces of happy people.

Never mind the buildings and the surroundings. Look at the human material. There is a vitality and enthusiasm as if life doesn't have enough hours for all that has to be done. Stand in the huge dining hall, like an overgrown armory, without tables or chairs, and watch the crowded little knots standing and eating from bowls which will be rinsed under a tap outside. Forget the drabness and look at these young people, and you will begin to understand China.

"What are you studying, what do you want to be?"

Physics, language teacher, hydroelectric engineer, geology . . . the answers would come quickly, all stated proudly and directly. How many of them are sons and daughters of peasants, I wonder.

"Where do you want to work?" The answer, in different words, is always the same: "Wherever my country needs me most."

To me this at first seemed naïve and even perhaps a little insincere. But when I heard it many times I began to believe that they indeed meant it. Again the desire for collective advance rather than personal gratification.

I did not know then that I would, before many months, hear another young voice, in a very different country: "Ask not what your country can do for you, but what you can do for your country."

Next day I started my tour of scientific work by driving to the Institute of Geophysics and Meteorology of the Academia Sinica.

I went to the director's office, and there, over the customary and comforting cup of green tea, I was greeted by the senior scientists: the director, Dr. Chao Chin-chan; the vice director, Dr. Chen Tsung-chi; and Dr. Lee Shan-pang. All spoke English and Dr. Lee had certainly visited the United States. I gathered that the other two had studied in Germany. It seems that the institute has about a hundred employees of all ranks in Peking, but it directs the work of many others. Dr. Lee, for example, has 150 seismologists working for him in stations scattered about the country. Many of the scientists are college graduates, but it also seems possible for a bright apprentice to become engaged in research and to obtain a bachelor's degree or diploma later. I think that the institute has research students and can award degrees roughly equivalent to Ph.D.'s, but I was never quite clear on this point, perhaps because the policy is changing. Some such institutes in the U.S.S.R. and in China, even though they are not related to universities, certainly do have the power to grant high degrees. For this reason the senior staff members of institutes may be called professors, although they are not at universities. To people with our point of view, all this is a little confusing.

This institute is located in a newly developed region of north-west Peking, in which is concentrated a great collection of new institutes, universities and similar buildings. Over a large region there is tremendous activity to replace the former fields of vegetables with hundreds of new laboratory and office buildings and with dormitories for the workers employed in them. These are laid out along brand-new avenues planted with trees. It seems quite possible that as many as 100,000 scientists and students may be working in that area. The institute that I visited is only a very tiny part of this cultural centre, but its one new permanent building is typical of so many others that I shall describe it.

It is well built of grey brick three stories high, with a tile roof. Few buildings, except hotels, have elevators, so that they are rarely more than four stories in height. Inside there are three stairways connecting central corridors that run the length of the rectangular building. On each floor and in the basement are a couple of dozen rooms. The building is plain but well built, with white plastered walls, terrazzo flooring, electric lights, running water, a few coils for steam heat in

winter, and doors and windows that open and shut properly
The senior scientists have bare and simple offices of their
own, equipped with the necessary furniture and plenty of
books. Laboratories have good benches, blackboards, and
sinks, also adequate outlets for electricity, water and gas
These buildings are in fact quite satisfactory for their pur
pose, but without any frills. I went all over the building
going into most of the laboratories and vaults to inspect pro
ects.

Housed in this fireproof building is an excellent library
The scientists pointed out that they have the responsibility
of answering a lot of questions upon which large expenditure
may depend; for example, about the construction of dams
bridges or buildings. They need a good library, and they are
proud of the fact that over the past thirty years they have
built up an excellent one.

By counting the shelves, I estimated that the reading room
held about four hundred current journals on geophysics and
related subjects. It was impressively complete and up to date
having, for example, four Italian geophysical journals, five
Japanese ones, and all the well-known journals published in
English, French and German. I also went carefully through
the stacks and opened a variety of volumes there. The sets of
all important geophysical journals were complete and there
were many marginally related publications such as the *Pro
ceedings of the American Society of Civil Engineers*, which
would be of value when considering the design of earthquake
resistant structures.

The library and its indexes are all in three parts, for there
are large Russian and Chinese sections, as well as that for the
Western languages. The Chinese publish about fifty scientific
journals at present, but the number is increasing. All may
be obtained by subscription. From my own observation
but the most popular ones have at least abstracts, and often
whole articles, in Russian or in some Western language.

Although this library is larger than most that deal with on
one field, there were good libraries to be found in every insti
tute and university I visited. Back and current numbers of
the more widely read journals, which might otherwise be dif
ficult to obtain in China, have been multilithed, and I re
peatedly saw copies of some of the standard American, Eng
lish, German and Russian journals, and of textbooks, in this
form.

I was also taken through the workshop where they made
some of their own instruments. Crowded into a temporary
building were fifty men and women who were operating

twenty lathes, a milling machine, a planer, and some other tools, mostly of Chinese manufacture. Each operator was training a young apprentice.

The chief mechanic explained to me with the help of Mr. Tien, "We have stopped all regular work for two months in order to make thirty more lathes. We will soon need them and cannot obtain them in any other way."

Pieces of a standard Chinese lathe were being copied all over the shop.

This Institute of Geophysics and Meteorology had been formed, I was told, in 1928 as an Institute of Meteorology with much the same functions as today. It is concerned with meteorology, seismology, geomagnetism, and geophysical prospecting. In 1935 there had been only fifty meteorological stations in China and only two seismological stations. (One was at Shanghai, founded by the Jesuits, and the other was at Nanking.) There are now said to be 1,500 meteorological stations reporting four times daily through local centres, of which four hundred are pilot-balloon stations and seventy are radiosonde stations. The Chinese make daily, three-day, and monthly forecasts by the use of computers, but I did not see the facilities for this work.

They have thirty seismological stations, of which they later showed me three and offered to let me see others. In Moscow the Russians had said that they received bulletins from twenty-three Chinese stations, and that sixteen more were under construction or contemplated. The Chinese also have temporary mobile stations.

In the vaults and scattered around this institute, I saw many Chinese seismographs, of seven types. There are three varieties of the so-called 1951 type, a simple instrument designed by Dr. Lee for the purpose of getting stations started quickly when he was told to do that in 1951. There are small Russian Vegik, standard Russian Kirnos and high-sensitivity Russian Kharin seismographs, all of which are copied and made in China. They have a portable instrument operated from batteries which can be used for preliminary investigations.

The chief job in the seismological division was preparing a map of China, indicating the frequency and intensity of earthquakes, so that suitable precautions might be taken in building dams, bridges, buildings, railways, and so forth. As is well known, many parts of China (but by no means all parts) have severe earthquakes from time to time. Because only two seismograph stations had been operated for any length of time, the old instrumental records were not complete enough for this purpose. Only in those regions where earth-quakes are numerous had there been time for collecting ade-quate data in the few years since the network of new stations had been installed. By good fortune these data sufficed in the mountainous parts of southern and western China, which had always been thinly settled. For the plains where earthquakes are less frequent but may, nevertheless, be dangerous, Dr. Lee obtained the services of 150 historians who in two years re-viewed the whole literature of China and found about 10,000 useful references to individual earthquakes occurring between 1189 B.C. and the present. By careful analysis of these varied and imperfect data, Dr. Lee has prepared the required maps in preliminary form. Two out of the three volumes of his remarkable report have already been published and favour-ably reviewed in the *Bulletin of the Seismological Society of America.* He showed me his work on the final volume.

It seems appropriate to mention two peculiarities common to all institutes; one concerns physical exercise. In the past, intellectuals in China looked down upon physical work in any form, an attitude that tended to make them impractical and completely divorced them from the labourers. To avoid any continuation of this custom, the present Government is very insistent that everyone engage in both forms of activity. In the middle of the morning and again in the afternoon, at all offices, institutes and colleges, bells ring, loudspeakers are turned on, and everyone troops outside for ten minutes of physical exercises to gay music. In many ways this seems to be an improvement on the coffee break. I always suggested that we go too, but my hosts never allowed this, so I do not know whether the professors normally join in or not. It is taken quite seriously, for I have seen charwomen stop scrub-bing and stand up and do ten minutes of exercises before resuming their scrubbing again. For similar reasons there is emphasis on sport, chiefly basketball, for which the nets can be seen all over China. They are so numerous that it seemed to me that it would have been more suitable if the secretary had referred to Canada as the land of Dr. Naismith, born in Ontario and the inventor of the game, rather than as that of Dr. Bethune. In those institutes that have not yet got play-grounds, it is usual for the employees to go out with shovels and baskets and work until they have. Some were doing that at this institute.

The second curious feature is the wall posters which can be seen in varying numbers in the halls of most buildings. These large sheets of white or coloured paper are covered with Chinese writing which, I was told, are statements of criticism or of praise which anyone may put up, directed against the director or anyone else in the establishment. I take it they are frequently detailed, personal and pointed, but I feel it improbable that they are very spontaneous.

In most of the places that I visited, the directors seemed to be chosen for their scientific or technical experience, and I suppose that from time to time some of them may be regarded as less politically mature and correct than they ought to be. Likewise some of the employees may from time to time stand in need of correction. It seemed to me that the wall poster was one ingenious method of keeping technically competent directors, and indeed everyone, on the correct political path without destroying their authority. Another method was interminable political discussions, and I noticed meetings wherever I went.

This particular institute had its share of these posters on the walls and stairways, although they were not nearly so abundant as in some other places. The director admitted with a wry smile that he was the target, but I was interested to observe that his authority had not been lost. As we went around the laboratory, everyone was most polite and deferential. When I later addressed the members of the institute, I could not have asked for a more polite and attentive audience, and when the director and I walked in, everyone stood up. Nevertheless, I often wondered what the dean thought in the university, which was so plastered with these posters that there was no more room on the walls, and posters were hung on strings across the corridors, until it was a little like an obstacle race to visit the laboratories.

These visits occupied all the morning, and I returned to the hotel for lunch alone, where I copied these items from the menu:

Cold Dishes

Chicken in red oil	$ .36
Spicy giblets	.30
Mixed cold noodle with chicken shred	.18
Spices pork	.34
Spices chicken fins	.20
Fried Phoenix fish tails	.32
Black eggs	.08
Vegetarian macedaing	.20

Vegetables

Sauté of rape	.10
Sauté of cauliflower and snow eggs	.22
Sauté of green pumpkin with dry shrimps	.16

Any Kind of Soup

Consommé of spongy bamboo and peas sprout ...... .14
Consommé of three-deliceous .... .26
Consommé of pork and eggs and fungus .... .10

Fowls

Mixed soft chicken in piece .... .42
Fried spice duck .... .72
Fried duck livers .... .32

Fish and Prawn

Fried Mandarin fish and paunch in sweet and sour
sauce .... .32
Sauté of prawn in small piece .... .34

Meat

Sauté of pork and green pepper in does .... .32
Slice of pork in fish-tasted sauce .... .22

Marin Products

Stewed bich-de-mer with slice pork .... .46
Sauté of fish tripe-shred in snow eggs .... .42

Deserts

Stewed lotus seed in sugar candy .... .12
Almond Bean curd in sugar candy .... .10

Pastry Foods

Noodle in soup with three fresh .... .24
Boiled noodle with hashed meat in bean paste ...... .16
Stew vegatarian dumpling (each one) .... .02
Rice congue (each bomb) .... .02

While the occasional misspelled words are amusing it is
more pertinent to reflect that most of the much longer menu
from which these excerpts were taken was entirely correct,
and to consider how few North Americans could translate
even a word, let alone whole menus, into Chinese.

I was reminded of the incident of Dr. A. D. Tshkakaya, a
charming seismologist from Tbilisi (Tiflis), Georgia, who
came to a convention in Toronto with other scientists from
the U.S.S.R. The advance cable listed only the visitors' sur-
names, Confident that "kaya" is a feminine ending in Russian
and not realizing that his name was not Russian but Georgian,
we listed him as "Miss Tshkakaya."

When he arrived and complained, a correction was made.

Unfortunately, the result was that on the revised list his name appeared as "Mrs. Tshkakaya." Ten months later when I visited him in Tiflis, he and his friends were still laughing over the old gentleman's jest that he had lost his virginity in Toronto.

5. Medicine and Health

[SCHMID, 76–81]

Dr Hsu Cheng-wen was showing me over the new Children's Hospital outside the city walls, to the west of Peking, when suddenly, out of an atmosphere of white-clad nurses, airy rooms, and surgeries with the most up-to-date equipment, we stepped into a little room which resembled an antiquarian's collection rather than a modern hospital. Old, yellowing books covered with handwritten squiggles adorned the shelves.

"This is the library of traditional medicine," explained Hsu. "You are aware that the traditional methods of curing the sick in China can look back to an experience considerably longer than Western medicine can. We are convinced that they could include much that is true and useful, and which could be applied with some advantage even in our own day. That is why, in addition to the modern medical faculties we have set up here in Peking a Research Institute of Traditional Medicine, where a number of selected students, after completing their medical training, are given an additional course of instruction in the traditional methods of curing the sick. Naturally, the old, uneducated village quacks will disappear in time. We have already forced them to undergo instruction in the most basic medical knowledge and to pass certain examinations—and in due course they will be entirely supplanted by the trained physician, a man who knows the positive sides of their cures and uses them to supplement his modern medical knowledge."

We had passed a group of young house surgeons who, behind their white masks, listened attentively to the explanations of a middle-aged woman doctor, and now found ourselves in front of the traditional apothecary's shop. From its door came a strangely pleasant aroma of dried herbs, and some assistants inside were weighing out the most curious roots, grasses, and animal remains—all according to medical prescription. These traditional potions and powders, Hsu explained to me, were often no less effective, and occasionally more effective, than modern drugs. At the same time they were considerably cheaper.

One of the most determined exponents of this symbiosis of traditional and modern medicine is Dr Jen Shou-chung, a young doctor of only thirty-seven, who holds something like a pioneering post in the drive for the recapture of traditional medicine in China. I called on him at a branch establishment of the new Children's Hospital, in an old building in the old city, which is enjoying increasing popularity as a department for acupuncture. Almost accidentally Jen had made the epoch-making discovery that one of the scourges of mankind, infantile paralysis, against which an intensive struggle is now being waged all over the world, can be treated by acupuncture. Jen, the son of an acupuncture practitioner, had learned the skill as a boy, but had given it up entirely after completing his medical studies at the university. Just then, in July 1953, a two-year-old boy, Chie Peng-lu, was received into the hospital. He had been totally paralysed for several weeks and was regarded as a hopeless case. There was no response at all to the usual treatment. It then occurred to Jen to test the 'quack method' on this otherwise hopeless case: acupuncture, or, to use the Chinese term, the Tsuntsiu therapy. The result was startling: after a few months the hopeless case was cheerfully running about the garden. Since then the new-old treatment has been extended far beyond infantile paralysis, and is now applied to some thirty-eight different complaints.

At the same time acupuncture is the simplest and cheapest method imaginable. The equipment of Dr Jen's surgery consisted of an examination couch, a table, four sterilized silver needles about an inch long, a few wads of cotton-wool, and some sticking-plaster for covering up the punctures in the skin. A mother was just then carrying her little girl in. The thickly padded trousers were slipped off her left leg, and the child was lifted on to the couch. Three weeks before she had been brought in for the first time. This was her ninth treatment, and she had by now lost all fear of the long needles, which are apt to frighten anyone seeing them for the first time. She was lying quite still on the table, merely clutching her mother's hand as the needle was sunk into her thigh and vibrated lightly in the doctor's hand. The pinprick, Jen explained to me, caused no pain whatever. His hand was probing down the leg, from the pelvis to the little foot. With the help of an old medical book he explained to me exactly where each nerve had to be 'stimulated'; every point had its Chinese name: Fon Szie in the thigh, Yang Lie near the knee, Tso San Lie close below the knee, and San Yun Tsio in the calf. When the little girl was dressed again and I distracted the mother's attention by asking a few questions the child suddenly slipped away and ran about a dozen steps quite unaided —naturally to everybody's delight.

The next young patient received a treatment that was less spectacular, but possibly even more magical and mysterious. The girl was suffering, not from poliomyelitis, but from dyspeptic diarrhœa, and in her case the treatment was not Tsun, the needle drill, but Tsin, a heat therapy. Jen lit a green rod which looked like a giant cigar and the inside of which glowed in much the same way—only it was not to-bacco, but the leaves of *Artemisia vulgaris*. With this thera-peutic cigar he described strange figures above the back and the knees of the little girl, without ever touching her. The effect of the heat, he maintained, was sufficient.

What was happening here? Since, as a consequence of the political alliance between the two countries, Chinese biology and medicine are based on Russian theories, Jen explained to me his treatment on the basis of Pavlov's theory, ac-cording to which the entire vegetative nervous system is governed by the cerebral cortex. Another Russian, by name of Baikov, had investigated in particular the relationship between the cerebral cortex and the intestines, and had found that the cortex determined their entire functioning. The effect of the pinpricks or the heat treatment on the nerve affected was not so much of local importance as that the shock produced was transmitted by the nerve to the cortex, affecting its function either by stimulating or by tranquillizing it, and thereby in-directly influencing the activity of the organism.

The points of stimulation have frequently no discernible connexion with the affected organs. Tso San Lie, for instance, which is situated below the knee, makes it possible to affect a person's digestion by way of the cerebral cortex. In other words, chronic diarrhœa is cured not by treating the intestines, but by restoring the upset balance and resultant disharmony in the sympathetic-parasympathetic nervous system. Analo-gously, enuresis can be cured by stimulating San Yun Tsio, in the calf; according to my informant Dr Jen, this reactivates the dormant alarm-post in the cerebral cortex, which normally wakes the sleeper when his bladder is full.

Generally speaking, a short and slight 'nerve-tickling' has a stimulating effect, and a more intensive and prolonged treatment a tranquillizing one. As a result, acupuncture is equally suitable as a treatment for infantile paralysis as for a condition which might almost be regarded as its opposite, the uncontrollable convulsions of St Vitus' dance—except that polio requires a brief, weak stimulation of certain nerves and St Vitus' dance an intensive, prolonged, tranquillizing treat-ment. Other frequent diseases which are successfully treated by acupuncture, not only in children but also in adults, are paralysis of the facial nerves, epilepsy, bladder cramps, rheumatic arthritis, neurasthenia, chronic headaches, and aphasia —*i.e.*, speech impediment—resulting from meningitis or encephalitis.

The most important aspect, however, is the treatment of poliomyelitis, where Dr Jen has achieved remarkable successes. It is already possible to say that the result of his treatment is excellent in 77 per cent. of all cases and discernible in 97 per cent.

Treatment starts ten to fourteen days after the onset of the disease, as soon as the patient's temperature and the number of cells in the cerebro-rachitic fluid are back to normal. Treatment is given three times a week, at intervals of two or three days. The duration of the treatment varies from case to case: the minimum is one or two months; the normal length is six to twelve months; and in difficult cases it may be as much as two years. Slight cases sometimes show a cure after only ten treatments. It is most important that treatment should begin as early as possible. If it is only resorted to one or two years after paralysis has set in a cure is inevitably much more difficult, or even impossible, because by then serious deformation and muscle atrophy will have occurred. But even such children have made remarkable progress under acupuncture. Jen told me the case-history of a boy of four, named Sze, whose legs had been paralysed for two and a half years, and, moreover, so badly that not only could he not walk, but he could not even stand up or crawl, and had to spend his time pitifully lying on his bed. Both his feet had already become deformed, and the muscles, especially in his left leg, almost totally atrophied. Knee and heel reflexes had ceased. In this case acupuncture had worked real miracles: after only three treatments—*i.e.*, after a week—the boy could stand again, though only with support. After six treatments he even managed a few steps. After twenty-one treatments he was able to pull himself up by a form and, holding on, walk the length of it. Jen had every hope that eventually this boy would be able to lead a normal life, though not perhaps as a long-distance runner.

To-day Jen's little hospital is one of the most hopeful spots in Peking. His waiting-room is always crowded with mothers and their children; while they wait their turn they do walking exercises with the little patients. Jen works overtime, without special pay. His salary is 130 yuan a month, and he can support his family only because his wife also works as an acupuncture practitioner. Each treatment costs 20 cents— which is about sevenpence. I could not deny myself a subversive remark: "In the United States," I told the doctor,

"you could earn your monthly salary in half an hour. You'd
be a millionaire. . . ."

[BOYD ORR, 81–87]

Sometimes, going down a street, we would see passers-by
wearing gauze masks like those a surgeon uses.

"Whatever is that for?" we asked.

"He's probably got a bad cold. Something infectious, at
any rate."

Inspecting a co-operative farm we came on two young
women feeding the hens—wearing masks; and in factories
and food shops we saw them too. Not only masks. There were
injunctions to children: "Keep your hands clean. Dirt means
disease." Notices in restaurants and public places read: "Do
not spit. Spitting spreads tuberculosis." (Apparently spitting
had been a national habit. The dust in some districts made
it almost essential). Posters told in pictures the awful progress
of dysentery, from an enormous fly crawling over a dish to
the end-product, a cadaverous sufferer squatting in a toilet.
(The Chinese are much less embarrassed about such things
than we are. One bold and popular poster shows, in great
detail, the development of an embryo in the womb up to the
moment of childbirth.)

We were at first inclined to regard this strident, as over-
doing it, until we saw some of the frightening statistics of the
incidence of disease.

Consider these examples. Typhoid and dysentery were
endemic. Cholera periodically spread inland from the seaports,
or along the river valleys. Typhus, carried by lice, was frequent. The incidence of malaria, hookworm and kala-azar was
relatively high. Smallpox killed 15,000 people in 1946. The
following year, rat-borne bubonic plague accounted for 30,000
lives in a single north-eastern province. Estimates, necessarily
only approximations, suggested that half the population suffered from one or other of these sicknesses every year. About
2.5 per cent of all deaths resulted from venereal disease; 10
per cent from tuberculosis; and 30 per cent from intestinal
diseases caused by infected food or water.

Consider also the slender resources which could be de-
ployed against these diseases a decade ago. Then there had
been fewer than 20,000 scientifically-trained doctors. The
majority were in the big cities and coastal ports. Most were
in private practice, and their patients were largely drawn from
the well-to-do. One U.S.-trained doctor, who is now responsi-

ble for health services in an outlying province, admitted that he had been able to charge upwards of U.S. $1,000 for delivering a child when he had a private practice in Shanghai. Apart from these, there were a few hospitals; a scattering of medical centres run by missionaries; 400,000 practitioners of what is called "Chinese medicine", who used herbal remedies and acupuncture (the treating of illness by pricking different parts of the body with needles); untrained midwives who, in the words of one doctor, "would go scrabbling up after the child with dirty nails"; and charlatans best described as witch-doctors who made use of charms, exorcisms, and the calling back of ghosts.

There was every excuse for painting dirt and disease in the most appalling colours, and this policy had brought tangible results. Peking itself was one of the cleanest cities we had ever visited. It was, as the Chinese claimed, practically flyless, though there was something slightly absurd about watching men armed with fly-swatters chasing flies through the market places with all the zeal which other men in other countries devote to chasing game. The villages were impressively clean. So were the new hospitals. Those responsible for them had evidently studied the medical advances of Western countries, as well as of Russia. Operating theatres had the latest equipment, and hygiene precautions were strict. Before going round we would be issued with white sterilized coats, gauze masks, and slippers, so that we could not carry any infection. There was also no over-crowding, and in one ultra-modern establishment seriously-ill patients were in single-bed wards, less serious cases in wards with two or four beds, and the biggest wards, for convalescents able to get up and about, had no more than eight beds.

These facilities were supported by a considerable training scheme, which had already turned out more than 7,000 fully-qualified doctors, and was then coping with nearly 37,000 medical students, 40 per cent of whom were women. This in turn was supplemented by the manufacture of pharmaceutical products and a considerable range of medical and surgical equipment, some of which is even being exported. Standardized vaccines and sera were being produced in sufficient quantities, though antibiotics were still imported in quantity from Europe.

The provision of such facilities on a big scale is expensive. Peking now has three hospital beds per 1,000 of the population, and it is probably better provided for than almost any other Chinese city. Such methods are also slow to take effect. Meanwhile, the bulk of the population has to be attended to. The obvious answer is preventive medicine, and Mme Li Tehchuan, the Minister of Health, made this abundantly clear to us when she talked to us. She devoted little of the time to talking about curing disease. But she talked at length about preventive measures.

Mme Li is a round-faced, easy-mannered, middle-aged woman, whose early life was spent in welfare and Y.W.C.A. work. Her husband, the late "Christian Marshal" Feng Yu-hsiang, was one of the most remarkable of the many remarkable men that modern China has produced. Starting out as a poor, illiterate peasant boy, he joined a warlord's army and himself rose to be a warlord. But being a warlord of unorthodox tastes, he earned the devotion of his troops by living, eating, and fighting in their company, and by insisting that his officers did likewise. Neither was his Christianity orthodox. He once baptised a company of his troops by having a hose-pipe played on them.

Before going to China we had heard a good deal of talk about China "turning her back on the West" and there are probably some ultra-nationalists in the country who regard anything that emanates from "imperialist" countries with aversion. Those whom we met, however, were eager to learn from whatever source they could, and Mme Li and her senior officials were certainly in this category. They were well primed in what health services in Britain and America were doing, and in recent years they have visited several European countries for this specific purpose. The measures they are taking to control preventable diseases are, in fact, very much the same as those in use in the West.

Smallpox, for example, is being eliminated by wholesale vaccination, and all children are vaccinated in infancy and twice again before they reach the age of twenty. Intestinal infections are reduced by the introduction of modern sanitation, and especially by the provision of a supply of pure water. Peking and some other cities now have an ample supply, and it is safe to drink, and the infected wells which formerly supplemented the inadequate piped-water system have been filled up. (One of Mme Li's assistants gave us an interesting sidelight on this question. People had been so accustomed to boiling all water before it could be used for drinking, she said, that when at last tap-water could be drunk with safety it took a lot of persuading before people would make use of it.)

These measures, combined with a war on dirt and carrier insects, a campaign for personal hygiene which began at primary-schools level, and, where necessary, inoculation to confer immunity, had, claimed Mme Li, brought a striking reduction in intestinal infections. Cholera, she said, was wiped out. Bubonic plague was nothing like such a serious matter as it had been. But one of the most difficult to eradicate, she went on, is schistomiasis.

Schistomiasis is caused by a fluke, whose eggs are excreted by sufferers from the disease. The eggs develop in small fresh-water snails which live in stagnant or slow-moving water, and the adult flukes bore through the skin of people washing or working bare-foot in the paddy fields. The disease is particularly common in South China, and its control is made more difficult by the use of night soil as manure. The life-circle of the fluke can be broken either by eliminating the snails or by eliminating the parasites. Both methods have been adopted, and since 1951 prevention and cure centres have been set up in badly-infested areas.

Perhaps the most dramatic step was the forcible closure of the brothels, the chief source of venereal disease. Their inmates were taken to convalescent homes, and the Minister had reports, made at the time, of the background of many of the girls. The majority had entered brothels because of poverty. Many had been bought in famine-stricken areas by the brothel-keepers. At the time of the closure, a good many of their owners were given heavy prison sentences, and the more vicious ones were shot. The girls themselves were treated for venereal disease and given training to fit them for a job—tailoring, weaving, and the like.

This whole health campaign had got under way very rapidly. The recipe was people—"we put large numbers of medical field workers on to short courses, anything from a few weeks to two years, and sent them out again"; propaganda; and an organization that reached into every household. Municipal wards and villages each had their health committees, whose members inspected every house and told the occupants what must be done to bring them up to reasonable standards of cleanliness. When age and infirmity prevented a householder from following these standards, then neighbours would clean their rooms and courtyard for them.

With considerable ingenuity those who might have been expected to oppose an approach so "scientific"—how often the Chinese use the word!—had been won over. "We could have disregarded the practitioners of 'Chinese medicine',," said the Minister, "but then, we would have alienated them. So we decided to have our doctors work alongside them, and study their methods. We knew these herb doctors had used ephedrine long before anyone else. They may have other things to teach us. In this way our doctors could also give them simple instructions in scientific methods. We did the same with the old-style midwives. They never bothered to wash their hands. They took no precautions against sepsis. Instead, we offered to give them a few weeks of training. This gave them great prestige, and when they went back to their villages we supplied them with scissors and gauze, and showed them how to sterilize them."

Some indication of what difference this could mean was contained in the figure for infant mortality in Peking. It had dropped from 145 per 1,000 in 1952 to 45 in 1955. (In England it had fallen from 60 in the 1930's to 30 in the 1950's.) Even allowing for a higher rate in the rural areas, this implies a fall in the death rate, and unless the birth rate falls the population is bound to increase. This must also be placed against an increased life expectancy.

A hundred years ago the death rate in the West was about 40 per 1,000, and the expectation of life at birth rather less than forty years. Now deaths have dropped to 11 per 1,000, and the expectation of life has risen to seventy, an advance more wonderful and of more benefit to mankind than all the more spectacular achievements of physical science. In China the death rate was higher, and the expectation of life no more than thirty years. But these statistics are improving, and given the wide adoption of scientific practices, they could improve at a striking rate. Then the population problem could become a nightmare. Each year 15 million people are added to those the country must support. This can rise with ease to 20 million. Within twenty-five to thirty years, there may be 1,000 million Chinese.

Theories of Communism and birth control do not usually associate with each other. Very wisely, however, the Chinese Government has not committed itself about the population question. They have placed emphasis on the potential expansion of the economy, and there is a natural reaction against the callous outlook of those who argued that floods and famine were necessary to keep the numbers down. On the other hand they were flexible enough not to denounce birth control outright, and Mme Li herself we found to be a strong protagonist of the right of the people to have access to methods of birth control. Not only, we gathered, because of the growth of population, but because women have a right not to grow old bearing many children, as have so many Chinese women.

But at the back of her mind, and of the minds of those who are pioneering a birth-control campaign in China today may well be the thought that fifteen to twenty million more mouths a year must be fed. More housing must be found. More clothing will be needed. To say nothing of the heavy drag on industrial development.

6. Industry and Mining

[CHANDRASEKHAR, 56–67]

"Industrialization is the key to our economic advancement and the weapon with which we shall defeat the American imperialists," said the Director of China's Export Commodities Exhibition in Canton with some animation, after presenting me with numerous finely printed brochures and leaflets describing all the industrial and other goods that People's China today manufactures and exports.

"In the past we were industrially one of the most backward nations in the world, thanks to the greed of the imperialist nations and the lack of interest of the Chiang clique. Now you have seen for yourself our exhibits. These are not merely for show. Within less than ten years of the Liberation, thanks to Chairman Mao, we have been able to produce goods which were beyond the dream of all past Chinese governments."

It appeared to be true. I had spent the entire forenoon after an early breakfast going around the wide variety of agricultural, industrial, and other exhibits at China's Export Commodities Fair at Canton, not far from the Ai-chun Hotel on the banks of the Pearl river, where I was staying. A modern six-story building had been put up for the special purpose of housing the exhibition, which had been on for a few weeks. Hundreds of buyers, businessmen, and traders from Communist and non-Communist countries had been visiting the fair to sample and test the goods that China was producing and order them if possible. Several businessmen from countries which had not recognized People's China had been given special visas just to travel to Canton to visit this exhibition. The commodities exhibited could be ordered through Chinese government agencies or certain joint enterprises (a combination of private and State ownership).

I was particularly interested in the exhibition of machinery and modern industrial goods. These ranged from bicycles and wheelbarrows to cars, trucks, and buses, textile machinery, radio and television sets, gramophones and hi-fi's! There were electric stoves, frigidaires, various kinds of laboratory apparatus and precision instruments and, last but not least, locomotives! This was indeed an impressive array of manufactures for a country that had been notoriously backward and underdeveloped until a decade ago.

Was it possible that China had manufactured all this in less than ten years—that she had changed from a feudal, agrarian economy, and one that was a shambles on the eve of the Communist usurpation of political power, to an industrialized economy able to produce these goods? I raised this question with a knowledgeable British businessman, an old China hand who had for many years been a prominent resident of Shanghai and who had come to the exhibition from Hong Kong to look it over and find out if he could order some machinery. He said that, though all the exhibits bore the label "Made in People's China," he thought only a few, such as bicycles and wheelbarrows, were really the products of China's factories. And a few others were certainly made in China with Soviet engineering skill, but only in experimental quantities. They were certainly not in use in China, and if any foreign buyer should order even a thousand of any of the exhibited items, China would probably take at least five years to deliver them.

"What about the prices?" I asked.

"They are attractive enough," he conceded. "In fact, lower than Japanese prices. But no foreign firm has tried their machinery, and we don't know how good it really is."

Later in the evening, at the hotel, I learned over tea with a Pakistani industrialist who occupied the room next to mine that some exhibits of modern textile machinery (which appeared to be an improvement over its British counterpart) were actually imported from the Soviet Union. But the Chinese had removed the labels indicating the origin of manufacture and replaced them with "Made in People's China"! This, of course, shocked me, for I had come away from the exhibition considerably impressed. But I had no way of verifying the Pakistani gentleman's statement. However, a Sikh businessman of our party from Hong Kong, who had been born and bred in Shanghai and spoke both the Mandarin and Shanghai dialects fluently, agreed with the Pakistani industrialist.

"I don't know about this particular textile machinery," he said, "but I am inclined to agree with you. I visited this exhibition last year and ordered some drugs, but I never received them. Later on, through certain private channels, I discovered that the drugs exhibited were of East German origin but packed in Chinese containers! This exhibition is put on not so much to do business as to impress foreign visitors."

Whatever might be the truth in the allegations of these seasoned businessmen that China has been indulging in these less-than-honest tactics for propaganda purposes, no one can seriously deny her tireless effort to industrialize her economy. She has made an industrial start. She is trying in every way possible to forge ahead. And it is likely that she will catch up with India and Japan in another decade. There is in China a new spirit, an ardent desire, and a grim determination to become an industrial power. Nowhere is this to be seen more clearly than in Wuhan.

II

Wuhan, a city of some 2,000,000 inhabitants in the heart of China on the middle reaches of the Yangtze, has become symbolic of the new China's determination to industrialize the nation, revolutionize her transport, and integrate her plans for a centralized and regimented economy.

In the past, Wuhan represented the general confusion and medievalism so characteristic of China. The three cities of Hankow, Hanyang, and Wuchang were separated for centuries by two rivers, the Yangtze and the Han, and there were no bridges to link them together. One could not travel straight through from the south to the north, from Canton to Peking, by train or automobile, for Hankow, Hanyang, and Wuchang came in the way, and, through the ages, the only communication between them was a primitive ferry boat. But now the Communists, with the technical assistance of Soviet engineers, have built a great bridge across the Yangtze river, connecting the three towns and linking the north with the south.

As soon as I arrived in Wuhan, I was taken to see this bridge. I was driven across it, and at the other end we stopped and took a lift down to a hall where the Superintendent of the bridge was ready with a speech, tea, and fruits.

He rapidly recited how the Yangtze is the largest river system in China and how, in Wuhan, the confluence of the Yangtze and its tributary, the Han, has divided Wuhan into three parts, and how the flow of communications, trade, and commerce was interrupted and hindered. The Canton-Peking Railway had to halt here, and one had to take a ferry that could not be used when the river was in flood, which it was more often than not.

For centuries Chinese emperors had dreamed about a bridge over the Yangtze, but nothing had ever come of it. The Kuomintang twice appropriated huge sums of money to build such a bridge, but, while the money disappeared from the coffers of the State, no bridge materialized. According to the

Communists the Kuomintang ministers built villas with the money instead (though actually nobody knows what really happened to the money).

There was another difficulty. It was not easy to build a bridge across the turbulent Yangtze. Chiang Kai-shek's American engineers had not been bright enough to devise a way of doing it.

I interrupted the Superintendent to point out that American engineers had built great bridges in the United States and other countries and I didn't see why they couldn't have built this bridge if the Chinese government at that time had been in favor of it.

"You can blame the Kuomintang if you want to," I said, "but you surely cannot believe that American engineering skill, which is responsible for so many marvels in the world, couldn't build a bridge like this." However, my remarks provoked no answer.

(The Yangtze bridge is of steel, is some 1,156 meters in length, and looks something like the Howrah bridge at Calcutta or the bridge over the Godavari at Rajahmundry. No one in India gets especially excited over these bridges—the product of British-Indian engineering skill.)

The Superintendent went on with his speech. The Soviet engineers took two years to plan this bridge. It was constructed entirely on a new principle called the "colonnade foundation method," which is purely a Soviet innovation. This was suggested by a Soviet specialist, and the advantages of it lie in the fact that it is relatively free from the controlling factor of flood-water level and free from the effects of seasonal fluctuation, enabling work to be carried on throughout the year. Compared with the time required if the pneumatic caisson method were used, the construction period was shortened by almost two years. As all the work was carried out above water, the health of the workers was safeguarded.

He went on to tell me that this great steel bridge is a two-storied structure designed for the conveyance of both railway and highway traffic. The railway deck, with a double track, is underneath and the highway deck above is eighteen meters wide and accommodates six lanes of traffic. There are sidewalks on each side of both railway and highway decks. At each end of the bridge is an eight-storied abutment filled with lifts. The basement of the bridge is a spacious hall where visitors to the bridge can be entertained by the authorities.

The steel for the bridge came from the Anshan Steel Works, all the way from northeast China. Part of the steel frame came from the Soviet Union. The whole project, concluded the Superintendent, had been completed, like every other undertaking in People's China, ahead of schedule. In this case, the bridge was thrown open to traffic two years ahead of schedule.

"I could tell you much more about this great bridge built by the people for the people, but I learn you are pressed for time," concluded the Superintendent.

As I rose to leave, the Superintendent told me that through the centuries spanning the Yangtze river had been but a dream, and the people, out of their long years of suffering from neglect and misrule, had made up a ditty about the Yangtze bridge:

> The waters of the Huang Ho—
> They never can be tamed.
> A bridge across the Yangtze—
> It never will be laid.

But now, thanks to Father Mao, the children of China do not have to sing this ditty any more. The impossible has been accomplished.

III

There are three sights of Communist achievement in Wuhan which it is almost compulsory for every foreign visitor to see. One is the great steel bridge over the Yangtze, the second is the Wuhan Heavy Machine Tool Plant, and the third and perhaps the most impressive is the Wuhan Iron and Steel Corporation. After seeing the bridge, we drove to the Heavy Machine Tool Plant, a huge factory rather neatly laid out. The Deputy Director, an engineer (the Director, who was a Party man, was away), received us at the entrance and took us to the reception room, which looked exactly like all the other reception rooms I had seen across the length and breadth of China. (I wondered whether there was any Party dogma about the size of reception rooms, the settees and tables that furnish them, and the portraits that hang on their walls.)

After the inevitable welcome speech and the equally inevitable cup of tea, the Deputy Director asked me whether I would not prefer to hear him speak before going around the factory. I said that I would.

He told me that the Wuhan Heavy Machine Tool Plant produces a large variety of machine tools. The construction of the plant started in April, 1956, and was completed in July, 1958, which was, as usual, one year and a half ahead of schedule. (I often thought to myself during my travels in China that, since everything in the country is finished at least a year or two ahead of schedule, there must be something wrong with their schedules! They obviously underestimate the power of Communism. Or maybe the planners in charge of schedules are bourgeois!)

The plant covers, the Deputy Director said, an area of 500,000 square meters and it houses nine workshops, including the forging shop, the first machine assembling shop, the second machine assembling shop, the material-preparing shop, the foundry shop, and the tool-repairing shop.

There were some 2,000 machines in all, half of which were imported from the Soviet Union and other Communist countries. There were a planer four meters in width and three hundred and sixty tons in weight and a vertical lathe with a bench five meters long, and other heavy machines. There were some 5,000 workers in the plant, and the average wage was about fifty-six *yuan* a month.

The plant produced vertical lathes, planers, milling machines, horizontal boring machines, gear hobbing machines, and seventy other types of machinery. The plant is capable of producing a 2,000-ton lathe, if the domestic market needed such a lathe.

With his introduction over, the Deputy Director took me around the factory. I was surprised to find many women workers, most of whom looked young, though one cannot be sure of their ages. On inquiry, I learned that the women did as well as, if not better than, their male counterparts.

"There is complete equality between the sexes today in China, as you must have noticed," the Deputy Director told me. "Women are permitted to work in factories and mines on the same terms as men."

As I did not notice a single Russian expert anywhere in the huge factory, I asked the Deputy Director whether there were any Soviet technicians around.

"Only a few are left here now, and they are in the offices," he said. "Once they have trained a few Chinese, their role is over. The Soviet-trained Chinese have now trained all the workers in the factory. This way we have solved the language problem."

The fact that Russians are not to be seen in factories and offices is true not only of Wuhan but of China as a whole. For though I did meet Russians in hotels and theatres, and at art shows and exhibitions, and on trains and planes, I never ran across a single one working in a factory or instructing Chinese workers, much less ordering Chinese about. The

Russian technicians were all apparently well behind the scenes, their presence as inconspicuous as their aid was impressive.

The last but not the least important sight of Wuhan is the large and sprawling plant of the Wuhan Iron and Steel Corporation. This corporation runs the rising new steel city of Wukang—a suburb of Wuhan—on the banks of the Yangtze. I spent a day driving around several square miles, visiting the blast furnace which had just gone into production, the ore-dressing plant, the open-hearth furnace plant, the rolling mills, the refractory materials plant, the huge kitchen and canteen, the workers' homes and grounds, and the halls and houses used for the various social services of the workers.

The Director, who accompanied me in a jeep, told me how they have created this stately steel city from almost nothing, thanks to Chairman Mao, the imperishable Chinese Communist Party, and, of course, the unselfish aid, technical and otherwise, of the Soviet Union.

The plant has been designed according to the latest technical achievements of the Soviet ferrous metallurgical industry. The Russian experts had helped in prospecting for resources, in the selection of a plant site, assembling of materials, drawing up of plans, and assembling and training the manpower. The entire plan of the steel town at Wukang was designed by the Leningrad Metallurgical Designing Institute.

This plant is the second largest integrated iron and steel enterprise in China, the first being the Anshan Iron and Steel Corporation started by the Japanese.

At the end of my tour of Wukang, I realized how much Russia had contributed to the beginnings of Chinese industrialization. If the Anshan Iron and Steel plant was the product of Japanese technical knowledge, the Wukang steel city was clearly the product of Russian knowledge and a witness to Russia's impressive technical aid to China.

I visited the Number One blast furnace and watched the hot, lustrous stream of molten iron flowing out. The furnace had just gone into production a few days earlier, and there was still great jubilation in the plant over its successful beginning. The Director reached for a tiny red flag which had on it Mao's picture superimposed on a steel furnace and pinned it on the lapel of my coat.

As we stood watching the molten metal flow by, the Director could not contain himself. He turned to me with a big smile and said: "This will be our answer to the American imperialists on Taiwan!" It was obvious that the Director took a very personal pride in this new steel city. It was but natural that he should do so, for his fate must have depended on his administrative ability to organize the entire project.

Wukang's ore and raw material base consists of eight ferrous and non-metallic mines. The Tayet mines, some miles away, are the first iron ore base. The quality of the ore is of a fairly high order, the average iron content being about 50 per cent. Modern methods of mining are now adopted, and an electric railroad connects the mines with the Wukang plant. A large, modern ore-dressing plant is located right near the Tayet mines. But the 5,000,000 tons of coal consumed annually at Wukang for smelting and power have to come from six provinces—from the far north, east, and central China. Despite the lack of some of the advantages of localization as far as coal is concerned, Wukang seems to be on its way to becoming eventually China's Pittsburgh. Wukang's present production is about 1,500,000 tons of iron per annum, but they hope to increase it to 3,000,000 tons by 1961.

Before I left, we returned to the small and unpretentious office of the Director.

"We started from scratch three years ago, and already the molten iron is flowing out," he told me proudly.

When I asked him what was the secret of Wukang's success, he said there were several reasons. "First, this plant is set up and run by the Party and not so much by the government."

"But doesn't that amount to the same thing?" I asked.

"Not quite," he pointed out. "While the Ministry of Metallurgical Industry in Peking is in over-all control of this plant, it is really the product of the great efforts of the Hupei Provincial and Wuhan City Committee of the Communist Party.

"Secondly," he went on, "the secret behind the rapid and successful completion of this plant is that here we used a whole division of the Liberation Army for purposes of industrial construction. The question of utilizing an army division for purposes of building a steel plant or plowing the land or laying bridges is usually a controversial one. Here in Wukang we have shown how the Liberation Army could change its profession of fighting and become an army of industrial workers. I think the soldiers themselves realize that, without iron and steel, there can't be much of an army or equipment to fight with.

"And thirdly, here we have more or less tried to abolish the division between worker and cadre. It is true there are numerous specialized tasks and different degrees of technical skill. But here in the steel plant, whenever necessary, cadres have joined in physical labor, and workers have participated in administration. The solidarity between the masses and leaders is complete, and the distinction between intellectual and manual labor has been virtually abolished."

"How many regular workers are there in the plant?"

"About 6,000."

"Their wages?"

"The regular workers receive salaries of between fifty and 100 *yuan* a month, depending on their skill. The staff is paid between 100 and 200 *yuan* a month. My own salary is 200 *yuan*," he volunteered.

I noticed the small gap between the salary of the Director of the whole works and the average worker. The ratio of emoluments between the average worker and the Director of the plant in Wuhan was 1 to 2, but in India the ratio is in the neighborhood of 1 to 20. Perhaps this lack of a big gap between the salaries of workers and heads accounted for the greater loyalty of the workers. Anyway, this probably was one of the factors.

As we were leaving, I asked the Director where he had received his steel engineering training.

"I never went to any school, much less to an engineering college," he answered. "All my life I have been a soldier in the Red Eighth Route Army. But I picked up some facts about steel when I was posted here!"

This was the man behind Wukang—the steel city that epitomizes China's struggle to industrialize her economy overnight.

[CROFT, 132–144]

I was in Manchuria, or what, for emotional and understandable reasons of their own, the Chinese now call Northeast China, for ten days.

It is, I suppose, mile for mile, the densest industrial area of the earth. It has been ravaged and exploited, plundered and despoiled, first by the Japanese invaders and after them by the Russians but, since 1949, with gigantic aid from the Soviet—an ironic compensation for the estimated £500 million worth of looting and dismantlement during their postwar occupation—its productivity has multiplied four and five times over. It represents not only the industrial heart of China but also the lifeline by which the Second Five-Year Plan will stand or fall.

For students of industrial development, perhaps, a crowded week in this part of the world would amount to an experience of almost poetic intensity; for me, it was a journey into caverns of ever-thickening darkness which I entered with reluctant acquiescence, and left with a sense of exhausted futility.

To say I was unmoved, however, on this heaving industrial ocean is not to say I was unimpressed; only that I had no means of measuring the significance of what was going on. I could register abstractly the fact that China was now building her own jet planes; that the Anshan Iron and Steel Combine was producing nearly three million tons of pig-iron and two million tons of steel products per year; that metal turning lathes and planing machines, now being produced for the first time in Shenyang, were (according to Crabb, who claimed to be an expert on the subject) 'as good as anything produced by America'; that the output of the automatic seamless tube factories, the first of which had opened only a year ago, was nothing short of miraculous; that stainless and rolled steel had not been produced at all before the Liberation; that it was a remarkable achievement for a country as scientifically backward as China to be producing up-to-date turbines and transformers, locomotives, twenty-four-row sowing machines, refrigerators, X-ray equipment and electrical sterilising machines. I could believe all this and more, and take it on trust, as they proudly insisted you should, that in every town except Harbin, they were now developing their own industrial plants without technical assistance from the Russians; but what it all amounted to—or might amount to when they complete the process of transition in another ten years or so—I could only begin to guess. But even if they were running too fast too soon, and neither their machines nor their economy will stand the pace—a possibility which they themselves refused to acknowledge in public— I had the sharply uneasy feeling that, sooner or later, the gaunt chimneys belching black smoke into the skies of Manchuria are going to provide a more formidable threat to western prosperity than any ideological edict issuing from Peking.

To suppose, as some commentators have done from afar, that the rigours of the totalitarian yoke have induced a spirit of restlessness among the workers is wishful, if not dangerous, thinking. In Manchuria at least, possibly, of course, only by contrast with the conditions they had suffered under the Japanese, they seemed more than contented with their lot. It is true that many of them look dog-tired, for, although they keep rigidly to an eight-hour day for six days of the week, there are no annual holidays, and they are subject to the continual strain of increasing their productivity 'in the cause of national construction'—with all the accompanying palaver of factory slogans, labour heroes, model workers, wall newspapers and workroom statistics to spur them on; nor is the day's work over when the factory siren sounds, for then there are literacy classes to attend, lectures on 'Current Events' to listen to, trade-union meetings and sessions of criticism and self-criticism to take part in.

On the other hand, working conditions compare favourably with the average in England. The new factories are centrally heated in winter and air-cooled in summer. There are clinics and recreation-rooms; well-run nurseries and canteens which serve meals a great deal more nourishing than many I had in the delegation hotels. Many factories run their own operatic and dramatic ensembles, and in every town there are Palaces of Culture and Sport where the air of abandoned enjoyment hardly suggests that the workers have anything particularly pressing on their minds.

Everywhere new housing estates were going up in feverish profusion, although I was told that, despite heavy appropriations, the authorities could still not afford to re ouse all the workers from the dank hovels of pre-Liberation days. Even so, they seemed to be accommodating a fair number. The new red-brick tenements were neither more ugly nor less habitable than similar establishments I had visited in Brixton and Camberwell, albeit they were a great deal more overcrowded.

I spent a moderately instructive afternoon in one of these in Shenyang (or, as it was formerly known, Mukden), talking to two young houswives, Mrs. Chen Yi-hai and Mrs. Wang Shu-mei.

Mrs. Chen lived on the first floor with her four-year-old son. She saw her husband only at week-ends because he slept in the steel mill where he worked, outside town. Her flat consisted of a single living-room-cum-bedroom and a kitchen and lavatory which she shared with the family next door. 'This,' she said, 'is the allowance for a family with one child.' When I enquired about a bathroom she explained that baths had to be taken communally in a separte building.

With its whitewashed walls and concrete floor the ill-lit living-room could hardly be called inviting, but she had done her best to brighten things up. Flower-prints, family photographs, pictures of birds and animals—and of course, of Chairman Mao—were pinned to the walls, and she had allowed herself the luxury of brightly coloured pillow-cases and a brocaded green coverlet for the bed. Chinese lanterns and red-and-green streamers hung gaily from the ceiling, but she denied that they had been put up specially for my benefit. 'When I first came here a year ago,' she said, 'I put them up to celebrate my new-found happiness, and they have been there ever since.'

'Don't you feel lonely,' I asked, 'with your husband away all week?'

'Not really lonely,' she said, 'though sometimes I feel sad. But there is always too much to do to be lonely.'

I saw her point when she explained that she belonged to the Street Committee.

'There are many things to do,' she said. 'I organize crèches for the children of neighbours who are out at work, and I try to educate other housewives in hygiene and cleanliness. Some days I go out to nurse sick people, and other times I have to visit disorderly tenants and tell them to improve their behaviour.'

'What happens if they take no notice?' I asked.

'I have to report them to the leader of the Committee.'

'And then?'

'Then she will rebuke them and persuade them to show more respect for their neighbours.'

'Supposing they still go on misbehaving?'

For a moment she seemed to hesitate, but then the reply came pat: 'Such cases are very rare. There have been none in my experience.'

The most surprising thing about Mrs. Chen was that she was a fourth-year pupil at the local primary school, which she attended two hours every afternoon for lessons in Chinese, mathematics and 'General Culture.' She had received no education as a child and now she was trying to catch up. Her neighbours apparently were equally industrious: some attended the same school; some went to evening classes; and those with large families received visits from the teacher in their own homes. When Mrs. Chen completed her course it was her ambition to become a teacher herself in one of the literacy classes.

The interview finished on an abrupt and painful note.

She had explained in some detail how she budgeted her husband's monthly income: twenty *yuan* for his food and pocket-money, six *yuan* for rent, sixteen for herself and her son, six for milk and eight to be put in the bank—and then, when I enquired how this compared with family spending in the old days, she suddenly broke down in tears.

It seemed that my question had reminded her of pre-Liberation conditions, and of her father, who had died of sickness and hunger. He had never known what it was to be happy, she said, to have regular wages and enough for clothing and food for the family. 'He was the slave to a cruel landlord, who beat him and stole most of his earnings. I shall never forget what he suffered.'

She lifted her young boy from her knee and tried to wipe away her tears. Pan murmured soothingly to her; but I could think of nothing to say, for while I felt instinctively moved by her grief some mean political whisper within warned me that the tears might be merely a trick.

Mrs. Wang lived on the floor above in a less tidy, undecorated room where the homely smell of oatmeal and baking seeped through from the kitchen.

She was a duskily handsome woman with sparkling brown eyes and a trim figure neatly enhanced by tight-fitting slacks and a gay flowered blouse. She also belonged to the Street Committee but her main interest seemed to be less in welfare than in the discussion of Current Affairs. Her greatest enjoyment, she said, came from reading the daily newspapers and discussing the world situation.

Since she volueteered this information cheerfully I felt no compunction in taking her up on it.

'What do you think should be done,' I asked, 'to improve relations between China and the western countries?'

I could have saved my breath, for though, as she said, she had never been interviewed before, she could beat the professionals at their own game. 'I have only just begun to study,' she apologised, 'so I can say nothing of international affairs. This is something I do not yet understand. All I know is that China wants peace with all the world.'

She did not belong to the Party, but her husband was a member of the Youth League and she was studying hard to gain membership herself. Previously she had lived in a slum with her husband's parents and family. Her father had been beaten to death by the Japanese in the mines and her mother had died of T.B. She stated these facts dispassionately, as faded memories which bore no relationship to the delights of the new life she had discovered.

Later, when I saw the damp and primitive squalor of the slums, I could understand better how she felt and could appreciate the jubilant impulse which had caused Mrs. Chen to go to town on her decorations.

As China possesses the longest wall in the world, so it can boast one of the largest holes.

The open-cast coal-mine at Fushun is nearly four miles long, half a mile wide and six hundred feet deep; and within five years, they say, it will have have been dug a further seven hundred feet. With the aid of pneumatic drills it now produces ten thousand tons of coal a day, an output nearly five times greater than in 1949, with substantial by-products of synthetic petroleum, cement, and—a recent discovery—*Han yaa*, a medicine for the treatment of blood disorders. Under the Japanese and Kuomintang, they said, the mine was so badly mismanaged that casualties from fires and floods were high; now they rarely occurred, and three days were set aside each month for the repair and examination of machines.

The miner, with an average wage of seventy-five *yuan* per month in the open mine (eighty in the three closed mines), is approximately twenty per cent better off than the administrative worker. A trade-union official expressed this improvement succinctly: 'Nowadays nearly every miner is a married man. Before, only twenty per cent of them married because the womenfolk knew that they would never earn enough to bring up a family.'

I tackled this official on the question of holidays. 'The country is backward,' he said, 'and we feel that production will fall disastrously if we restore annual holidays. This happened in 1952, but production went down by five per cent, and since that time we have given up holidays. The workers do not raise the demand because they realise the country's needs.'

'But surely,' I said, 'if they are given no rest at all their output is bound to suffer anyway.'

'I agree,' he conceded dubiously, 'that holidays are necessary, and perhaps in the Second Five-Year Plan we shall re-introduce them. But meantime we have made very big improvements in welfare and canteen facilities so that the miners don't suffer from the strain.'

The main function of the trade union, it appeared, was to criticise the municipal administration. 'For instance,' he said, 'last year the miners needed more houses, but the city bureau refused to build them. The union complained, and so the houses were provided. Then there are commodities. Sometimes the miners are dissatisfied with the quality of goods in the shops, but we complain to the government and the quality is improved.'

'Has any issue arisen when the miners have threatened to strike?'

'That is unlikely to happen so long as we look after their interests and so long as they realise their duties in the cause of national construction.'

One miner who genuinely realised this was Liu Yung-tang, who had worked in the Dragon and Pea-hen—the biggest of the three closed mines—for fifteen years.

I made my way to his home through a maze of wooden and straw hovels, down bumpy lanes where labourers tugged and hauled dilapidated carts laden with stones and bricks and children squatted over crude sanitary fixtures on patches of waste land. He was not expecting me and, despite the inhibiting presence of Pan, I think his family and myself equally enjoyed meeting each other.

With his wife and young son he lived in a small room in a Japanese-built house and shared the kitchen with another family. His two eldest sons were strapping lads of sixteen and eighteen who worked in an ammunition factory and slept in one of the town dormitories. When I called, the evening meal was being prepared on a little table propped up on the bed.

Yes, said Liu, he could certainly do with a holiday, but he didn't worry too much about it because working conditions were so much better than they used to be in the days when nobody even mentioned holidays. Now he worked a regular eight-hour day and he could go down the mine without wondering if he would ever come up again alive; he could bring up his young son properly, buy two suits of clothing a year, and even invest some of his wages in national bonds.

'Is Mrs. Liu happy about this?' I asked.

Yes, Mrs. Liu, a buxom, beaming woman in her early fifties, took time off from kneading liver balls on a wooden board to confirm that she was very happy. It would have been difficult indeed to imagine a housewife who could possibly look happier, with her young son bustling about the kitchen to help her, her elder sons coming in from work, greasy, begrimed and affectionate, and a stranger from a remote country suddenly arrived to sample the pleasures of her board.

No, she had no problems besides looking after her family, although living in such a tiny room always bothered her. Yes, she took an active part in the cultural performances in the town and she also belonged to a women's organisation which specialised in sanitation and hygiene work.

She went to evening classes with the rest of the family three times a week, and she was gradually learning to read. Some nights they also went to film-shows or they might invite other families to visit them—'to play games amongst ourselves and study the newspapers'.

'Do you take any interest in politics?' I asked her husband.

'Yes,' he said, 'but not in the big things. They are too big for me. I think only of my mine and what I can do to improve it.'

'Do you belong to the Communist Party?'

'Yes. I qualified for membership in 1952.'

'Do many of your workmates belong to it?'

For some reason he replied that they did, but Pan assured

me privately that this was impossible—'There are fifteen thousand miners in Fushun, and it cannot be imagined that even one half of that number have been admitted to the Party!'

However, we did not venture any further on the ideological front, and the meeting developed into a gay family party, typified by Liu's interjection when I asked the eldest son if he had yet started courting: 'No,' said his father, while the rest of the family hooted with laughter, 'but he's trying hard to.' As our smart Molotova car pulled away from the cramped but happy home, Pan turned to me and said, 'I think you have enjoyed for the first time your meeting with the Chinese people.'

'Yes,' I said, 'I think I have only met them for the first time.'

There could be no conflict of feeling about the merits of the Old Miners' Home at Fushun. Its purpose was solely to provide for its occupants, in the evening of their lives, the ordinary material comforts and consideration which had been denied them for longer than most of them could remember.

It accommodated one hundred and fifty men who were too old or too worn out for further employment and who had no homes to return to. They were given State pensions which covered all their wants and they lived in conditions of comparative luxury, two to a room, with central heating, spacious windows, cheerful wallpaper and an overall atmosphere of relaxed comfort and well-being.

Without exception they had suffered terrible hardships under the Japanese, the marks of which they would carry to their graves. They were the only men I met in China who looked a good deal older than they were. Listening to their stories of the occupation, I wondered how some of them had survived at all.

Huan Liu was a typical example. He was only sixty-three, but with his lined and battered face, punched-in cheeks and tight-drawn eyes he looked nearer to ninety. He spoke with a stammer and his shrivelled hands twitched continually beyond his control.

When I asked him about conditions under the Japanese he winced and trembled as though from a blow. As he spoke of the gruesome conditions in the mines, of the floggings and barbarities and the slavery of the fourteen- and sixteen-hour day his voice rose sharply in anguished recollection.

'When we had no strength to lift our picks,' he said, pulling back his sleeve to show the scars and wounds on his arm, 'we were whipped and beaten with spiked clubs till our bodies were covered with holes and our backs dripped with blood. We were treated like dogs, like horses'—his voice rose higher, half-strangled with pain—'like cattle—not like human beings. Every day we saw our workmates beaten unconscious, to be kicked and trampled to death, and every day we fought to keep on our feet because, for every dead man, there were twenty more waiting to work to keep themselves from starving.'

There was no need to look at his wounds to believe him implicitly; his pathetic, broken figure told its own tale. Pan, who had accompanied me, was moved almost to tears, and for some minutes, ignoring his official duties, he talked tenderly to the old man in his own language. 'I have heard of such sufferings before,' he told me, 'but it is the first time I have seen them face to face.'

When we rose to go Huan shook hands and thanked me for calling to see him. Then he added something else which Pan chose not to translate. When I asked him what had been said he tried to brush the matter aside. 'Oh, he just made some sentimental remarks,' he said. 'Not very interesting to you.'

'Even so,' I said, 'they were meant for me to hear. I should be glad to know.'

'Very well,' said Pan, 'but it was not my wish to tell you. He said that without the help of the Communist Party he would not be alive today. From his own experience he believes that socialism is a good way to go.'

Tsing Ching-shan, a bald-headed, withered little man of seventy-five, told much the same story, but he had not been so broken by his sufferings. He had a hearty sense of humour, with twinkling eyes, and was remarkably lively in his movements. His room was the tidiest and most cheerful in the home. The walls were covered with pictures of innumerable children and richly coloured scenes from Chinese Opera, with a multi-coloured quilt on the bed and goldfish bowls and large pots of chrysanthemums on the window-sill.

He had started in the mines as a boy of six, looking after the mules and gigs, and had never once been outside his native Fushun.

When I asked if he had met any foreigners before, he suddenly winced and jumped from his chair, in a state of great agitation. Apparently he had taken my question as a joking reference to the Japanese and it took some time for Pan to persuade him that this was not what I meant. When the misunderstanding had been cleared up he asked me to excuse his behaviour and then surprised me by saying that the Home had recently been visited by a Japanese Trade Union Delegation.

'I should hardly have thought they would have been welcome,' I remarked.

'It was a different matter,' he said. 'They were people who wanted peace, not war. We had no grudge against them.'

'Do you separate the men who ran the mines from the Japanese people in general?'

'You cannot compare the two. Our old taskmasters were beasts, evil men who were amused by our suffering. They were only interested in themselves, but they did not represent the people. The real Japanese are like the people of every other country. They want only to live in peace with all the world.'

'Do you,' I asked, timorously—and idiotically in the circumstances—'take any interest in political matters?'

The question had to be repeated because at first he could not understand it. When at length he did he shook with laughter.

'Nobody has ever asked me that before,' he said. 'I've never given the matter a thought. I can only say I want the general prosperity of the whole country.'

So I left politics alone for the rest of the afternoon and joined Huan and Tsing and their friends in the games-room where they taught me to play mah-jong and told me stories about their early days in the mines, and of the changes they had seen from the start of the century onwards, and of the furore there had been one day in 1913 when a peasant, digging his land, had struck unwittingly upon the surface of the huge vein which was to be opened up as the Lung Fung open-cast mine, and of the coming of the Japanese in 1931, and of the joy of the Liberation . . .

'In 1949, when the Home was opened,' the Director told me, 'many of these men were too weak even to climb up the stairs. They had worked many years as slaves, receiving no pay and only enough rice to keep them from starving. They lived herded together in huts, eighty and ninety to a room, with neither fresh air nor fuel, in a space barely sufficient for twenty. In Europe I don't think you have anything with which to compare these conditions, and though we might still seem backward today you must compare everything with our past standards—and remember that in China there is much in the past which can only be left to the imagination.'

There was nothing backward, however, about the Liberation factory at Changchun. It represented China's first atempt to produce its own motor vehicles and had been of-cially opened two weeks before I arrived.

The Director admitted that it had been built 'with con-derable Soviet help' and that a number of Soviet technicians ere still working there. In addition, over five hundred Chi-ese employees had been sent to Russia to study 'special chniques'.

The target was to produce thirty thousand Liberation lor-es a year, but at present technical and economic difficulties ad restricted the number to ten thousand. Even so, here as an achievement about which you felt the Chinese had very right to be proud.

The place had been built on a large scale. It had thirty-our workshops which covered every aspect of production xcept tyre manufacture, glass-work and upholstery, with ecial electrical and hydraulic power units and a direct con-ction with the main-line railway.

'Because this is our first motor factory,' said the Director, e have to study at the same time as we produce. We have ver eighteen thousand workers, who have come from all arts of the country, eighty per cent of whom are under enty-five.'

Their influx along with their families had brought into ing what was practically a new town, with a population of er forty thousand. Tenements, dormitories, schools, can-ens and shopping centres had been built around the fac-ry, although, as always, there was the sharp contrast with e outer surroundings of tumbledown huts and gloomy com-unds. Even more striking was the contrast between the ining five-ton vehicles sliding off the assembly line at the te of twelve a day and the Mongol ponies and broken-down rts being used for internal transportation.

Within the workshops, despite the giant banners exhort-g the workers to study advanced techniques and the rousing essages from labour heroes urging on the production ef-rt, there was no evidence of any great sense of urgency. It ay have been that the requisite tempo had not yet been ablished, that neither men nor machines had clicked into ar, or simply, perhaps, that there was a shortage of raw terials, but groups of men stood staring and smoking in iet corners with time on their hands and, well before the ch break, a crowd had gathered near the canteen with ddy bowls—and some with packs of cards—in their hands, r did the arrival of the Director seem to disturb them. For moment I could almost have imagined I was back in gland.

[GREENE, 77–85]

Changchun: Facts, Figures, and Slogans

I suppose the Changchun truck-factory visit was jinxed from the start. That incredible man who turned up as my interpreter! I should have taken that as an omen. I am as irritable as most people, and this fellow annoyed me from the moment he met me at the station. "You have arrived late and you shouldn't have come on a Sunday morning—everything is closed." (He sounded as if I were responsible.) These were his first words. Dressed in white shirt and white trousers he made me feel underdressed in my blue polo shirt and baggy flannel pants. He ordered a porter to take my heavy bag but didn't offer to help with the two I was carrying. "Unreconstructed Shanghai type," I thought. He told me his name was —well it *sounded* like *Nng,* and that was the nearest I ever got to it. Definitely, we didn't get off to a good start!

The next morning began badly, too. I was about to take a photograph of the largest, shiniest automobile made in China today—the Red Flag (like a slightly enlarged Lincoln)—which was standing outside the hotel. "You must get permission to photograph that car"; it was Mr. Nng at my side, "is a private car and we should get the permission of the owner." Hell! I didn't even trouble to reply.

Arriving at the truck factory, because time was so limited, I suggested to the officials who met us that we leave the "background" briefing until afterward and get straight into my questions. I hoped to eliminate the political stuff and get some facts if I could. This insistence on reversing usual procedure may well have touched off the difficulties.

Our conversation, according to my notes, went as follows:

QUESTION: What are the principal products of this factory?
ANSWER: Heavy-duty trucks, the new Red Flag sedan, some variations on the basic design for trucks for special use, engines for combine harvesters, motors for pumping, for irrigation. . . .
Q. How many units in each category did you make during the last three years?
A. The factory was designed to make 30,000 trucks a year.
Q. Have you achieved that?
A. Due to leadership of the Party, Mao Tse-tung . . . et workers showing tremendous enthusiasm for increasing production, technical innovation, the Great Leap Forward, etc., etc., etc. . . .
Q. (breaking in) How many trucks did you make in 195

A. There was a slight shortage of material last year so we just about filled the capacity of the plant.

Q. You mean you produced 30,000 trucks in 1959?

A. I do not know the exact figure. . . .

Q. What about 1958 . . . it must have been in the neighborhood of 30,000?

A. But the figures are controlled by another department, I really couldn't be certain.

Q. (trying another tack) How many people do you employ here?

A. I'm not sure, I don't have the figures. I think the number of women is increasing. The Soviet government gave us all-round and unstinted help in setting up this factory —a large number of our technicians, as well as the administrative staff, went to the USSR, to study their methods; a great many Russians came here.

Q. How can I get the figures of production and of personnel?

A. A great many of the technical innovations were initiated by the workers, especially since 1958 when the general line was laid down and the Communist Party of this district . . .

Q. Who can give me the figures? May I see the Director —could he give me them?

A. We didn't know when you came which figures you would want so that we were not able to gather the right facts together.

Q. Look! I have been to a number of factories since coming to China—they have always known exactly what their production figures were. As for not knowing what questions would be asked, it's surely obvious when one goes to *any* factory, it doesn't matter *what* it is—shoes or toothbrushes—one of the *first* questions is "How many of these things do you make?"

I am here to write a book about China. I want to write a fair and honest book. How can I if I can't get any facts?

You say you don't have figures about the number of trucks you make or people you employ. Let's be frank. Every factory knows how many people it employs—at least approximately—and how many units it manufactures. . . .

A. But this factory is so much larger than others—it's dif-

ficult to assemble the facts . . . if we had known thi
is the sort of information you require . . .

Q. (I just had to!) I have been round automobile plant
twenty times the size of this one and they know how
many people they employ.

At this a huddled, whispered conversation between the chief
and one of the "silent men" (Party members?) who always s
in. The chief then says that the production figures would b
difficult to get unless the chief of the planning department
available. However, the number of employees is available an
his colleague would go to phone the personnel department.

While waiting I tell them that I understand that *ever*
country has certain figures which it doesn't make public fo
security and other reasons. If their production figures a
not given out for such reasons I would understand and re
spect that. But I think we ought to be frank and say so.

That's about as far as the conversation went. We were n
too friendly, though on the surface things were all right.
didn't like being told untruths and they didn't like my pres
ing them and making them admit it.

Eventually the man came and said that as far as he coul
determine the round figure of employees was about 23,000

As time was growing short, I broke off the questioning an
asked to see the plant itself. We walked quickly throug
nearly all the main construction departments, hurrying, n
because they set the pace but because of the enormous si
of the factory.

Designed and equipped by the Russians, the plant beg
operations in August 1956. It is self-contained; it has its ow
foundry, forging plant, motor-tools and assembly unit, boo
works, and main assembly lines.

Because this was the first factory in China to turn out mot
vehicles, the Chinese are immensely proud of it. To them
represents a step into the age of mass production. Perhaps
may stack up well by Russian standards; by our standards
has a long way to go.

I listed in my notes nine weak points in this factory.
An array of parts lying about between the buildings, many
them rusting. 2) Too many people not doing anything, a ge
eral lack of drive and precision. 3) Too much being carri
by hand; a single part would be tugged along by a couple
men while other parts are moved on electric carts. All
this through a good deal of disordered rubbish. 4) Whe
there is good equipment it isn't being properly used. For e
ample, main body frames are pressed out on a 3500-ton pre

The press itself is fine; but a lot of time has to be spent prying the part loose from the press, by hand with levers. The pressing takes five seconds while removing the part takes half a minute. A few well-placed automatic punches from inside could eject each part instantaneously. 5) Too much single-occupation work: a man fixes one part with a welder and turns to do something else. 6) Poor lighting—even though it *was* a rainy day. 7) Assembly line moved so slowly it was difficult to see if it was moving at all. I timed it: a foot every twenty seconds. Trucks were spaced twenty-five feet apart so this means that maximum output would be only 115 per sixteen-hour shift, or 34,500 per three-hundred-day year. Even this is more than estimated. 8) Sloppy assembly-line techniques include passing tools from one side to another—not enough tools—and lack of testing, no checking anywhere. Lights were not adjusted for alignment, brakes not tested, and it took a long time to work gas into carburetor; I saw water leaking from a hose pipe insecurely fastened. 9) Lack of minimum safety precautions, e.g., there was no fire extinguisher visible near the gas supply.

I stood for ten minutes watching trucks being driven off. If this general carelessness was the case at this final stage, it can be assumed that a general lack of precision is true all along. The appearance of the factory supports this.

In general I would say from what I saw that the equipment in the factory is at least fair, if not good, but is not being used to best advantage. Given some technical planning advice and know-how by a crew from Detroit or France, a general cleaning-up of the factory, and a rearrangement of feed-ins, etc., my layman's guess is that with existing equipment plus some minor auxiliary stuff which could be made in China, and given an adequate and continuous supply of raw materials, this factory could turn out several times its present production, which is probably only one-third of the total capacity.

The trip to the Changchun truck factory was a useful reminder. The industries in the communes, the developments in heavy and light industry, the colossal human effort going into production all over China still do not add up to a thoroughly industrialized nation.

If the Chinese believe this plant shows that they are ready to turn out all the trucks needed, they are simply deceiving themselves. With tremendous muddle and waste they are producing in a year what Detroit could run off in a single day without turning a hair.

As to the product itself, by examining the truck, bouncing on it, listening to the motor, seeing it in operation under all kinds of loads, I would say it is a sturdy, no-nonsense vehicle without frills to go wrong; rather rough in the engine. I imagine it could stand a great deal of abuse and poor driving, bad gas and overloading. Probably what is most suited to China's present needs.

About a month after I was there, in August, another correspondent visited the factory. He told me afterward that it was operating much more efficiently than when I had seen it. He said they were expanding production and now expected to turn out 70,000 trucks a year. I think our diverging experiences proved to some extent the variability and inconsistency of so much of Chinese industry at this stage of development. Considering the lack of technological experience the Chinese had ten years ago, progress has not been inconsiderable.

Shenyang: Pittsburgh of China

The final stage of the train journey to Shenyang—once known as Mukden—the largest city in the Northeast. Population nearly three million. As the train nears the city new factories, new blast furnaces, poke up through the rice paddies and kaoliang fields; then the scene becomes a jumble of industrial plants, smoking chimneys, and endless gray streets.

Shenyang is the main rail center for the southern part of the industrial Northeast, and is the focus of nearly a dozen major cities. In 1952, on the eve of the first Five-Year Plan, more than 50 per cent of China's industrial production came out of the Northeast. In terms of sheer industry, Shenyang makes Harbin and Changchun seem small-scale. There is simply no comparison. One could spend weeks here going through factories. I went through many—some as muddled as the Changchun truck plant; some in a curious state of transition, factories in which age-old hand methods were combined with modern streamlined techniques ("walking on two legs" the Chinese call this); and some that I think could, as smooth running operations, compare with any in the Western world.

The Shenyang Number 1 Machine Tool Factory presents a sharp contrast to the truck factory I saw a few days ago. It took a bit of doing to discover the number of lathes being manufactured. I had hardly sat down when Mr. Nieh Tseng-kuo, deputy-director of the factory, confronted me with base of 100 for 1956 and then proceeded to rattle off yearly increases to 180 per cent, 280, 350, etc. I shook my head, and asked him for something more concrete. After all, percentages

ased on a hypothetical 100 base are quite meaningless. I
ame right to the point and asked Mr. Nieh how many lathes
vere being turned out.

The first response to this was, "Our objective this year will
e overfulfilled," and so forth.

"You must understand my difficulty," I broke in. "You give
1e a base of 100 for 1956 and then tell me that production
as increased and you expect to overfulfill your plan. Really,
1at means very little. Supposing your production one year
vas five lathes, and the next year you made ten. Production
vould have gone up 100 per cent. It might sound good, but
ou still would only have produced ten lathes!"

We were sitting (a refreshing change) in his office, not in
1e usual reception room. A secretary sat at another desk and
ccasionally answered a phone call, but was otherwise busily
ngaged, and paid no attention to what went on. No one else
ere this time taking notes. In a bowl on the table before us
vo goldfish were swimming inexhaustibly round the Temple
f Heaven.

Mr. Nieh was looking at me steadily.

"You are right. We are not revealing our annual figures, but
can tell you this. Our factory at present is turning out more
1an a thousand lathes of all sizes in our standard patterns
1ch month (and he here listed the dimensions and capacities;
1e smallest of the standard lathes was five tons in weight).
'e hope to continue to increase this number during the rest
f the year, provided supplies of raw materials continue to
: made available. I can also tell you that a thousand lathes
month is 50 per cent more than our average production in
)59."

I felt like a winner of an international chess match who
1ins an unexpected victory. I had been given an actual fig-
e—and I believed it to be a true one. This man was an engi-
er, not a propagandist.

"Is this the largest factory of this kind in China?" I asked.

"No, no. There are many far larger. This is not a large
ctory. It is listed as a medium-sized factory. I have seen
any much larger than this."

I liked Mr. Nieh. He was direct. He hardly mentioned "the
rrect line" or the "inspiring leadership of the Communist
irty." He answered my questions promptly and always to
e point. Here are some of the facts I was given as I jotted
em down in my notebook:

Twelve per cent of the six thousand workers are women,
1d they get the same pay as men. There is no piecework at
in this factory. The wage scale is comparable to other fac-
·ies—the average wage for the entire factory is 70 yuan

($28) a month, the lowest wage for unskilled beginning workers who are being trained is a little over 30 yuan ($12), and the highest-paid technicians get something over 100 yuan ($40). The director gets less than his chief engineer, the highest-paid individual in the plant, who gets 200 yuan ($80). There are the usual welfare schemes—free medical aid, eight weeks' maternity leave on full pay, etc., as in other factories.

The educational facilities provided by the factory are extensive—there are spare-time schools for adults who missed schooling, from primary-grade level through college, and technically more advanced courses for those who want to go further. Writers from the Shenyang Writers' Union hold classes for creative writing; there is an amateur drama group; a sports and recreation club, and a documentary-film unit for those interested in making films. Ninety-five per cent of the workers make use of the educational facilities. There are the usual nurseries and kindergartens.

"Percentage of illiterates?" I asked.

Mr. Nieh (with a grin): "In this factory now—none. The last group passed their literacy test two or three weeks ago. We have very few old people and the young are very eager. Of course 'literacy' is a vague term. Our standard here is not especially high—I believe we have set it at fifteen hundred characters."

The factory itself is almost fully self-contained. Some smaller components and some electric motors are made by the commune workshops in the neighborhood, supervised by the factory technicians, who set rigid quality standards. Rejects from the commune workshops were high at first. "After all," Mr. Nieh said, "the workers were almost all women who had never handled a machine before, but now rejects are comparatively rare."

Before starting our tour of the factory I asked whether I could take photographs. "Take whatever you like," Mr. Nieh answered.

I expected that the quality of directness and competence that Mr. Nieh showed would be reflected in the factory itself and I was not disappointed. If nothing else, my journey to this factory has revived my belief that the Chinese are capable of efficient large-scale organization. Watching the lathes roll off the line, the special train backed onto a siding for easy handling, and the general efficiency here, I feel that this factory really is producing lathes in considerable numbers. My guess is that the plant is working at 80 to 85 per cent of capacity. There were very few machines idle, and an absolute minimum of people just standing about.

The Chinese are not just talking when they talk about work

ers' innovations. Many were pointed out to me. There were automatic grinders which can now be attended to by one man instead of four, a bit clamp which can be tightened by one twist instead of being locked by tightening three clamps. A huge multiple plane was shown me as being a "technical innovation." I didn't understand, since it was of Russian manufacture. The answer was that the design was based on suggestions made by Chinese workers.

Quality and finish seemed excellent. The assembly line moved smoothly, seemingly without much pressure on those working the line. Every part was individually checked before assembly, checked after attachment to the main frame, and the completed machine is tested in a special room after coming off the assembly line. After this it is painted, greased, wrapped, and crated for shipment. Some of the lathes being crated were going to India.

There was a noticeable air of intense concentration on the faces of many of the workers. Each one seemed to pay close attention to the job at hand, with an eager look almost like students who have just mastered some new skill. I watched many at close range. They handled their tools well, seemed to know what they were doing—always with this eager quality. Perhaps this is just Chinese!

[GREENE, 91–93]

Anshan: Steel City

For the rest of the afternoon I went round the steel plant. It seemed in full production. There were no idle men, noth- thing that gave any sense of inefficiency or lack of direction. A constant pouring of metals, men sweating, steam, coal dust —a nightmare vision of what hell must be like.

The rolling mills seemed to be working full speed. Tre- mendous chunks of bright-red steel were being pushed around, flattened, squeezed through giant rollers till they went leap- ing, one hundred and fifty feet long, back and forth between the rollers like red serpents.

High above was the control room. The driving mechanisms below were operated by three men seated at the electric switches. Even here the heat was overwhelming, and the nineteen-year-old at the center controls was unable to pre- vent sweat running down his face. Over his head was a large mirror in which he could observe the incandescent snakes as they lashed out beneath him.

Below, the circular saws with a screech and a shower of

sparks parted the snake into five rails. Seventy kilometers a day, enough for thirty-five kilometers of track. I timed the cutting and figured out the equation. It came to almost what Mr. Liu had claimed. If one were to discount half that amount for replacement use, the availability of even seventeen and a half kilometers of track per day from this plant seems quite good.

At this point Liu said he wanted to run me out to one of the smaller steel plants which the mother-company operates on the outskirts of Anshan. I said fine, anything to get away from the dust, the glare, the crash of cranes. . . .

We drove thirty miles. On the way I asked Liu to tell me what had happened to the small back-yard furnaces I had heard so much about. He said that in the summer of 1958 there were hundreds of thousands of these small furnaces all over China. "Everyone was making steel in home-made furnaces, some of them just a meter or a meter-and-a-half capacity. Foreigners laughed at us about these furnaces, and of course they were very inefficient. But they missed the point. The iron and steel that these furnaces turned out were never included in the national production figures, the iron wasn't good enough for industrial use."

(In a thirty-five page report, the United States Department of the Interior, referring to the period of back-yard furnaces, stated: "As many as sixty million people were taken off the farms to look for minerals, work in coal mines and smelt iron. Although this program dislocated the country's economy as a whole . . . it served a useful purpose to the mineral industry with regard to the accumulation of information on resources and training a large number of persons in the fundamentals of mineral extraction. The by-product of this program was another great increase in mineral production, coal and steel output being respectively more than 100 per cent and 50 per cent greater in 1958 than in 1957. The back-yard program has since been junked, but it set the stage for many small and medium semi-modern industries."

This revealing report, which makes some of my conclusions about China's industry seem almost conservative, appears in Special Supplement No. 59, March 1960, Mineral Trade Notes of the Bureau of Mines, United States Department of the Interior, and is available to the public without cost.)

"It wasn't production that these furnaces accomplished," Liu went on, "it was education. Our people, especially our peasants, have never been around machines like your people have been. They were completely unmechanically minded. Many of them were in awe of technological processes. But now they were encouraged to make their own simple tools—wheelbarrow wheels, gate hinges, even their own ball bearing in a pestle and mortar—and out of iron they themselves had smelted! In one summer's hectic activity, our peasants learned not to be afraid of 'technique.' It lost its mystery. People who have actually poured their own steel and made things with it feel they can do anything. I don't know if that was really the reason why these furnaces were started—but the effect has been just what I said. In six months it was all over.

"There were other side benefits. The peasants discovered many unsuspected sources of ore and coal, which we can now exploit. Now integrated plants—medium-sized furnaces—have taken the place of the back-yard furnaces, and these are now dotted all over China. The steel they produce is as good as anything we turn out at Anshan. What we are going to see is one of the integrated plants which developed out of the little furnaces."

This enterprise (rising out of the rice fields) consisted of fourteen furnaces, each with capacity of fifty-five cubic meters.

The entire plant was set up in three months. Of the sixteen hundred workers—four hundred are women—almost all were peasants a few years ago, only eight men have any advanced technical skill. To construct these furnaces and produce steel with such an unskilled work force, my guides told me, would have been impossible except for the experiment with the back-yard furnaces. These provided a cram-course in applied metallurgy. Millions of peasants who had never conceived of making steel learned enough of the rudimentary principles so that they could now come into a medium-sized operation like this integrated plant almost without technical direction from above.

[GREENE, 53–55]

"This factory," the director was saying, "was started in 1918 by the war lord Tuan Chi-jui. Those were times of great strife and during the next three years only 36,000 tons of pig iron were produced. . . .

"During 1959 the plant turned out 740,000 tons of iron and 170,000 tons of steel. We have just opened a new blast furnace with an annual capacity of 500,000 tons. . . ."

This, too, is the pattern of all such discussions: *growth*—over the cups of tea the facts and figures of a fantastic expansion. And whether or not one cared to question the fig es, the *fact,* in broad outline, was indisputable. I needed nly to glance out of the window to see it: the chimneys, the olumns of yellow smoke slanting across the blue sky.

"We employ fifty-one thousand workers today! Two years go it was only twelve thousand! We are leaping forward year y year and the lives of the workers are improving every ay!" Everything was exclamatory. The director rocked for-ard on the edge of his chair, cigarette in hand, ejecting uffs of smoke like a forced-draft engine. I never found out vhether he was married or got along well with children, or vhat sort of problems he was having with his mother-in-law. ut this man was enjoying life. He was tough and hard and ital, like a successful Texas oilman. He was, one felt, an in-lividual functioning to capacity. His work was his life.

"To what," I asked, "do you attribute your advances?"

I was pitching him my slow ball. And back it came, as I xpected, without a second's hesitation. "The reasons? First: he correct leadership of the Party and Chairman Mao. Sec-ond: the unselfish assistance of our brother countries, espe-cially the Soviet Union. Third: the growing political aware-ness of the workers. . . ."

Imagine, I thought, a General Motors plant manager in Detroit telling a visitor that the success of his assembly line was due to the correct Free Enterprise policies of the Na-tional Association of Manufacturers! And yet, come to think of it, he just *might* if the visitor were Russian! And my di-rector here, I felt sure, would find he had more in common with an American manager than he would have expected, if political concepts could be set aside and *management* and *technique* were the subjects of their discussion.

After two hours of background briefing and questions we went on a tour of the plant. I have been through steel plants in Pittsburgh and Sheffield, and this one looked exactly the same—the same roar of machinery, the screech of switch en-gines from the shunting yard, the hiss of steam; the same huge cranes moving through the same kind of fiery glare and the same perpetual rain of soot.

The new welded steel tube plant was half a mile away. It was almost completely automated. In an enormous, cheer-fully lighted building, a handful of workers, several of them women, were minding sets of electric relay switches. Rolls of steel plate, fed in at one end, emerged at the other as com-pleted tubes, cut to length, counted, bundled, tied, and were whisked away to be loaded on flatcars. This monster was of Russian construction, and I actually saw one Russian there keeping a rather casual eye on the operations.

While we watched, one of the relays went out of whack

and the whole show came to a halt. A girl on the contro[
platform with a smear of oil across her cheek, and her cap
on the back of her head, flicked open one of the switch
panels, but obviously didn't know what to do next. The Russian, though he was standing nearby, made no effort to inter-
vene. The girl called to another man (Chinese), who strolled
over (there was, in all this, no sense of pressure, although the
entire assembly line was now waiting), produced a screwdriver
from a pocket of his coveralls, diddled with something inside, and closed the cover. The girl then pressed the warning
signal and the line began to move again. But she had forgotten to switch on the high-voltage welder. There was a good
deal of joshing, which I took to be the equivalent of, "Hey
there, wake up! Why don't you do your sleeping at night?"

She seemed not in the least abashed—she tripped the switch
and shouted some answer which set all the others laughing.

[ESKELUND, 122–127]

At daybreak the workers set out from their barracks. They
walked in a long row, silently, each man with a shovel on his
shoulder. In front of the administration building they stopped
to look at the thermometer. Fourteen degrees centigrade below zero! They shivered and went on towards the river.

"The other day it was twenty degrees below," said the engineer as we got into the car. "We told the workers that they
could take the day off, they would get paid anyway, but they
didn't want to. They know how much is at stake. Most of
them are farmers from the area that was flooded last summer."

"Don't you use forced labour also?" I asked. Despite my
thick gloves, my fingers were icy.

"No, not here. We keep them away from important projects
where we use machines or dynamite. Some of them still have
an unfriendly attitude, so we can't trust them. They are building dikes further down the river."

He pushed the self-starter. After an unwilling cough the
engine began to hum. We rolled down the road in a cloud of
dust. Several times we had to use the horn. The workers had
pulled down the flaps of their hats, so they could not hear us
coming.

"At the moment we have only twenty thousand workers,"
the engineer continued. "That is enough as long as we are
only doing the preparatory work. In a year or so, when we
start building the dam, we will have twice as many."

The engine began to stutter. He changed into second gear, then first, but even so we had trouble making the steep hill. It was a Czechoslovakian car of the type you see everywhere in China today. Most Chinese drivers agree that these cars have too weak engines, but the Communists praise them because they have been produced in a Peoples' Democracy. This has not prevented them from ordering eight hundred Mercedes from the capitalistic West Germans, however. These beautiful new cars, which arrived a few months ago, are reserved for officials. They always ride behind closed curtains— a custom which they have learned from their Soviet colleagues.

When we reached the top of the hill an invisible hand seemed to grab hold of the car and shake it. Up here the wind had free play. Dust came whirling like dancing dervishes. Chi-yun clutched my arm and I braced my feet against the floor, for we were driving along the edge of a ravine. The engineer nodded towards the water that was roaring deep down below.

"That is the Yellow River." He had to use the brake, for now we were going down a steep hill. "It is only a shadow of itself, but you should see it in a few months, when the snow melts in the highlands. Then it reaches all the way up there."

He pointed at the naked slope on the opposite bank. High above the yellow water was a faint line.

"I have seen the river rise sixty feet within a few hours. Then it sounds like thunder, you can barely hear yourself talk."

We came down to a suspension bridge that was nearly a hundred yards above the water. Here we got out and continued on foot. I did not dare to look right or left as we crossed the bridge. It seemed to me that it was swaying back and forth in the wind, but perhaps that was only my imagination. From a tower-like scaffold, the bridge reached out to a gigantic rock in the middle of the river and then across to the opposite bank. Chi-yun and I ran the last few yards, and we drew a sigh of relief when we again had firm ground under us.

The path on which we stood had been worn into the rock by coolies pulling boats up the river. This was the Gorge of Hell—nowhere else along the three thousand-mile course of the river is the current so strong. It took the men several days to pull a boat through the gorge.

"Do you know why the Tang Dynasty fell?" The engineer looked questioningly at me. I turned to Chi-yun. She is not only my walking dictionary, she is also my Chinese encyclopaedia. The Tang Emperors ruled from the seventh to the tenth century, she said from behind her thick scarf. Under them, the culture of China reached its greatest heights. Finally the dynasty became so weakened by a rebellion that it fell . . .

"Yes, but the river was the real bane of the Tang Dynasty," the engineer said. "It was the cause of the dissatisfaction that made the rebellion possible." He explained that at that time the emperors had their seat in a town that lay upriver, west of the gorge. The farmers paid taxes in rice. There were no roads, so the rice had to be transported upriver by boat. Every year thousands of boats were lost in the whirlpools—the strength of the nation was sapped in the Gorge of Hell. The succeeding dynasty wisely moved its capital to a town west of the gorge.

A roar interrupted him. The earth shook, and a couple of hundred yards away there was a tremendous landslide. When the dust from the explosion had settled, the workers swarmed back to work. Their swinging hammers crushed the rocks into pieces that were shovelled into baskets and carried down to the place where the first section of the dam was to be built. Steel struck sparks against stones; the carriers moved in endless, untiring rows. Thus you move mountains in China.

The Yellow River waters about forty per cent of China's agricultural land. For three thousand years the Chinese have kept a record of the river, and during this period it has overflowed one thousand five hundred times. It is estimated that several hundred million people have drowned in its waters or starved to death during ensuing famines. There are no exact figures for this, but it is known that during the last big flood —that was in 1938 when Chiang Kai-shek's troops dynamited the dikes in order to stop the advancing Japanese— eight hundred and eighty thousand people were drowned.

Once the river had its outlet near Peking. Later it changed its course and flowed close to Shanghai, nearly one thousand miles to the south. Then it changed back to its present bed south of Peking.

No other river in the world is so muddy, the engineer told us, not even the Nile. If one takes a yearly average, it carries only one point seven pounds of mud per cubic yard of water. The Yellow River carries fifty-seven pounds per cubic yard, and when it rises after a big rain it can reach as much as nine hundred and seventy-five pounds!

"If you took all the mud which the river washes into the Yellow Sea during a year and used it for building a wall one yard wide and one yard high, it would encircle the world twenty-three times at the Equator," the engineer told us.

Most of the mud comes from the fertile loess areas of northwest China. This is hilly terrain, and at some places the rainwater washes away as much as half an inch of soil every year.

How can man put a stop to the floods and this terrible erosion. From the time of the first emperors, the rulers of China have pondered over this problem. For three thousand years it was the practice to build dikes, but they had to be made higher and higher, for the river kept raising itself by its own deposits, and sooner or later it would break through.

In 1946, Chiang Kai-shek flew a group of American engineers to the Yellow River. After a short survey, they declared that the only solution was to build a series of dams and simultaneously plant large belts of forest. This would take around a century, they said, and require more machinery than China could ever pay for . . .

The engineer smiled. "In new China we do not measure such things in dollars and cents. Perhaps that is why we have not let ourselves be discouraged by the difficulties. We are going to build forty-four dams altogether. The largest and by far the most important one will be here at the Gorge of Hell. This dam alone will be able to prevent floods. It will be completed in 1962."

A man with a red flag came towards us. In a little while there would be another explosion. We went under a ledge where some workers had already gathered. They nodded and made room for us.

"Most of these workers will soon be homeless," the engineer continued. "The wall of the dam will span the river just about where the hanging bridge is now." He made a sweeping gesture which took in most of the river valley. "All this will be under water. There will be a lake of more than five hundred square miles, so we will have to evacuate more than half a million people."

The artificial lake will easily be able to absorb the water even after a heavy rain, so the danger of flood will disappear. The mud will settle at the bottom of the lake, so the water will eventually run clear—"maybe we will have to change the name of the river," he added with a grin.

He explained to the workers what he had just told us. They nodded. Yes, the new dam would prevent floods. They would lose their homes, but the government had promised them new and better ones elsewhere. And all the people living near the river would be better off, all China would be better off when the dam was finished. This they had learned at the political meetings in the evenings . . .

"The dam here at the Gate of Hell will be the second largest in the world," the engineer went on. "It will have a drop of about two hundred feet. We have already ordered the turbines from the Soviet Union. They will produce four thousand six hundred million kilowatt-hours a year—more than enough to supply three provinces with electricity even after the towns become industrialized."

He looked out over the barren winter landscape and smiled. In his mind the hills were already covered with forest, water from the artificial lake irrigated fertile fields, humming turbines powered new industrial plants.

"But there are many difficulties ahead," he continued soberly—one of the latest political campaigns emphasized that a good Marxist should never underestimate his problems, he should be humble and criticize himself. "We figure that it will take around fifty years to complete the project. It will be considerably larger than the T.V.A. project in the United States. The beginning is especially difficult because we have so little machinery, almost everything has to be done by hand, but once we begin to produce our own machinery we will be able to speed up . . ."

The dams will form a gigantic staircase along the middle section of the river. Fields which now lack water during the dry season will be irrigated all year round once the artificial lakes are completed. Instead of bringing misery to the people, the river will give them riches—it will produce ten times as much electricity as the whole nation now consumes . . .

Again his eyes became dreamy. I could understand his enthusiasm. Never before had China attempted to carry out so great a project . . .

Again there was a roar. Chi-yun and I squeezed ourselves up against the rocks. The workers laughed, and even before the stones had stopped raining down from the sky they were hurrying back to the job.

[BOYD ORR, 118–122]

After Shanghai—Hankow. We had completed our set programme, with a week to spare, and we let our guide decide where we should spend it. We plumped for the biggest industrial town of Central China, set on the middle reaches of the Yangtze, a steel and textile city too hot in summer and too raw in winter for comfort, a sort of Black Country place whose pleasure-parks and boating-lakes cannot dispel the atmosphere of factory grime.

In reality Hankow is three cities, all located on the banks of the Yangtze where the river is joined by its tributary, the Han, and what it has to commend itself is some bridges. One

spans the Han; the other, then nearing completion and no
open to traffic, links the railway from Peking with that fro
Canton across the Yangtze, and has a mainspan of 3,78
feet, a six-lane highway for road traffic, and a double-trac
railway on the lower deck.

"The taming of the Yellow River, the bridging of th
Yangtze. . . . The one will never be done, the other wi
come to nothing" went a popular local ditty. The bridge
probably one of New China's most impressive constructic
works, built largely by Chinese engineers using Chinese m
terials. We talked with some of those responsible for it, amor
them a Dr. Mao Yi-sheng, a graduate of Cornell Universi
and Director of the Ministry of Railways' Research Institut
who has been in bridge building all his life. While they ga
credit to the Russians who helped with the design, one of th
most interesting features was the development of a pile-dri
ing method devised by the Chinese, which dispensed with th
need for caissons and allowed work to go on at depths of t
to forty metres for a good part of the year. This, they r
ported, had made it possible to schedule the opening of t
bridge to traffic at the end of 1957, instead of in 1959.

Hankow's bridge, in fact, is so impressive an indication
the importance of better transport routes to China that it
worth touching on this subject, for the era of railways ar
good roads has reached the country very late. Except f
about 14,000 miles of railway mostly built by foreign inte
ests for trade and military purposes, and certain trunk hig
ways laid primarily to allow for the movement of troops, ve
little in the way of improving transport facilities had be
done before 1949. The people had to depend on primiti
means to move their goods, and this not only hindered ec
nomic development, it also contributed to famine conditio
Food shortages could devastate a district when a nearby
gion had a grain surplus which could not be brought in b
cause bulk transport was impossible.

Much of the carrying of goods still depends on primiti
means, of course; upon mule carts and donkeys; on pannie
slung from a shoulder pole; above all, on sampans and jun
River craft crowd the Yangtze, the Pearl River of Kwan
tung province in the South, and every waterway we sa
Rowed by long oars, with one at the stern doing duty as sc
and rudder, they accommodate the owner, his family, a
three or four sailors, and a square sail stretched on bamb
rods replaces the oars when there is a favourable wind. Th
usually move only by day, and a return Shanghai-Hanko
voyage takes about two months. Something is being do
about the welfare of the sailors on these craft, and their wa

e fixed by the seamen's union, which also gives scientific
planations of how wrecks occur, and how they can be
oided. (Old superstitions required blood sacrifices to ap-
ase evil water spirits, though this came to be no more than
e killing of a fowl so that its blood could drip into the river,
the burning of joss sticks, or the casting of money into the
ters. The thrifty sailors used "false" money, on the as-
mption that the evil spirits were too stupid to tell the differ-
ce.) But the work is arduous, particularly for the trackers
o haul the boats over rapids, and while Chinese-built steam-
s are making their appearance it will be a long while before
ese picturesque vessels are seen for the last time.

One of the things which must strike any visitor to China
how back-breaking is such toil. For local traffic in and
ound the cities, buses, motor cars and bicycles are replac-
g the rickshaw, partly on the grounds that a man is humili-
ed when he has to act as draught animal for another human
ing. Pedicabs—bicycle rickshaws which seat two passengers
are still allowed, though they are now more often used for
rrying goods than people, but as no new ones are being
ade they will soon be museum relics, superseded by power-
iven passenger conveyances. The cities are fairly well serv-
d by buses, and there are numbers of automobiles—includ-
g many American models, some of them new, but most, we
derstood, loot captured from Chiang Kai-shek. It is out in
e countryside, however, that one sees evidence of the strenu-
s, tiring way in which goods are taken from one village to
other, or into the market towns.

This same back-breaking work is expended on road mak-
g. In the neighbourhood of Peking and urban centres mod-
n road-making equipment is on hand, and we heard that
aders, earth removers and other machines were being used
the trunk roads which are to link the interior provinces
th the coast. A great deal of hand labour is still involved,
wever, and north of Nanking, along a 200-mile stretch of
ad, we came on squads of men and women slowly carrying
nes for bottoming and gravel for surfacing in baskets
inging from bamboo shoulder-yokes. The material was
nsolidated with a big stone roller pulled by about thirty
n. With trucks and a power-driven metal roller half a dozen
n could have done the work of fifty of these road-makers.
ey were paid three *yuan* a day (about 8/6), and this wage,
ich augmented their farm income, made it easy to recruit
skilled labour for the job, but we were saddened at the
ht of these men and women bearing a burden of harsh
ysical labour which modern technology, when applied, has
ed from mankind's shoulders.

These hands and this hard labour have had to suffice, and with them the Chinese have laid or repaired some 6,000 miles of railway track and doubled the mileage of serviceable road. Priority in railways has been given to routes which will make the country an economic and political unit—to the north-west line which reaches across the Gobi desert to the newly-opened oil fields and will eventually join the Turk Sib Railway over the border of Sinkiang province; to the rail link with Outer Mongolia; and those lines which make available the resources of rich regions hitherto largely inaccessible to the rest of China. The most obvious example of this last is Szechuan province in the west, whose eighty million people dwelling in one of the most fertile districts, had no railway until 1952.

The same priorities have governed road-making. Here the most difficult construction jobs were the making of the two highways into Tibet, which join at Lhasa, from where another highway now runs to the Indian border. They have economic as well as political importance, for the Chinese believe that Tibet may have coal, iron and other minerals, and road builders had to work at heights of 5,000 metres above sea level, in temperatures of 20 degrees or more below zero, to hack their way through mountain barriers.

Except for Manchuria, which the Japanese developed, China had no real communications system ten years ago. Today there is a reasonable network, supplemented by air services at first jointly operated by Chinese and Russian and now wholly in Chinese hands. It falls far short of any West European system, however, though it does make possible a centralised political administration and the country-side distribution of goods, as well as giving China overland outlets. By all reports the Government is also pushing rationalisation of the existing facilities, and quantities of signalling and other equipment have been bought abroad—in, for example, Denmark. But there are plenty of bottlenecks, most of which stem from the shortage of trucks, freight cars and locomotives.

When one thinks of the number of these in Western Europe, which has a smaller area and a smaller population, one gets an idea of the enormous number China must need. Steam locomotives are being manufactured there—but less than 200 in 1957, together with rather more than 6,000 freight wagons. Trucks are being turned out at a Manchurian plant, but far too few to meet requirements. There are one or two aircraft factories (Japanese experts who have visited them report that the latest Chinese models are an advance on Russian Migs), but in very small numbers. All diesels are

el-electrics have to be imported, and for many years to
e China will have to buy in great quantity transport
ipment—from Russia, Eastern Europe, Western Europe,
wherever she can get it—if the transport system is to be
:ient enough to answer the requirements of so vast a
ntry.

[WILSON, 237–238]

t the corner of the Pearl River Bridge is a large, hand-
e new hotel for overseas Chinese visitors and next door
t a five-story exhibition building belonging to the Export
st. It was barely finished and the management were busy
anging a new fall showing, but we were made welcome
escorted all through the building.

he goods displayed covered a wide variety of needs, but
hout frills and without the competing lines of a free-
erprise economy. It was like a mail-order catalogue with
choices, designed to meet the essential requirements of
dern Western civilization in as economical a fashion as
sible.

he exhibits for export were all neatly arranged on stands
in showcases, and all were said to be produced in China.
oticed one bus, a line of machine tools, small electric
tors and tools, bicycles, a few light steel girders, rails, iron
e up to six inches in diameter, other common metals in
ious shapes, raw materials such as sulphur, talc and barite,
d galore, lacquer, good furniture and chests, carriages,
s, rugs, cloth and clothing (much of it beautifully em-
idered), household utensils, dyes, stationery, surveying and
fting instruments, microscopes, radios, electronic com-
ents, telephones, electric meters, chemicals, glassware, 35
motion-picture projectors, cameras and film, typewriters,
es, rope, leather and straw goods, tires ("Rubber is the
y raw material imported into China"), paints, brushes,
s and shoes. In the best style of Western salesmanship
were presented with lithographed catalogues and copies of
onthly sales journal.

t was in this building at half past three that a bell rang,
twenty scrub-women stopped washing the floor and
ted a tirade. The younger and more enthusiastic stood up
ong their mops and pails and did the rhythmic physical
s approved by the Chinese authorities in lieu of a coffee
ak, meanwhile keeping up a running fire of abuse at the
d, older women still on their knees who obviously con-
red the whole performance silly.

[WIZNITZER, 66–78]

Chinese industrial capacity has been vastly over-rated on th basis of Chinese figures and production statistics. Western ol servers based in Hong Kong have not been foolish enough t accept statistics published on the mainland at face value, b they have often taken off 25, 30, or 50 percent without reali ing they must sometimes take off 99 percent. A visit to th plants upon which some of the Chinese production figures ai based is revealing.

The Chinese seem to underestimate the western newspape man's understanding of industry, and naively try to convinc him a factory is working by moving cranes aimlessly back an forth and making a lot of noise. I don't know many detai about specific industries, but when I see a huge crane mov back and forth carrying nothing and only making a big noi with its cables hanging loose for 15 minutes, I know th nothing is going on.

For example, when I visited the huge new oil refinery th Russians built for the Chinese in Lanchow, I was assure it was in operating order. When we looked at the automat control board, however, all but one of the 12 productic gauges showed zero. On one of the gauges the needle w off zero, so I asked the guide, "How come all the others a showing zero?" And he said, "Oh, that doesn't mean an thing. They are to be repaired." Back in Peiping foreign tec nical experts confirmed my suspicions that when these gaug show zero it just means there is no production.

The refinery was not an exception. At the oil-well equi ment plant in Lanchow I was told that they have 12 enginee —four of them Russian, the rest Russian-trained—and 4,00 workers. Though the plant was not yet completed, th claimed to have several shifts engaged in actual productio The workers I saw were busy all right, but they were bu in a very strange manner—people going about hammering nailing or doing things on the floor or running one machi to learn how it operates, but there was no production at a The American expression for this type of labor is "bus work."

Another example was the ammonium bicarbonate pla in Shanghai, which was supposed to be making chemic fertilizer. They were reluctant to show it to me, and I to them this was the sort of plant we don't have in Brazil an wanted to see it especially. When they finally agreed, th warned me it had been shut down for 24 hours for repai and indeed I found not one worker. It was like a ghost tow

One Chinese chemical engineer showed me a very impr

sive comparison between the formula the Americans use to make ammonium bicarbonate and the one the Chinese use. He said the Chinese variety was much better and gave me figures of how much more rice it would produce per acre. The catch was that they weren't producing any ammonium bicarbonate at all. Not only was there not one man working when I was there, but there was no coke—an essential in their production process. If the plant had been working the day before or a week before, there would be some trace of coke, but the whole plant actually had been shut down for months. Western businessmen and technicians living in Shanghai told me this was typical of a great part of the Chinese industry.

Even in small factories, they said, production is sporadic, continuing for a week or a month, then shutting down for a month or two, according to the amount of raw material coming in, the amount of fuel, or perhaps the availability of transportation.

The reasons for this inefficient method are numerous, but the one greatest problem is undoubtedly lack of skilled labor. The heavy-machine-tool plant in Wuhan employs 6,000 workers, most of them trained right there on the job. They have 2,000 "technicians", but by technicians they just mean skilled labor—someone who can use a hammer or has a little more knowledge than an ordinary illiterate worker.

A second problem is lack of transportation. China has no transportation as we know it. As you travel through China—north, west, south, east, to as far as Sinkiang—you never see a truck on the road. You never see a tractor on the landscape. They do produce a few thousand small trucks, but they don't know where to use them first. Thus the iron and steel plant at Wuhan presents one of the maddest contrasts I have ever seen in my life—a modern iron and steel plant where thousands of men carry things on their backs.

The third and fourth problems are a shortage of raw materials and power.

Inefficient planning is, of course, a serious handicap in itself, and if the Chinese can be accused of any one thing it is that. At the huge "Tractor No. 1" plant at Loyang, for instance, one third of the factory was empty, completely empty. One third was half equipped, and one third was fully equipped. Construction of the plant was started in 1955 and finished in 1959 at a cost of 200 million yuan, or 50 million dollars at the unofficial rate of exchange. By the time of my visit they claimed to have produced 200 54-horsepower tractors but they had no assembly line. In many rooms heavy Soviet equipment lay unpacked or not working. I asked why they had no assembly line in a factory employing 22,000 workers, and they said, "Well, we don't have an assembly line yet. Some of the equipment is still missing."

The only activity that I could really see was training in the small workshops. People were sort of busy with hammers. They were trying to bend iron. In the middle of all these machines, they had places to bend iron by hand. I asked to see a tractor and they were not able to show me one. At the very end of the visit, after three hours, they said that there was one tractor, but it was circulating around the factory and they didn't know where it was. I finally saw it. We happened to bump into it outside.

This lack of production in many Chinese industries is covered up by so-called "percentage gains", reported in the "Hsinhau (New China) News Agency Bulletin." They will always say that "Factory such and such," or "plant so-and-so has increased production by 20 per cent," or "40 per cent." Often, of course, the production is so small that an increase of 20 per cent means 20 per cent over nothing at all.

7. Can We Believe It?

[LOH, 80–84]

Ever since I succeeded, two years ago, in leaving the Chinese mainland, I have read with much interest the books and articles written about Communist China by visiting foreigners. Whatever their nationality, politics, religion, or profession, most of these travelers seem to have one point in common: they are favorably impressed by what they have seen.

I do not doubt the sincerity of these visitors. In their position, I would have had the same reactions, for they were the audience. I, on the other hand, was for seven years on the other side of the footlights, sometimes on stage, sometimes behind the scenes, in Communist-directed theater meticulously designed to woo the onlooker.

Overseas visitors to China can be classified into several groups. The first consists of heads of state, invited by Mao Tse-tung or Chou En-lai and treated as honored guests of the regime. Among these have been Clementi Voroshilov of the U.S.S.R.; President Sukarno of Indonesia; Jawaharlal Nehru, Prime Minister of India; and Prince Norodom Sihanouk of Cambodia. The second group is composed of those who come to mainland China as private or more or less private individuals. In Shanghai, as in other selected cities, the Communists organized a special Committee for Reception of Visitors to receive these "friends." It employed a large number of college graduates as interpreters and receptionists, whose qualifications were, in order of importance: 1) membership in the Communist Party or Young Communist League, wholehearted devotion to socialism, and political alertness, 2) good presence and manners, 3) knowledge of at least one foreign language.

After they were engaged, they attended frequent political lessons; on duty, they were extremely busy. They had to go early in the morning to receive instructions from the reception committee; each night, after saying good night to the visitors at the official guesthouse, they had to submit a written and verbal report to the committee and discuss any problem which might have arisen during the day, such as unsympathetic attitudes or questions by the foreigners or clumsy behavior by any Chinese.

Visitors like Mr. Clement Attlee, former British Prime

177

Minister, and M. Faure, former Premier of France, were classed in between the first and second group.

Of those in the first group, the Communists gave the most elaborate reception to President Sukarno, in September, 1956. Feverish preparations were made for many weeks before he came. Along the route he was to take, numerous arcades were erected with slogans like "We salute President Sukarno, hero of anticolonialism!" "Long live Sino-Indonesian friendship!" I was one of about 500,000 people chosen from schools, government bureaus, factories, and other organizations to welcome him, and at the outset we were briefed on the political significance of Sukarno's visit. "To win over President Sukarno is tantamount to winning over the people of Southeast Asia in their struggle against imperialism."

All of us participating were instructed not to wear uniforms, but to put on our best clothes and remove our badges (in Communist China everyone who is employed wears a badge of identification), so that Sukarno would not notice that we all came from certain units and therefore suspect that his welcome was not spontaneous. The point was stressed that President Sukarno preferred to be called Brother Karno—in Indonesian, *Bung Karno*—instead of President. Before the meeting broke up, all of us practiced shouting *"Bung Karno."*

On the day the Indonesian chief of state was due to arrive, buses and trolley cars began at 6 A.M. to move the half million "friends" to designated points along the route from the airport to the official guesthouse where Sukarno was to stay. Everyone carried fresh flowers and small flags of Indonesia and Communist China. All windows facing the route were ordered closed, to prevent any attempted assassination. By 9 A.M. everything was ready. Suddenly it began to rain. Nobody dared to seek shelter or to show any signs of reduced enthusiasm, because the crowd was under the watchful eyes of innumerable cadres. All 500,000 of us waited in the pouring rain until noon, with no sign of Sukarno's arrival. Then we learned that bad weather had forced the President to travel from Nanking to Shanghai by train instead of by air. Cadres gave each of us about 12 cents to buy something to eat, while the Party mobilized every available public vehicle in the city to transport the crowd of half a million from points along the way to the airport to the vicinity of the railway station at the other end of town.

At 3 P.M. Sukarno, Chen Yi, then Mayor of Shanghai, and Madame Soong Ching-ling, the widow of Sun Yat-sen, drove from the station in an open car, to the accompaniment of loud shouts of *"Bung Karno"* and the fluttering of flags and somewhat wilted flowers. The President waved, acknowledging the applause, happily unaware that because of his changed plans the Communists had spent at least an extra 200,000 American dollars and that half a million people had stood for hours in a downpour waiting for him.

In every case, the Communists made the most thorough and meticulous general arrangements for visitors. First, the Party selected certain cities where the travelers could "freely choose" to go: Canton, Shanghai, Hankow, Tientsin, Hangchow, Mukden, Changchun, and Peking. The first four were centers of commerce and industry. Hangchow was renowned for its scenic beauty; the motorcar factory at Changchun and the Anshan Steel Works at Mukden represented achievements of socialism. Peking was the capital and the center of culture and historical relics.

In these cities, the best hotels were chosen for official guesthouses. Many of these, such as the New Overseas Hotel and Peace Hotel in Peking, were new. In Shanghai, older ones—the Peace Hotel (formerly the Cathay) and the King Kong Hotel (formerly Cathay Mansions)—were taken over by the regime. Local people entered these premises only by special permit. First-class attendants, cooks, hairdressers, and beauty specialists were employed after careful scrutiny and approval by the Security Bureau. Top quality consumer goods such as tea, silk, brocade, and works of art unavailable in the open market were sold to visitors at ridiculously low prices.

The forethought of the party in assigning accommodations is illustrated by the case of former British Prime Minister Attlee. After long deliberation, the Communists put him in a suite in the Park Hotel. The reason for this decision was that the two customary guest hotels—the Peace and King Kong—had formerly belonged to a British citizen. If Mr. Attlee stayed in one of them, the authorities reasoned, he might be reminded of the unpleasant fact that, like most other British property in China, these hotels had been virtually confiscated by the regime. So Mr. Attlee was quietly ensconced in a building that had not been seized from the British "imperialists."

The Communists are well aware that most overseas visitors, especially those from non-Communist countries, want to visit places other than those designated by the Government. So, in every city the authorities made careful arrangements to give the illusion that nothing was prearranged and staged. In Shanghai, for instance, they chose one or two of the biggest and best-run factories from each industry to serve as show places; the personnel of each were specially and carefully trained. Among the cotton mills, Sun Sing Number 9, representing private mills, and Shanghai Number 1, representing state mills, were selected for visitors. If a foreigner said he wanted to visit cotton mills, the Communists would take him to one of these in the most casual manner. At both places, overseas visitors were bound to be impressed by the ardent enthusiasm of the workers. Labor heroes would make most encouraging reports, and satisfactory answers would be given to any question.

Buddhists or persons interested in religious freedom would be taken to Shanghai's beautiful Yu Fe or Bubbling Well Temple. There the monks would earnestly inform visitors that before the Communists came the temple buildings had been in a very dilapidated state, with almost no worshipers. Since the Communist take-over, they would say, the Government had spent a great deal of money on renovations. They explained, too, that it was only under the leadership of Mao Tse-tung and the Communist Party that real freedom of religion was assured. What the monks never mentioned was that more than 90 per cent of Shanghai's Buddhist clergy had already left priestly for worldly lives because of Communist persecution.

In fact, before the Communist victory there were about a thousand Buddhist temples in Shanghai. Less than ten remained when I left the mainland. The Yu Fe Temple and the Bubbling Well Temple had been at first requisitioned by the Government; it was not until the Dalai Lama visited Shanghai in 1954 that the regime released them completely. At that time, it spent about 240,000 American dollars in hurriedly repairing them to make the Dalai Lama believe that the Communists not only protected religious freedom but also helped restore and rebuild the temples. These two temples were actually state operated. The Government forced the monks to study Marxism and Leninism and gave them robes and salaries, since ordinary worshipers no longer had money to contribute to their upkeep. Naturally, no visitor guessed any of this.

To meet the request of overseas "friends" for contact with private Chinese individuals, the Reception Committee made arrangements for visitors to call on people in every walk of life, to have a meal or cup of tea and chat with them. These model homes of scholars, factory workers, peasants, and capitalists were the show windows of socialism.

An increasing number of visitors from non-Communist countries were interested in the way in which Chinese Communists treated their capitalists and in the reasons why China's capitalists agreed to be reformed by the Communist Party. Peking knew that a satisfactory answer to these questions would have an immense bearing on the sympathy and support of Communist China's international friends. Comrades from

Eastern European countries have also been impressed by the success of Mao Tse-tung's policy for the peaceful reform of China's capitalists. North Koreans and North Vietnamese were eager to learn from Mao Tse-tung's experience in order to apply it at home. In 1956, the year the Government took over all private business and industry, North Vietnam sent a score of their young capitalists to Shanghai to learn from their Chinese counterparts their experiences on this "peaceful transformation."

The Communist Party chose about half a dozen big capitalists or directors of large enterprises to serve as typical examples of contented capitalists who had voluntarily given their enterprises to a socialist regime. The chief exhibits were the Chen brothers, leading figures in the textile and flour businesses and the biggest capitalists in China; David Koo, an Overseas Chinese from Australia, managing director of the great Wing On Textile Mills in Shanghai; L. S. Koo, managing director of a well-known department store; C. Y. Wu, a British-trained textile specialist and mill manager of China's largest private cotton mill; and J. Liu, a graduate of Cambridge University who had been the managing director of Shanghai's biggest match factory.

The Party allowed—or, rather, arranged for—these capitalists to enjoy a high standard of living, with servants, big mansions, and cars, so that from time to time they could entertain and impress overseas visitors. However, these men were far from free. They were subjected to severe indoctrination. The Party regularly rehearsed them, and the other members of their families as well. In fact, in one of Shanghai's few lavishly furnished bourgeois sitting rooms, the wives of China's show capitalists were often gathered around a handsome young man. He was the son of a vice mayor of Shanghai, indoctrinating the women on how to play their parts correctly when called upon to meet overseas visitors. These few remaining Chinese capitalists and their families, well trained, were the friendly hosts with whom unsuspecting visitors lunched or spent a pleasant evening in Shanghai.

When receiving visitors from so-called "imperialist" countries, the hosts were to make it quite clear by their demeanor that Communist China's position had been raised. The politeness of the Chinese was combined with dignity and a touch of mild arrogance. Most important, the guests were made to realize that the welfare of all Chinese had greatly improved since the advent of the Communists. The hosts would explain that, although they had had money before the Communists came, the currency had never been stable. Their enterprises had been shaky and uncertain; even their lives had been in danger because of the unsettled social conditions. The Chen brothers would tell their guests how their father had been kidnaped and they had ransomed him for 500,000 American dollars under Kuomintang rule right after World War II. They carefully avoided telling their visitors that the old gentleman after his retirement had died almost penniless and broken by Communist treatment.

Whenever women overseas visitors appeared, it fell to the hostess to do most of the entertaining. The callers invariably received an impression of an extremely contented family unit, which removed any doubts the visitors might have had about the prospects of a happy family life under Communist rule.

One autumn afternoon, a man in uniform called on the Chen brothers at their home. He was an important member of the Committee for Reception of Visitors and also one of the most accomplished directors of the acts put on to impress foreigners. That evening, two distinguished French industrialists who had just ended trade talks in Peking were to call with their wives on the Chen family. The Frenchmen were considered to be difficult to impress because they had not troubled to hide their disbelief of the Communist statements that Chinese capitalists had accepted renunciation of their enterprises and socialist transformation voluntarily. They had requested a visit and an opportunity to talk directly to a Chinese capitalist.

The Communists had given even more than usual thought to this particular visit because of the high intelligence of these Frenchmen and their considerable influence at home. The committee had already spent some days studying the various aspects of the reception with the Chen brothers. But the director of the play, still doubtful, had come again just before the arrival of the guests to give his final instructions and see that every detail had been taken care of.

At five in the afternoon, the two French couples arrived, with the usual pig-tailed Communist girl interpreters. When the guests were admitted to the sitting room, they could not hide their amazement at the luxurious standard of living these ex-capitalists were enjoying under Chinese Communist rule. Through a French window, they could see a large garden full of flowers. A neatly dressed governess was wheeling a child across the lawn, with two dogs frisking about them.

In the adjoining room, the eldest daughter was practicing the piano. Everything seemed so peaceful and natural that no one could possibly guess that each of these details had been carefully planned and rehearsed. No wonder one of the French ladies remarked, "I have never seen a more contented family."

At the guests' request, the hosts took them through the

house. In their immense garage there were three cars: a Singer, a Buick, and a Mercedes Benz. Actually, two of the cars were borrowed for the occasion. The French saw two giant-sized Philco refrigerators in the kitchen and a second piano in another room. In the study there was a fine selection of books, not only by Marx, Lenin, and Stalin, but also Shakespeare. On one wall of the children's room hung a cross (to show that religious freedom existed on the mainland).

After viewing every room with real admiration, the guests sat on the balcony drinking cocktails. They asked their host, "Mr. Chen, how is it that a great capitalist like you finds it possible to endorse Communism and to abandon willingly all your property to the state?"

I had heard this same query from visitors and Mr. Chen's reply more than ten times previously. He had rehearsed it well, and his acting was perfect. He assumed a serious expression, paused for a moment, as though for thought, and answered slowly: "When the Communists first occupied Shanghai, we were very apprehensive, if not for our lives, at least for our property. We were also not sure we could rely on the Communist promise to protect national capitalists. However, they have kept the promise; we have come to realize that the Chinese Communists never deceive people. As a capitalist, I have worked in the past for several things: for my business, my country, my living, and my children. Now the country is prospering; within a few years it has achieved things which it could not do before in many centuries. My business, which was drifting before, is now growing and developing. As to my personal mode of living, it has remained the same since my business became joint with the state. Every year I receive dividends which are more than adequate. Eventually, when I have completely turned over my property to the state, I know I will receive due compensation and a good position.

"I have nothing to worry about. The education and careers of my children are all taken care of by the state. The younger generation, imbued with the ideals of socialism, realizes that gain without effort is shameful. So even if I were able to bequeath my property to them, they might refuse to accept it. Under such circumstances, there is no reason why I should not support the Communist Party and accept socialist transformation."

The French visitors nodded again and again. They did not know that since the Communist victory Mr. Chen had been forced to close down four flour mills and to sell cheaply to the Government two textile factories and a flour factory because of massive taxes or losses incurred through Government control of raw materials and prices. He had owned a modern iron works capitalized at more than two million American dollars. By cutting down the supply of raw material and at the same time imposing a heavy fine for "late" delivery of goods they had ordered, the Communists had deliberately driven the iron works onto the rocks. It had become a "joint state-private" concern, but the private shares had dropped to one tenth of their original value.

Mr. Chen still had, indeed, a large income. However, every item was known to the Communist Party, which had no difficulty in taking most of it by means of "voluntary" purchase of national bonds and all sorts of "voluntary" relief contributions. Not much was left him.

The Frenchmen asked whether the mode of living of other capitalists on the mainland was similar to Mr. Chen's. His answer was, "As a rule, the standard of living of the capitalists is not as high as mine, but basically it is not very different."

This was certainly a lie. It was generally known that there was not another capitalist in Mr. Chen's circumstances. In Shanghai, China's chief commercial and industrial city, for instance, there were 165,000 business units; by the time they became joint state-private enterprises in 1956—that is, were taken over by the Government—90 per cent of them had assets of under 2000 Chinese dollars (about 830 American dollars) each. The yearly dividend to private owners was not enough to pay for their cigarettes. Many other capitalists whose liabilities had exceeded their assets had become bankrupt long ago; their living conditions were no better than those of an ordinary factory worker. But when Mr. Chen made his remarks, his manner was so sincere that he won the confidence of visitors. The outsider cannot be critical of Mr. Chen's integrity or character; nobody who sticks to the truth can survive under Communist rule.

In any case, the French visitors were extremely pleased with all the answers. A banquet followed, and the two French industrialists, completely won over, shook Mr. Chen's hand, saying: "If the French Communists adopt the policy of the Chinese Communists, we shall have nothing to say against it." This phrase was printed in all the newspapers on the following day. Even Mao Tse-tung used it in one of his speeches many months later.

One day, the Committee for Reception of Visitors informed the Chen brothers and me that we were to entertain two English businessmen at the house. We were told that we must be extremely careful in our conversation because one of the guests intended to write a book on Communist China. A single slip could cause a great deal of damage.

The visitors arrived, and at first everything went on as usual. The men toured the Chen house and asked the questions we expected and were used to answering. But when we were having tea on the veranda, suddenly one of the guests said to me, "Mr. Loh, would you mind accompanying me to the next room? I want to have a few private words with you."

My eyes automatically turned to the interpreter. She smiled and nodded very slightly, a sign of approval. So I said, "Of course, of course," and went into the next room with the foreigner.

The moment I closed the door, he said, "Look here, Mr. Loh, we are away from the others. Whatever we say will be just between the two of us. Now, tell me frankly. Are you really a capitalist? Or are you just a Party member pretending to be a capitalist in order to win over the visitors?"

I was startled. How could this man be so naïve as to think that if I were a Party member I could betray the Party by admitting the truth to him, a capitalist from an "imperialist" country?

I spent some time convincing him that I was not only really a capitalist but in fact an American-returned student. The guest was greatly interested. Finally he said, "Since both of us are capitalists and not Communists, will you tell me honestly whether you are really in favor of the present regime or simply forced to pretend you are?"

At this point, I felt real resentment at his naïveté or selfishness. He was naïve if he thought I or anyone else could afford to say anything against the Party or Government and if he did not know that cadres minutely questioned every Chinese who had talked with foreigners. He was selfish if, without caring what would happen to me, he planned to write when he returned to England that the Chinese progressive, Mr. Loh, was really bitterly anti-Communist.

My job was to save my own neck. So I told him emphatically, "I love the Communist Party and Government more than my own life." Our private conversation abruptly ended. He seemed disappointed in me. I was certainly disappointed in him. I do not understand how a really intelligent foreign visitor could expect to have private conversation with anyone on the mainland of China.

[GREENE, 111]

Are things especially arranged for foreigners?

Yes and no. *No* in any significant sense of changing things to impress a visitor. Often the foreigner is alone, as I am. Are they going to disrupt a factory employing 25,000 just so one person will be pleasantly surprised by what he sees? I have often at the last minute changed my plans and decided to see *this* instead of *that*. Are they going to go to much trouble for a plan that might be changed by a foreign visitor's whim?

Secondly: They simply don't care! They are not overly concerned with what we think. They are enormously busy—as a nation at war is busy. We don't care in the middle of a war whether some foreign journalist gets the "right" impression or not. It is part of our self-importance to think that our opinion matters so much to them.

But *yes* in a different sense. Preparations are made; a hotel room is booked; certain plans are arranged for, the picnic lunch is prepared. The most "casual" day, you can see afterward, was most carefully thought out—mostly for your own comfort. The Chinese have a rare sensitivity about a traveler's needs. They seem to know exactly when he's had enough, when he wants to be alone, when he needs a nap, when he needs a beer.

8. Bureaucracy and Propaganda

[SCHMID, 18–19]

My interpreter from the China Travel Service, Mr. Chin, was a charming young man. He was the son of a teacher in the provinces, and only twenty-two. He was obligingness itself whenever it was a case of organizing some permitted excursion. But for those not permitted he remained rigidly unrelenting. Not permitted, for instance, was such a harmless request as driving out of the city to have a look at a village. The villages of Kwangtung Province, as I had established from the train, are particularly picturesque. From among the white cubes of the houses there rise up, as in little medieval towns, tall towers, belonging, no doubt, to the houses of the landowners—or, rather, the *former* landowners. The peasants were busy tilling their fields: winter here does not condemn them to inactivity. No, explained Chin, such a visit was out of the question so long as I had no permit for it from Peking.

"Surely," he remarked, almost indignantly, "even in Switzerland a foreign journalist can't simply drive out to the villages and talk to the people!"

"No," I agreed gloomily, "he must first pass an examination in Jassen [Swiss card game] at the Press Department in the Federal Government Building."

"There you are," Chin said triumphantly.

There it was, the invisible wall which immediately surrounds every foreign visitor. The wall of language, which can be surmounted only with the help of an interpreter who is close to the police. The wall of appearance, which immediately singles out the stranger and causes him to collect crowds of onlookers at even the briefest stop. As for the hesitation of my good Chin, I do not believe that it sprang so much from any real intent to keep certain things hidden from me, as from a panicky endeavour not to allow anything that might conceivably be forbidden. As to what is, in fact, forbidden there exist the most diverse ideas. Especially where taking photographs is concerned.

It is forbidden to take photographs of strategic objects and installations serving communications—such as railways and bridges. This does not, however, prevent lesser brains—which

exist also among the Chinese police—from nurturing truly
fantastic ideas about the nature of strategic objects. Once, for
instance, I met with obstruction when trying to photograph a
'Palace of Culture' in Canton—a massive theatre built by the
regime and adorned with a statue of Mao.

Another time a reactionary fortune-teller in the street
proved a highly strategic object. When I tried to snap the
colourful life aboard a train a horrified guard clapped his
hand over my lens. In vain I tried to explain that people playing cards and dozing on their bunks, or small children crawling along the corridor and climbing over the seats, could not
possibly be military secrets. He remained unshaken: regulations were regulations. And then, all of a sudden, I experienced
an unexpected triumph. After a stop at one of the larger
stations the guard suddenly entered my compartment, cere-
monially sat down facing me, and embarked on a long speech
which was translated for me by my English-speaking travelling
companion. I learned that the good man had consulted his
superior at the station we had just left and had found that
I had been right. He now apologized with genuine contrition
in his features, just as if he had committed a capital crime,
and I for my part consoled him, much touched, and assured
him that I greatly appreciated his devotion to duty and, even
more so, his readiness to correct his mistake.

[WILSON, 86–87]

I did consider photographing another class of people also
there in great numbers, but I decided it wise not to do so.
On the sides of the courtyard a battalion of soldiers were
sitting sheltering from the rain. While photographing the
Temple of Heaven I noticed that when I turned my camera
towards the soldiers an orderly was dispatched in my direction, so I surmised that it would be prudent to refrain.
Conspicuously and intently, I photographed the central architecture and elaborately put my camera back into its case.

By the time we had finished seeing these things and returned
to the head of the ramp, the worst of the shower was over
and on the causeway many soldiers were parading to the
music of a hidden band. Mr. Tien and I walked slowly down
its whole length to another palace a quarter of a mile away.
The road was just wide enough for twenty men abreast to
march by us on either side as we walked down the centre,
brushing past fierce and angry drill sergeants while the

lumns of troops swung past on either side, only two or three
et away.

"Mr. Tien," I said, "how is it that in your peace-loving
d progressive country there are so many soldiers about?"
For a moment he hesitated and then replied, "I believe
at they may be a cadet corps from one of the universities
dergoing holiday training."

"Congratulations!" I said. "I do not think I have ever seen
tter-trained cadets."

I thought back to the spring of 1940 to a parade ground
Aldershot, England, where with the help of experienced
rgeant-majors we Canadian engineers had desperately sought
prepare ourselves for a general inspection before a trip to
rance, which never came.

How Mr. Tien could have imagined for a moment that I
ould believe that these were cadets, I do not know. These
en, far from being half-trained youngsters casually parading,
ere magnificent troops, well drilled and disciplined and prac-
sing a precise and exaggerated goose-step in phalanxes of
ur hundred. It was a tremendous sensation to feel the ring
' the stone beneath one as these khaki-clad men stamped
st in tight formations twenty wide and twenty deep. They
ere clearly the *élite* of the Chinese professional army, prac-
sing for some ceremonial parade.

Much as I would have liked to do so, I did not take pic-
res, but walked slowly down the parade admiring the excel-
nt discipline that was being driven home by tough sergeants.
he latter looked at me with hatred, but they knew that I
as not there by chance and said nothing.

[CLARK, 118–121]

In Peking, I requested the information department of the
Iinistry of Foreign Affairs to arrange an interview with the
inister of health. The minister, I was informed, was not
vailable, but the propaganda chief of health was; and so I
ent along, accompanied by Mr. Chen, my interpreter of the
revious few days. Mr. Chen is a native of Shanghai and, I
n convinced, can hardly speak Mandarin, let alone English.
once asked him to express my gratitude to an official with
hom I had spoken at length. But even a simple "thank you,"
anslated by Mr. Chen, emerged as something else; the
ficial, misled into thinking I had asked for the time, glanced
his wrist watch and said it was ten minutes past four.

In any event, we now had a chat with a man named Chan Chao-shen. For an hour, while the usual cups of tea wer poured, Mr. Chang stared at me peculiarly and struggle politely but vainly to answer some general questions abou public health.

"How many doctors are there in China?" I asked.

"I don't know," said Mr. Chang, "but I can tell you abou sparrows."

It was only then that we discovered that Mr. Chang was n the propaganda chief of the Ministry of Health. He was, i fact, the chief statistician for the Patriotic Sanitary Movemen Mr. Chen, the interpreter, blinked his eyes in some consterna tion. But, since we had already lost an hour, I decided to sta a while and hear about the Patriotic Sanitary Movemen China is still engrossed in the all-out campaign against th "four pests"—flies, mosquitoes, and rats because they sprea disease, sparrows because they nibble at precious grain. Th flies are relatively easy to cope with; millions of Chinese ar issued fly swatters, and these instruments of destruction han conspicuously in hotel lobbies, rail carriages, public building and private residences. Sparrows are a bit more difficult t handle. The Chinese cannot issue air rifles to six hundred an fifty million people; so they've thought up an ingenious alterna tive. People bang away on cymbals and drums, frightening o the birds that need occasionally to alight on trees to res Sparrows drop from the sky out of sheer exhaustion.

After relating the thorough preparations for the shock tac tics, Mr. Chang handed me a prepared bulletin:

Peking's headquarters for the war against the sparrow pes ordered a general offensive to start at 4:30 A.M. on April 19 An army of millions of Peking residents went into action Every house and tree was turned into a fortress. At the ap pointed time everybody was at his battle post. At five o'cloc sharp, men and women, old and young, began the attack They beat drums, gongs, cymbals, pots and pans, let off fire crackers, and raised a deafening clamor. All over the city scarecrows and bright-colored flags fluttered on roof top and trees. After a few hours, large numbers of sparrows scared out of their retreats, starved, and with no place t rest, perished. Some fled into areas where it seemed to b quiet only to fall into snares and concentrated gunfire Operations continued late into the evening to capture thos that had somehow escaped the daytime offensive and gon into hiding.

There was a grim seriousness about Mr. Chang, and so th

bulletin had to be accepted at face value. He did not care to elaborate on how some sparrows managed somehow to go "into hiding." But I had already heard from British embassy people how they had turned their own compound into a sanctuary, permitting millions of bird refugees to use the trees there. Such is the perfidy of which the British are capable. But the British were highly criticized for granting diplomatic immunity to Chinese birds; eventually the Chinese staff of the embassy shot off firecrackers, and the terrified sparrows flew off.

What happened to them? Statistician Chang, in all earnestness, said: "In the last six months the people have eliminated 1,600,005,000 sparrows." What about rats? Statistician Chang said: "In the same period the people eliminated 1,500,007,000 rats." Mr. Chang swore that the figures were deadly accurate, hence the specific 5,000 and 7,000. As for flies and mosquitoes, 118,000 tons of these were exterminated in the six months.

"How are you so sure it was 118,000 tons and not 120,000 tons?" I asked. "Did people weigh each fly or mosquito as they caught it?"

"Oh, no," said Mr. Chang. "The way we do it is to spread papers on floors and in bushes. We collect the dead flies and mosquitoes in batches, and then weigh them."

At least I think Mr. Chang said all this. I will never know for certain, thanks to the ineptness of Mr. Chen as an interpreter. China has plenty of older men who speak good English, but they are never employed as interpreters. It is much more sensible to take a young man like Mr. Chen, who is about twenty-six, give him a thorough indoctrination course, with English as a sideline, and then turn him loose on helpless foreigners. Really, on reflection, you don't have much fun in China even as a visitor. But if you are patient you can learn a little about Chinese logic. For instance, a diplomat's car was in a collision with a government vehicle, and he was afraid his Chinese chauffeur would be considered at fault. The state insurance company said it would have to wait for a ruling from the traffic court. Finally it informed the diplomat: "Since your driver is held 80 per cent responsible for the accident, you will receive 80 per cent of the compensation."

The diplomat, so far as I know, is still trying to figure it out.

[WILSON, 128–130]

I was up at 7.30 and went to the European dining-room upstairs for breakfast of an omelette and tea. I felt that I was not cheating too badly in my resolve to eat only Chinese food, for I had learned by now that black eggs, sour pickles and stewed rice were not the only form of Chinese breakfast. I could have had an omelette and tea downstairs. The waitress was rather astonished when I refused a knife and fork and asked for chopsticks.

Going down to my room I noticed that the elevator was of a make well known in North America, but it had on it in English "Made in Switzerland." It worked well, either with an operator or in the evening by automatic buttons.

"*Wu lou*," I said to the elevator operator. Whether he understood that I was trying to say fifth floor, or whether he merely recognized me and knew where I should get off, I do not know.

In my room I was preparing to go to the University of Peking when Mr. Tien phoned and said that there had been a change in plans. I wondered whether this delay was because of some real difficulty or whether I had asked to see too many institutes. In any case I was glad of the chance to write letters and to get my luggage organized. It was nearly noon before Mr. Tien arrived. He was rather brusque and asked me for two passport pictures.

"It will be necessary for you to get a special police permit to stay in this country."

"That is absurd," I said. "I have been here a week already and no one ever mentioned the matter before. This is a ridiculous piece of red tape."

I was puzzled, but the reason soon became apparent when Mr. Tien produced my passport and said,

"Why does your passport refer to 'Mainland' China? There is no 'Mainland' China. There is only one China, not two Chinas. It is most insulting."

I asked to see the passport and discovered that he was referring to a slip of paper, giving instructions to Canadians intending to visit Communist countries. It had been pasted in the back of my passport by the Canadian authorities when I had asked their advice and help in getting visas for this trip. The notice warned Canadian travellers on entering or leaving Communist countries to report to Canadian consulates on both sides of the border, for their own protection. If there was none, Canadians were advised to go to British consulates; and it gave a list of these countries and addresses of the consulates.

No doubt with the best of intentions, and because Canada does not formally recognize their governments, it referred to two of these countries as "Mainland" China and "East" Germany, instead of by their proper names, "The People's Re public of China" and the "German Democratic Republic." The whole thing seemed unnecessary and a great nuisance.

Fortunately, I realized that the offending paper was not part of the passport but merely a note of advice. I therefore ripped it out and tore it to small pieces.

"Stop!" said Mr. Tien. "You can't do that. You are defacing your passport."

"Nonsense," I said. "It is not part of the passport, and I've done it." I gave him back the passport and, muttering, he went off to the authorities on the mezzanine floor. I realized that I had caused the Canadian Government and myself a considerable loss of face, but it was a small price to pay for the resultant restoration of my passport and Mr. Tien's equanimity. Thereafter, all question of an internal passport was dropped.

[GREENE, 114]

Letter to Elena   June 24

. . . Another appallingly frustrating day. I phoned the Ministry again today, but couldn't get anywhere; no answer, not even "no." The Chinese have a highly developed sense of *timing*. They will wait until *they* think it is time to act. And then, if need be, they can act quickly. But they *won't* be *pushed!*

I have never in my entire life come up against this in quite the form it takes here. It is like being pitted against a solid wall of rock. There is no way to climb it or push it, or to get around the ends. It is just there; a colossal disregard for anything but that which they consider important. There is tremendous strength in this and it creates havoc with anyone who cannot bend a bit.

This is what the early Europeans found when dealing with the Emperors. This is what the Americans found when negotiating with the Chinese in Korea. This is what has been going on for more than five years of ambassadorial meetings in Warsaw. The Chinese are ready to meet, ready to talk, but not ready to compromise a single basic principle.

It has been a difficult lesson for me. I'm usually impatient to get things *done*. But the Chinese refuse to be hurried or made to do something in a way that is not right to *them*. One sees it, too, in the ordinary people everywhere. They are never rushed, never petulant, never impatient; they go their own way and at their own speed.

[SCHMID, 16–17]

One feature of Chinese trains is the loudspeaker which blares in every carriage. It blares, at full volume, from the start of a journey to its end, fortunately with a few merciful breaks. Wonderfully sensitive as the Chinese are in the visual field, they are quite insensitive in the acoustic field: they must have calluses on their eardrums. I had tasted this delight in noise to the full in countless sleepless nights in Chinese-owned hotels throughout Southeast Asia, and was therefore not surprised by the box above our heads, especially as I did not understand its message. The songs it offered had a decidedly Eastern ring: at times I felt that I had heard them before, in some choral scene from an opera by Mussorgsky or Borodin. At other times the loudspeaker seemed to present scenes from classical Chinese plays: a nasal female falsetto, half speaking and half singing, accompanied by those fiddles and tinny drums that are found whining and bleating behind every Far Eastern stage.

All this was just a mask for a more essential message. Later, when I shared a compartment with an English-speaking traveller on the long trip from Canton to Peking, I asked him the meaning of those songs, and discovered that they were propaganda tunes for the regime. This stirring marching song extolled an heroic feat of the Chinese Red Army during that famous Long March, when an advance-guard found a suspension bridge destroyed but its chains still intact, and, under the enemy's bullets, worked their way across hanging by their hands from the chains, thereby securing the river crossing for their comrades. That other little song, breathed lightly by a girl's voice, expressed the raptures of tea-pickers at having exceeded their production target. A woman's choir, elegiac *ma non troppo,* sent its greetings to the soldiers on the frontier, who were guarding the country against the imperialist beasts. And here—oh, yes, quite unmistakable—this exciting revolutionary outcry, throbbing with almost impatient optimism, called for the liberation of Formosa. Even the falsetto-voiced prima donna in the classical play spoke of the joys, and even more so of the duties, of the Communist Paradise.

The traveller's reaction to the continual blaring above his head is like every human protest that is not settled by force: for a few hours he curses the thing which makes impossible all conversation, and even the flow of his own thoughts, or concentration on his reading matter. Then he surrenders, sitting underneath that ceaseless stream of tones and words, apathetic like a hen in the rain, all his mental plumage ruffled.

But all the time, even if he is not listening, the thing seeps into his soul. After a while I knew the two dozen songs by heart; after another while I was humming in tune to them. And if I had been a Chinese—who knows, I might even have believed them.

[SCHMID, 147–151]

It may seem a little strange to start some observations about the building of the new China with complaints about Mr Li. Li was my interpreter in Peking, and he was one of the most stupid people I have come across in my whole life. I have never quite understood why Peking, which in every other respect endeavours to be a display window of a perfectionist Utopia come true, should be the meeting-place of the worst interpreters in China. Li, I discovered, was no exception: a British colleague was having a terrible time with an interpreter who wrote down every word during an interview and subsequently translated it for her with the help of a dictionary. But even Li was bad enough to drive a person to distraction. To quote one example: when I intended to inspect the Great Wall I declined the customary lightning tour in the car of the Travel Service and announced that I wanted to go there by rail. Mr Li made eyes like saucers. "There is no railway going to the Great Wall," he said.

I proved to him by the map and the guide-book that there was a railway, and asked him to look up the departure time in the railway timetable. Li declared that there was only a train in the afternoon, which would make it impossible to get back. It needed the interpreter of the Swiss Legation to establish that there was a train which left at half-past seven in the morning, and that it was perfectly feasible to return by a train at three o'clock, with five hours to devote to the Great Wall. All this was unknown to the official Travel Service. It is so incredible that one is led to seek the explanation not in stupidity but in excessive cunning. But Li did not confine himself to this isolated proof of his genius. Every Communist, one would assume, ought to know Picasso's name, considering that his dove of peace adorns not only every shop-window, but also many a tea service in China. When I asked the Director of the Art Institute what his opinion was of Picasso's work I had to spell out the name for Li. The Director's reply, in Li's translation, ran as follows: "The Chinese comrades are enthusiastic about the work of the great Soviet painter Picasso."

I have a reason for recording these incidents. The stranger in China has not the slightest hope of casting a glance into the inner workings of the administration, or of discovering how this all-powerful bureaucratic machine deals with the Chinese who have got into its maw. His only experience will be that of the official Travel Service, which, unless he resolutely frees himself, will hold him firmly in its clutches and control his every movement. This is done with smooth efficiency so long as the visitor keeps to the well-worn path, and breaks down completely the moment he moves an inch off it.

Admittedly there are many other countries in the East—and even in Europe—where every attempt to cope with the slovenliness and incompetence of the administration only results in torment. But there, nature as a rule provides its own cure: you can either lubricate the sluggish machinery with a tip or else you can use your initiative. In China these safety-valves are blocked: there is nothing for it—you have got to go through the mincing-machine. Similarly, in the event of a dispute there is no way of obtaining justice. The China Travel Service, to quote an example, presented me on the last day of my stay in Peking with a bill on which a sum of more than 40 yuan was set down for a less than three hours' tour of the outlying district—although on the day before a colleague had paid only half as much for a tour of about the same distance and, in fact, longer duration. I demanded a detailed statement of account. Mr Li disappeared to an upper floor, and after a while returned with the general assurance that everything was quite correct. No further explanation. No possibility of appealing to the Director for an elucidation of this absurd arithmetic.

The conclusions I have drawn from these experiences are obvious. If the management of agricultural, industrial, cultural, and Heaven knows what other affairs is functioning as incompetently and as arbitrarily as that of the official Travel Service—what colossal assets must be wasted by this bureaucratic machine! A foreign-language teacher in Shanghai with whom I discussed this problem gave me the reason for the inadequacy of the interpreters. "They could get thousands of Chinese with an excellent command of foreign languages," he told me. "But they don't trust them. They prefer to put some youngsters through a brief training course, while their brains can still be moulded to the pattern of Communism. For dealing with foreigners, needless to say, political orthodoxy is more important than real knowledge. Even our classes here have been ideologically streamlined to the point of absurdity. The other day I was going to develop a lesson from Kant's dictum 'Peace is the supreme conclusion of Reason.' The censor, to whom we have to submit in advance even our language lessons, cut out this sentence." "Why?" I asked him. "Surely this is a sentiment any intelligent person could subscribe to?" "Because Kant said so," was his reply.

China is thus faced with the same problem as troubles all other Communist States: at the very moment when the centralization and bureaucratization of all life demands the highest level of efficiency in the administrative brain of this super-organism, the organism finds itself short of the vigour it so desperately needs. The drive which it had been hoped would spring from centralization and Socialist control flags under the icy armour which lack of ability, fear of responsibility, and similar consequences of an all-too-forcible reorganization have clamped on the country. A journey across China is tremendously impressive even for a visitor in a hurry—or, perhaps, mainly for a visitor in a hurry.

The things that are springing up, not only in Peking, but wherever the Government wields its spade, are simply overwhelming in their scale. The whole of China, one might say, smells of cement. And it is not just a case of huge new factories, schools, universities, hospitals, and stadiums—those showpieces of an ideology which has inscribed progress on its banner. In Shanghai I met the East Berlin musicologist Harry Goldschmidt, who is helping, as a visiting specialist, to reorganize China's musical life. I met Hungarian footballers and Polish glider pilots who were working as instructors in China. This is what impresses the visitor so tremendously: that not merely a few sectors of life are being driven forward, but that the whole front has begun to advance. Or, to use another simile, that the shrivelled tree of a stagnating China is not only pushing out buds along its principal branches, but that here is new life stirring throughout its foliage.

But—and it is a huge But—the cost is simply staggering. In exchange for the modern machinery it imports from Russia and Czechoslovakia China must export such quantities of agricultural produce that the population has to be put on rations, and even unrationed foodstuffs are in short supply in Shanghai. The pitifully low wages make it possible to keep the cost of the vast projects low, and hence, in a State-controlled economy, represent a kind of indirect contribution from every individual. The result is that every urban family must work like fiends in order to earn even their barest livelihood; indeed, I came across several instances where both husband and wife practised a sideline in addition to their principal occupations. The whole nation, so to speak, is putting its last ounce of strength into the race, and, if I may believe the data given me by a foreign employer, the incidence of tuberculosis has risen alarmingly among his staff.

One thing is certain: the excessive demands of the process of economic growth are exacting untold sacrifices from the Chinese people, and these sacrifices are growing not proportionally, but with the square of any further stepping up of the pace—just as this higher pace must also magnify colossally any administrative blunder. Here, it seems to me, is the Achilles' heel of the regime. China, accustomed to counting in terms of thousands of years, now suddenly believes she must gallop through years and months, and accomplish an already exacting five-year-plan within the space of four years. More haste less speed is a proverb never far from one's mind.

[GREENE, 181–182]

Patterns of thinking are not easy to shake. The prevailing Chinese image of the United States is that of a country controlled by a few rich capitalists grinding down the poor. They refuse to listen when I try to correct that image and when I tell them that American society is far more varied, far more complex, far livelier than they imagine and that whatever fraudulence and exploitation does exist is more subtle, more hidden than their image would suggest.

When I tell the Chinese something that conflicts with their preconceived idea, they are bewildered but are too polite to tell me that they think I'm stringing them a line.

Examples of things they have had a hard time swallowing: that the Negro girl who comes once a week to help my wife with the housework comes in a car better than our own (Negroes are the most crushed of all the American poor); that I take the garbage to the dump and help with the washing up (a capitalist like myself, rich enough to travel, would have poor people laboring for him); that the unemployed are not lining up in the streets in New York waiting for the soup kitchens to open, and that they often have enough funds to keep running their cars for a while.

The Czech football team had a big party on the top floor of the hotel a few nights ago, celebrating a victory. There was much singing and drinking—an outburst like this, I am sure, hadn't been seen at the Shin Chiao for many a year. This completely floored the Chinese. They watched in amazement. Americans get drunk and become boisterous, but not Communist friends!

Three years ago the Indians had a magnificent exhibition here in Peking and I went along with my guide to see it. The Indian guides and I got talking (they all spoke perfect English) and they invited me and my interpreter to have lunch. My interpreter declined. Afterward when I rejoined him I could see that something was disturbing him. "Mr. Greene," he finally said, "how is it possible that these Indians could invite you, an Englishman, to lunch?" "Why on earth not?" I asked. "But you represent the cruel colonial power that has been crushing India for years!" My lunching with them just didn't fit the image!

[WIZNITZER, CBS]

The Chinese Communist Party is engaged in a 24-hour-a-day hate campaign which no party or government has ever equalled. On every train station, on every wall, posters show the United States as a rat, a snake, an octopus, a paper tiger, or a figure being kicked or hung. I spent seven weeks in Red China and traveled over much of the country by train. In every compartment a loudspeaker delivered a constant harangue against the "American Blockade," and "American bacteriological warfare."

Movies, operas, the press and radio are also used to spread this hatred. Other countries, particularly Britain, are also condemned, but the most poisonous attacks are reserved for the United States.

When I visited the sacred Buddhist mountain of Longmen, my interpreter kept up a running account of the Americans who had stolen this or that relic. When I visited the heavy machine-tool factory at Wuhan, my guides spent as much time making acid statements about the United States as they did talking about the factory itself.

At the universities of Peking and Wuhan I had a look at the books students used to learn French grammar; they were anti-U.S. books. One book of French lessons was called "A Marxist Interpretation of the Phillipine War." In Shanghai my interpreter spent half our time pouring out hate and resentment against the U.S., which had done this and that, and against the U.S. sailors who used to take Chinese girls. He added that it was a well known fact that Americans made love in the streets.

As a Brazilian correspondent I was not primarily interested in the feelings of China for the United States, but after a few days I could not help identifying as a westerner with the object of such hate. I had the headlines of the "People's Press" translated to me every morning and it was always the same repetitious insult.

Yugoslavia and Japan were also under fire, and even fellow Communist countries were at least indirectly insulted. In more than one hundred offices I visited in Chinese communes, plants, universities and ministries, there were always pictures of Marx, Engels, Lenin and Stalin, but never of Khrushchev.

In spite of official statements of friendship the Chinese seem to have little affection for Communist delegates in China. At the British Embassy I met even Bulgarians, Rumanians, Poles and Czechs, who came for some social life and relaxation from the rigidity of Chinese officialdom.

By sheer accident I ran into Chinese engineers, professors and scientists who had been educated in the west. One told me he was a Yale man. Another remembered the days when he studied at Illinois University, and wanted to know everything about life in the United States today. They spoke good English and often referred to the United States with friendship. There was a young boy at a post office who told me his professors had been Americans.

But there are, on the other hand, 600,000,000 Chinese who have never visited the United States, have nothing else to judge by, and can only believe what they are told.

9. The People

[CLARK, 41–45]

She came confidently out of the jabbering Peking crowd, still clutching knitting needles and yarn. The people stood aside to make room for her, and then she singled out the old man who leaned against a wall. Nodding and knitting, she listened to him, and then swung momentarily to issue a curt order to the crowd, to quiet the people so she could better hear the old man's complaint. She was obviously the head of the street committee, for the people obeyed her and fell silent. I had just taken the old man's photograph, with his own permission, which had been relayed through my interpreter. But now, for some obscure reason, he regretted having had his picture taken. The woman with the knitting needles objected, too, for she turned to my interpreter and said many heated things. The bystanders, clustering around us in a circle, approved of what was an apparent reprimand; they shook their heads solemnly.

My interpreter, a rather soft-spoken girl, was chagrined. She said to me, "They are superstitious about pictures. I told them you would not take any more here."

We walked away, but the woman with the knitting needles still was not satisfied. For a hundred yards or more she followed us down the *hutung*, the narrow alley or back street characteristic of Peking. When we paused to decide on our direction, she paused, staring at us, all the while continuing mechanically and coldly with her knitting. There was a vignette here, as I saw confirmed in other cities and in the countryside: the vigilance and influence of China's women, newly emancipated from ancient oblivion and thrust into a position of importance and authority. The woman with the knitting needles was doing only what she considered her duty, protecting the security and interests of the men, women, and children of her street. But she also had other, unspoken duties: to maintain the security and interests of the state. As head of street committee she was a Madame Defarge in miniature, filled with her own mission to further the revolutionary process of China.

While communes, with institutionalized controls, are solidly established in the rural areas, their introduction in the cities has been postponed. During the early days of the communal movement there was considerable speculation about how the principles of extreme collective life could be applied to the cities. For one thing, communes imply that everyone must be able to switch instantly from working in a factory to plowing the soil or gathering the harvest, and such a drastic transition would obviously dislocate operations and transportation in the more heavily industrialized areas. Vague efforts were made in one or two cities, such as Shenyang in Manchuria, to organize urban mess halls; but even these efforts were abandoned when the Communist party's Central Committee issued a manifesto chastising impatient local cadres and calling for less haste. Aside from the practical problems encountered, the slowdown in the cities may be attributed to the reluctance of urban dwellers, a more sophisticated people than the peasants, to throw themselves wholeheartedly into the anonymous existence of communal eating and sleeping and working. The Central Committee, after reasoning that much urban property, anyway, was already collectivized, confessed that "bourgeois ideology is still fairly prevalent" in the cities. The farmer may have had a brief taste of possessing property during the first period of land reform, but the little shopkeeper or even pedicab driver in Shanghai had commanded his own destiny for many years, and middle-bracket mentality takes time to eradicate.

In any event, city dwellers form only one fifth of the total population, and their partial regimentation is still ensured by the street committees while the constant process of "persuasion" or "re-education" goes on. The street committee is the all-enveloping weapon on the ground floor. Its function is to translate into action the doctrine of community thinking, rather than individual thinking, as laid down each morning by the *People's Daily,* which speaks for the men on the top floor. Committees, usually of thirteen members, are elected by residents of every street in every city in China. This minor degree of self-government, characteristic of the regime's desire to foster the impression of a "people's republic," brings material benefits, and also some pernicious practices. The chairman of each committee, usually a housewife who can stay home and keep an eye on activities and habits of her neighbors, has three main tasks: to explain the aims of the government, to reflect and transmit the opinion of ordinary Chinese to party workers, and to administer public welfare. Thus a two-way channel of communications is established. If, on one hand, something like a fly-swatting campaign is decreed, it is madame chairman who sees to it that the two hundred or so families under her wing get into the proper spirit. The usual start is at a street rally, with madame chairman and members of her committee exhorting the residents to toil for the common good. If persuasion fails, shame is employed. At one rally, attended by upward of three hundred men, women, and children, I heard the woman leader cry out, "The people's eyes are snow bright and are on you, Li Cheng." And Li Cheng, a shop clerk, crept away, presumably so mortified that he would promptly volunteer for a weekend of digging a dam site in the country.

On the other hand, madame chairman, through her daily personal contact with her flock, can sense if there is undue resentment against extracurricular labor; and if enough street chieftains report to the party that people are not yet ready for a major move, as they must have reported during the early attempt to communalize cities, the regime can declare a temporary reprieve while the educational process is continued. This is one of the great strengths of an old culture and still newer system that believes in infinite patience and gentleness. In China today, contrary to the popular Western misconception, they do not chop off heads; they reshape them. Madame chairman, who may not be formally trained in the fine art of propaganda, nevertheless plays an important part in sugarcoating the pill of indoctrination. She gives the impression that she is more interested in the welfare of her charges than in authority. If roofs are leaky, she makes certain that they are repaired. If garbage cans are not cleared by the usual 5 A.M. or 6 A.M., she complains strongly to the appropriate city department. If husbands and wives quarrel, she mediates. At the same time she has not been unknown to notify the police of "heretical" outbursts, against the party or the system, that she may have overheard. It is also her duty to impress on children the need to inform on their parents if they demonstrate "rightist" tendencies at home.

In Peking, madame chairman has a relatively simple job keeping in touch with her subjects. A *hutung* boasts of its own self-contained personality. Gray walls stretch from one end of the alley to the other, broken only by gates painted bright vermilion. From the street, usually unpaved, you can see only the tile roofs of the single-story buildings. The gates open not into one house but rather into a compound consisting of several houses; and here play hordes of children, who can easily be reached, and here gather the men and women to relate their problems. Madame chairman, after hearing them out, can also announce in person the next item on the agenda. While I was in Peking, committee people went from house to house and browsed around on the pretense that they were, as madame chairman had declared, advance inspectors for DDT squads. In reality, their mission was to decide which families had more furniture than they could legitimately use in new quarters being built for them. The result was a compulsory mass sale of antique furniture to state-owned shops, which, in turn, designated it for export to foreign markets.

But as against this kind of evil, madame chairman, in propagandizing the new social order, also preaches that old superstitions must be forgotten and that it is a noble thing, for instance, to submit a child to a doctor's needle. The result in this case is widespread immunization against diphtheria and the fast disappearance of smallpox. In Shanghai, where committees have less orderly streets, physically, than *hutungs* to cope with, I asked one housewife if she was ever subjected to intrusion by committee inspectors. "Not by the street committee," she said. "If the house is unclean, it is the neighbors who complain."

"But aren't you upset or angry if neighbors intrude and criticize your housekeeping?"

"We do not feel that way any more," she said.

The back streets in Shanghai are not much more than earth tracks between rows of hovels. But they are at least under hygienic control, with no litter and no offensive odors. People line up for drinking water at community taps. But, as one committee head pointed out succinctly, the taps are far better than the unsanitary open troughs of former days. "We have taught our people good health measures," she said. "See for yourself if there are any flies."

The flies had indeed disappeared, thanks to the zeal instilled by madame chairman into every man, woman, and child. And simultaneously, through corner meetings and personal persuasive talks, she was getting them to volunteer for public projects and to accept the regime's philosophy. And anything else? A Western-trained Chinese doctor told me: "After our hospital fluoroscoped everyone in the district, we didn't know what to do with all the active cases of tuberculosis we found; there simply weren't enough sanatoria to handle them. So we called on each street committee to choose a house and move into it all the neighborhood patients. Now they're isolated and no danger to anyone else. They're also getting, under our supervision, proper food and shelter."

[ESKELUND, 25–27]

I will never forget an experience I had many years ago. I had not been long in China then. Perhaps that is why it made such a strong impression on me. I was fresh from Denmark, not yet used to the poverty and suffering of the East.

It was a bitterly cold winter evening in Peking. I was on my way to visit some Danish friends, when I saw a man struck by a hit-and-run driver. A crowd gathered around the unconscious man who had a bleeding wound in the temple. A policeman dragged him up on the sidewalk and was about to walk away, when I grabbed him by the arm.

"But you can't leave him here—you must get him to a hospital!"

The policeman looked at the wounded man. It was an old farmer, probably a refugee from a famine district. I suppose he had come to the city to beg. His cotton gown was worn and patched.

"It costs money to stay at the hospital," the policeman explained kindly. "He can't get in without someone to guarantee for him. Most likely he has no relatives here in town. Who is going to help a stranger?"

I don't think the Chinese are more callous than people in other countries, but there was no public welfare in the old days. People only felt responsible for members of their own clan . . .

I didn't even have any money on me, so what could I do? When I arrived at my friends' home, distressed by what I had seen, they tried to comfort me. We were foreigners. It wasn't our fault that there was so much misery in China. There was nothing we could do—the problem was so hopelessly big.

Later in the evening, when I returned by the same road, the old man was no longer there. Only a pool of frozen blood remained on the spot where he had been lying . . .

Now, twenty years later, my wife and I came walking down the same street. It was early in December and the sun was shining from a clear blue sky—it does practically all year round in Peking. We were on our way to visit two places—an old-age-home and a prison.

Just as we were going to cross the street I saw an old man leaning against a wall. He has had too much to drink, was my first thought, but that was so unlikely. During all my years in China I have never seen a drunken Chinese.

We took another look at the old man and saw that tears were running down his face. Some people stopped and began to question him. Why was he weeping? He explained that he was from a village sixty miles away. He had come to the city to sell peanuts and had lost his earnings, and now he didn't know how he could get home—he was an old man, it was too far to walk.

In the old days I would have suspected him of being a

beggar playing a trick. At that time all the citizens of China were infested with starving wretches who exhibited their open sores or a sick child, or just stood with blind eyes, holding out a bowl. One tried to pretend that they weren't there and told oneself that they were probably professionals who didn't want to work for a living—people even said that the sick babies they carried had been rented . . .

One of the bystanders asked the old man how much a train ticket would cost. A little over one Yuan (about three shillings), the old man replied. Someone took out a ten-cent note —coins are no longer used in China. Someone else gave twenty cents, a third only five, but it quickly added up to more than a dollar. The old man smiled happily, bowing right and left, and hurried off to the railroad station.

"Imagine that this could happen in China!" Chi-yun said. "By the way, have you noticed that there are no beggars any more?"

I had—and not alone that. A couple of days ago I had given twenty cents to a shoeshine boy who looked as if he needed a meal. As I walked on he came running after me.

"I haven't shined your shoes," he said.

"They don't need it."

"Then I don't want your money—I am no beggar!"

Finally I had to stay and let him shine my shoes although I had just polished them at home . . .

[ESKELUND, 68–75]

If there is anything more boring than writing about a factory, it is to visit one. Chi-yun and I were therefore prepared for the worst that day we went out to the National Spinning Mill No. 2—but there was a pleasant surprise in store for us.

First there was the inevitable tour. We wandered past miles of clacking machines, accompanied by a female secretary who filled us with statistics. There were five thousand workers at the factory. They produced two hundred and forty thousand yards of cotton cloth a day. Each year the government was building four new cotton spinneries with the same capacity as this one. China, once an importer of cotton cloth, now exported it to several of the South Asian countries . . .

I tried to listen intelligently, but suddenly the secretary broke off in the middle of a description of a complicated chemical process.

"I am afraid this doesn't interest you very much. Is there anything special you would like to hear about?"

"Yes," I replied with a smile, "something less technical, something, uh—something romantic. But I suppose one doesn't find that at a cotton mill?"

"Something romantic?" She brightened. "Oh, yes—you could talk to Comrade Liang. I think the story of her marriage is very romantic."

We found her in the day nursery where she was suckling her baby daughter. Seen through European eyes it was not a very impressive place. The cement floor was bare, the stove smoked. But one should bear in mind that public welfare was practically non-existent in China before the liberation. It was not unusual for factory girls to work with their babies bound to their backs. Now there are nurseries and kindergartens at every large institution in the country.

Comrade Liang was not at all embarrassed by our sudden arrival. She just went on suckling her child. The Chinese are very natural about such things. She was small and plump, and two dimples appeared on her cheeks when she told us about how she had met her husband.

It was at a union convention. She had already read about him in the papers, for he was a famous workers' hero who regularly overfulfilled his quota. She was only a model worker, which is one degree lower, but nothing to sniff at for a girl of nineteen.

The papers said afterwards that their immediate interest for each other was due to "mutual admiration for their unselfish sacrifices in the service of the Chinese people". I wonder whether the dimples didn't have something to do with it, too. In any case it was love at first sight.

Did they get married right away? No—after the convention meeting she did not hear a word from him for more than a month. She smiled at the thought of how nervous and worried she had been. Her work even suffered—one day there was a fault in a roll of cloth from one of her machines.

"Her comrades offered to take the blame," the secretary put in. "They were proud of her record and wanted to keep it unblemished, but Comrade Liang firmly rejected this proposal . . ."

"Why didn't you hear from him?" I asked. She explained that he was a member of the Communist party. As soon as the convention was over he told his "cell" what had happened. They wrote to the chief of personnel at her factory. True, she was a model worker, but even so they wanted to know about her background. Fortunately it turned out that her attitude had always been correct, so the cell gave him its blessings, and then he came and proposed . . .

When Comrade Liang was through feeding the baby she

offered to show us her home. We accompanied her to a large group of buildings opposite the factory. They reminded me of the workers' dwellings that were built in northern Europe around the turn of the century. Though the houses were only a year and a half old they already had a slight atmosphere of slum. Here and there the plaster was falling down from the walls, the paint peeling off. When one considers how much the Chinese have built during the last few years, it is not surprising that the quality has suffered.

On the way she showed us the school, the clinic and the big dining-hall where you could get a good meal for less than a shilling. Some of the workers came over and chatted with the secretary and Comrade Liang. They were free and easy in their manners; there was none of the former servility of their class. Everybody was dressed alike. It was a classless society, void of tradition. It was China's new proletariat.

When you tell the Chinese Communist that many of their countrymen are afraid of expressing themselves freely, they reply that at least this is not true of the workers. No, of course not, for generally speaking they have nothing to complain about. They are the apples of Mao Tse-tung's eye.

Thus, Comrade Liang made twelve pounds a month, or about three times as much as a farmer. She paid only six shillings a month for her one-room apartment. True, there was only one small window, and the cement floor and bare walls reminded me of a cellar—but there was central heating, there was running water and even a flush toilet. Her husband, the workers' hero, made fourteen pounds a month.

She saw him only once a week, when he came to spend the night. He worked at another factory, and their weekly day off did not fall on the same day. "But maybe we'll get a summer vacation next year," she said hopefully. The Chinese workers only get a day off on October 1st, the anniversary of the People's Republic, on May 1st, and at Chinese new year.

Many of the married workers had their parents living with them. But the family relationship had changed quite a bit since the days when the young people brought their wages home to their parents. The old people now looked after the children, if they did not have a job themselves. They got food, lodging and a little pocket money. The young ones were their own bosses.

Around seventy per cent of the workers at the mill were girls. The unmarried ones lived in dormitories, six to each room. Most of the space was taken up by the beds, but the walls were plastered with pictures of film stars.

Only about seventy-five per cent of those employed at the factory did productive work. The rest were bookkeepers, clerks or political propaganda workers. At some Chinese industrial institutions the percentage of administrative personnel is even higher. Many of the offices I have been to were crowded with people who seemed to have difficulties in making the time pass. About a year ago, the Communist leaders vowed that they were going to reduce this army of personnel, but they have not done so yet. It is not easy in a country where everything is as centralized as in China.

All the workers belonged to the same union. Did this union have much power? Certainly, replied both Comrade Liang and the secretary, but when I questioned them further it turned out that the workers' rights did not go much beyond Article 4 of the Trade Union Law. The first and foremost duty of the unions is to educate and organize the masses of workers and staff members to support the laws and desires of the Peoples' Government and to carry out the policies of the Peoples' Government in order to consolidate the peoples' state power . . .

In the transition period before the state nationalized Chinese industry and business, the workers were encouraged to strike. "Now it is quite unthinkable that the workers should want to do so," the secretary said. "After all, we have a peoples' government in China—the workers would not want to strike against themselves."

Comrade Liang was a member of the managing committee of the union, and she told us about its social activities. There were recreation centres for sick workers. Once a week, the union organized a social evening with dancing. Uneducated workers could pass high school examinations by attending night school. There were daily meetings at which the policies of the government were explained. The union also helped workers who had large families and found it hard to make ends meet.

"Some weeks ago, the union started a birth control campaign," Comrade Liang went on. Chi-yun and I looked at her in surprise, and the secretary gave a start and protested. The leaders of new China are extremely sensitive where birth control is concerned. Not long ago they condemned it as "capitalist nonsense" and "a vicious way of killing the people without spilling blood".

For years the Chinese Communists have maintained that birth control is unnecessary. China is not over-populated, they say—it is a matter of under-production. All the densely-populated countries of Asia have such a low standard of living because the upper-classes exploit the poor, runs the Communist argument. The distribution of wealth is unjust—and that cannot be denied.

But Comrade Liang admitted that a problem remained although the distribution of wealth was now more just in China. Before the liberation, the mortality rate was one hundred and seventeen per one thousand in some Chinese cities. It has since gone down to forty-four per thousand. A survey among seven thousand female workers at a factory showed that one thousand nine hundred of them became pregnant in one year. Each woman gets fifty-six days off with full pay for her confinement, so this means a great loss of manpower.

The standard of living of the workers has not improved very much although their average monthly income has risen from eight pounds five shillings before the liberation to ten pounds sixteen shillings today. The main reason for this is the large number of children. Each year, there are fifteen million more Chinese than the year before. Despite all the progress under the Communists, the advances in production can hardly keep pace with the growth in population . . .

I asked the secretary why she had objected when Comrade Liang used the word *birth-control*. She claimed that it was an incorrect way of expressing it.

"The cultural standard of the workers has been raised under the democratic leadership of the Communists," she said. "Therefore, the workers have realized the advantage of not having too large a family. The people have asked their leaders for help, and the desire of the people now being the will of the government, a campaign to teach mothers proper spacing of children has been started . . ."

Comrade Liang told us about an ancient Chinese way of avoiding conception. One only has to swallow a couple of dozen live tadpoles. She had heard that it was quite effective, but as far as she knew it was hardly ever used any more.

She added that not only the unions taught birth-con . . . She checked herself in time. "Teach the mothers proper spacing," she said instead of the forbidden word. The farmers' associations have started a similar movement in the country. They show films which point out the advantages of planned parenthood. Several million leaflets with graphic illustrations have been distributed.

"Has it had any effect?"

It was too soon to tell. Comrade Liang said that the union now offered a course in planned parenthood. About one quarter of the married workers had signed up for this course.

"That's not very much," I commented.

"No, the desire to have many children is very strong in China." Life had been so uncertain in the old days. If a man had many children, there was more chance that one of them would get ahead and could support his parents in their old age. It was difficult to change this attitude . . .

Before we left, I asked Comrade Liang if she had signed up for the new course in planned parenthood. No, she replied, not yet . . .

"My husband wants to have at least two sons before we begin to think about that."

[SCHMID, 158–160]

Entering China from the countries of South-east Asia, one begins to doubt the evidence of one's eyes and ears. The Chinese inhabiting the Chinese People's Republic appear to have scarcely anything in common with their brethren abroad. The Chinese in South-east Asia are anarchists, whose every thought and effort are directed at cheating the authorities of their host country to the advantage of their own purse. They seem to underwrite the moral principle—not unknown among European taxpayers—that the laws of decency and business honesty apply only between man and man, not between man and the State. A curious result of this attitude is the fact that Chinese businessmen are honesty itself in all business arrangements—there is no need even to put them in writing; a handshake is enough—but these selfsame businessmen will not shrink from the dirtiest means if concerted hoarding, rumour-mongering, or some other machinations hold out the prospect of a profitable coup at the public expense. This applies all the way down to the meanest coolie, who will shamelessly relieve an inexperienced client of a multiple of the correct fare.

All this is totally different in Communist China. Take the most ingenious cheat of all—the rickshaw coolie. Elsewhere, unless you want no end of argument afterwards, you have to settle the exact fare before you start out. In Communist China precise tariffs have been laid down for all distances, and these are displayed at the rickshaw ranks where the cyclists wait for their customers. One day I wanted to get to a place of which I did not know the name: I just stepped into a rickshaw and directed the boy. He charged me 17 cents, which was exactly the fare he was entitled to under the tariff. Why did he not charge 20? I should have paid it without batting an eyelid. In fact, I should have paid 25. No one would have overheard us. Most likely we should never have seen each other again. The man would have risked nothing by overcharging. But he did not do so.

Another instance. I am occasionally a bit absent-minded in paying a bill, and am apt to leave without waiting for my change. One day I was passing a Peking restaurant where I had eaten a few days before when suddenly a waiter dashed out, made straight for me, and pressed a few cents into my hand—the change that I had forgotten to pick up.

In an hotel it is impossible to leave a pair of worn-out shoes, a torn shirt, or even a used razor blade or a pencil behind. Without fail the boy will take them to the porter, or, if necessary, breathlessly chase you to the station with them. Honesty is practised to a point of absurdity, where it almost becomes a surrealist nightmare. What a subject for a novel by Kafka—a man trying to rid himself of some troublesome object but finding it pressed upon him again and again. You cannot even give the things away, because no servant will accept a tip or a present—at least, not while somebody else is watching. In the shops, too, you can safely pay the price asked and rest assured that you will not be overcharged.

To my inquiries into the cause of this attitude I received contradictory replies. Sheer terror, said one set of experts. The poor blighters are so intimidated they will not even run the most infinitesimal risk of being caught and punished. Nonsense, said the others. There really has been a kind of moral cleansing, combined, of course, with rigorous discipline imposed from above.

[GREENE, 182–183]

I've noted many times indications of the trust that runs through Chinese relationships with each other. Yen, my interpreter, has a monthly ticket for the Peking bus and trolley-bus service—it's a reduced-rate card that's good for unlimited travel. On leaving the bus I give up my ticket to the girl who stands at the door, but I have noticed that Yen merely says "monthly ticket" and she accepts this and has never, while I've been with him, asked to see it.

Another example took place at the Central Telegraph Office. Sending cables from China is fiendishly expensive and, on this occasion, I was cabling the BBC in London, CBC in Toronto, and NBC in New York. The messages were all very long.

When the girl totted the total up it came to more than 350 yuan ($140). I only had half the amount and so I told her I would go back to my hotel to fetch some more. "Pay tomorrow, or when you come this way again," the girl said.

"I can't do that," I replied, "these cables have to go immediately."

"Oh, we'll send them right away, but pay us when you come by next time."

There are those who will say, "They know where every foreigner lives, they would quickly catch up with him if he tried to get away without paying." And that is quite true. But I don't think this went through the girl's mind at all. Here, they go on the assumption that people are *not* cheats.

[GREENE, 261–262]

Today, Ku (my interpreter) and I were having lunch together at the Shung Lung restaurant near the Tungan Market. We talked about some of the changes that have taken place in China—I was thinking especially of the disappearance of tipping, begging, stealing.

The absence of beggars, Ku told me, was easy to explain, everyone now has work so there's no need to beg. Those who are sick and cannot work are looked after. As for tipping, this is now a country that tries to share everything, he said. (The English would call it a "fair-shares-for-all" country.) The slices may not be very large but everyone believes he's getting more or less an equal share of the pie. So there are no longer rich people who can buy extra attention or flattery by tipping. And apart from this, though Ku did not put it into these words, accepting handouts would injure their pride.

But the lack of stealing? That puzzles me. Like everyone else who comes to China, I have grown careless about my possessions. I come back to my room to find I left money strewn over the desk; I never bother to lock my door, though in this hotel there are keys, which is more than can be said of the place I stayed in three years ago. The wife of one of the British Embassy officials told me the other day how she had some jewelry stolen on a visit to Hong Kong simply because she had forgotten that people elsewhere lock up valuables. I asked Ku how the regime established this moral sense, what fearful penalties are imposed on those who do steal.

He hesitated. He was obviously puzzled how he was going to explain it. "I don't think these changes have come because of laws. You can't change people by passing laws. We have laws, of course, against stealing and so does every country. And, don't think stealing doesn't happen, because it does, although not very often. I think your question shows that you haven't really understood the Chinese revolution. The change inside people that now makes stealing rare—well, that change *is* the revolution; that is what the revolution is, and what it did to us. We can't think of stealing from others any more than we would steal from our own family." And then Ku made a little gesture with his hands which conveyed much more vividly than any words how impossible it was to explain this to someone who had not been through it.

[GREENE, 111–112]

Chinese are among the best hosts in the world, and the least formal. You can have a good time and laugh with them. Or be silent with them. Silences are not uncomfortable socially as they are with us.

At Anshan, after a beer or two with Mr. Liu, who had been showing us around, we became rather cheerfully friendly and he told me some of the difficulties from their side. "You know," he said, "we Chinese like to be hospitable, but we often don't know how to be. We haven't traveled, we don't know your customs and we often don't have the faintest idea of what you really want to do. We try our best but we are never quite sure, especially as you come from so many different countries all with different customs. We never feel certain as to whether we are doing the right things for our guests."

Sense of Equality

This is an important aspect of Chinese life. I remember my surprise when I first came to America from England to see a senior surgeon in a hospital lining up at the cafeteria with nurses and orderlies—this simply couldn't have happened in prewar England—and, another time, seeing the head of a company having to wait for an elevator because the office boy got in first. China is like this, but more so.

It runs through their entire life. Yen, my current interpreter, feels perfectly at ease with cabinet ministers when I go for interviews. He shows respect, of course, but speaks as an equal. I have been told by one of the diplomatic people here that when Mao visits a farm or a factory people are eager to talk to him and do so at will, not fluttery and nervous. The judge at the court, the conductor on a train, the head of a factory, the senior engineer on a hydroelectric dam project, all of them I have noticed, walk around among the workers but never as "bosses." No one is obsequious. No one makes way specially for them—they aren't even noticed very much. They are another kind of worker doing their job.

[GREENE, 259–260]

This is an *egalitarian* society. You feel it everywhere. I watched some soldiers at drill one hot day. They were smart as could be, officers barking orders. Then drill ended and all, officers and men, raced each other to the tubs of fruit juice. No priorities.

Every foreign country here entertains on its "national day" and last week one of these receptions was held in this hotel. I was standing near Chou En-lai and I watched while a waitress with a large tray of drinks came up and offered one to the Prime Minister. They stood chatting together as easily and naturally as could be, the girl without a trace of shyness or servility. With respect, of course; but the respect, I felt, was both ways.

It was probably easier to maintain this sense of equality and comradeship when they were guerrillas in the mountains; more difficult now as this country becomes an elaborately organized modern state. But they are trying. It is a pretty well-established rule that everyone in authority must spend at least one month a year in the lowest rank of the organization of which he might be the head. The director of the steel company I visited told me he had just finished a month's work as a puddler. All officers, generals, even the chief of staff, spend one month a year in the ranks as ordinary GI's. I asked about this; it struck me as being a little theoretical and phony, and that the other privates would probably make it pretty easy for him. Not a bit, I was told. No special privileges. The point being that it gives the GI's a chance to see whether the general running their show is the kind of man they can trust. *They* are inspecting *him* for a change!

The other day I was with Yen in a taxi, and the driver seemed puzzled about the way, and I didn't think he was driving very well either. I asked Yen whether he was a new driver. "No," Yen said, "he isn't ordinarily a taxi driver. He's in the taxi administration office." This was one of the bosses, doing his month's stint.

[CROFT, 85–87]

No meeting, of course, was ever complete, no friendship went far beyond formality. The personal element could never enter into it because there were too many inhibitions on each side and, even if they could be overcome, there was always the language barrier or the interpreter standing in the way of direct communication.

One morning, however, there was a meeting with a difference. It was nothing very much—casual, inconsequential, unfruitful, but it stays in the memory with a warmth and poignancy which other encounters, of weightier significance, were never able to evoke.

I had set out with Galal and an interpreter on a tour of the Temple of Heaven. Galal did not stay the course for long but suddenly complained that his feet were aching and sat down outside the Hall of Prayer for Good Harvests, refusing to go any further. I made my own way through the Temple grounds, mingling with the crowds, looking in at one building to watch an exhibition of advanced techniques in coal-mining, joining a crowd of students in another to study a demonstration of glass-blowing. It was a relief to arrive at the Circular Mound Altar, where the only techniques on view were those of the craftsmen and architects who had built it five hundred years ago, in three concentric terraces, bordered with marble balustrades and supported upon three hundred and sixty magnificently carved pillars which symbolised the degrees in the celestial circle.

The Chinese were too interested in the buildings and exhibitions to take much notice of me, the solitary westerner present, until, coming out of the Imperial Vault of Heaven and stopping for a moment to whisper, according to custom, along the Echoing Wall, I had the uncomfortable feeling that I was being followed. I walked on slowly down the temple steps and then stopped on the Triple-Sound-of-Voice Stone and looked suddenly behind me.

About ten yards away a boiler-suited Chinese youth stopped too and stood watching me rather shyly. He was by no means disturbed at being caught out, but on the contrary broke into a bashful smile and, when I smiled back, ambled towards me, beaming delightedly, and took my hand in his. He was about twenty-one, big and broad by Chinese standards, with a relaxed, easy gait and strangely tousled hair which gave a touch of the gamin to his robust good looks and cheerful, honest eyes.

For a moment, in fact, I wondered if I had stumbled upon someone the Street Committee had missed, a Peking *ragazzo*, a lad of life who refused to conform to the 'correct attitude.' With profuse smiles and nods of cordiality he led me away by the hand to admire the gardens and altars, babbling happily the while and smiling regretfully whenever I reminded him that I could not understand a word he was saying.

After proceeding all round the Temple grounds in this fashion we arrived back at the Hall of Prayer for Good Harvests, where Galal and the interpreter were waiting. Now at least, I thought, I can find out the young man's name and thank him for his company—but it was not so simple as that. After a few minutes, the interpreter had to confess that he himself could not understand the dialect in which the young man was speaking. This was the cue for uproarious laughter all round, during which, with a great deal of gesticulation, shouting and nodding of heads, we all did a sort of communal rock 'n roll down the Temple steps. At length the interpreter reported that the young man came from the province of Kwangsi, which was 'somewhere in the south.' After further parley and pantomime he discovered that, far from being a vagrant, he was a teacher on holiday, although what he actually taught could not be ascertained.

For some time we lingered together on the Temple steps in a spontaneous kind of chummery, compounded of smiles, hugs, hoots and shrieks of laughter, which nobody seemed to enjoy more than the young teacher. I could not find out anything more about him and I was certain I should never see him again. When we moved away he followed us towards the Temple gates, not walking beside us but always a few yards behind, with his relaxed, easy stride, smiling and shyly waving his hand whenever we turned round. I never knew what to make of this meeting, but I remember that when eventually he disappeared into the crowd the Temple of Heaven seemed a colder, less joyous place.

10. Sex in Red China

[GREENE, 115]

China is going through a period of intense sexual morality. They are determined not to have foreigners make sexual liaisons with Chinese girls. This is less likely to happen with Russian and East European technicians who come for a year or more with their wives and families. The problem is with foreign students. There's a rumor (I distrust rumors) that seven or eight foreign students are now in jail in Peking awaiting transportation back to their own countries because of illicit sexual relations with local girls.

A Hungarian technician (this is another story that's going the rounds) who was here fell in love with a Chinese girl and wanted to sleep with her. She said she had to get permission from her organization first. The next thing the man knew was that his visa had been cancelled, and he's now on his way to Budapest.

An African student (this I think is a true story) who traveled to school every day on the bus was attracted by a girl conductor. He made sure he caught the same bus every day. An after-work meeting was arranged and he invited the girl to his hotel room.

The girl arrived accompanied by a friend, whom she hoped to leave downstairs. However, the hotel management wouldn't allow a single woman in a foreigner's room, so both went up. They all had a pleasant time—but perhaps not the kind the man had hoped for.

The incident got back to the girl's superiors and she was reprimanded. She didn't lose her job, but was transferred to another route. The student soon discovered that his studies were being rather mysteriously curtailed and his visa was not extended. He sent the girl a letter and a small gift, offering his apologies. The gift was returned and the letter remained unanswered.

[SCHMID, 105–114]

The creature who was introduced to me at the headquarters of the Chinese Women's Union in Peking as a typical

218

representative of modern Chinese womanhood was not exactly attractive. She was dressed in one of those padded suits of blue cotton which turn the wearer, male or female, into a sort of indefinable sausage devoid of all sex characteristics. Her hair hung down in strands like overgrown garlic, and her face was as flat as if her mother had run an iron over it immediately after birth. She was a creature who instantly banished all thoughts of caress into the deepest recesses of the subconscious. Yet this person had been picked by the Women's Union to talk to me about love—about the new love which has awoken in China since her "Liberation."

Lan Sho-fang was a child of the people, the daughter of a rickshaw coolie, the lowest social category, from a little town near Peking. She came about half-way in the numerous poverty-stricken crowd of brothers and sisters. Two elder sisters had married before "Liberation"—or, rather, had been married by their mother to small shopkeepers. These shopkeepers, if Lan Sho-fang was to be believed, had been real fiends, who never treated their wives otherwise than with a kick in the rear, and the poor women had, moreover, been plagued by mothers-in-law who regarded them simply as slave labour or outlets for their foul tempers. Neither of these loveless marriages had been blessed with children. Little Sho-fang had grown up with a secret fear of what must lie ahead of her.

But then came the miracle of "Liberation"—*i.e.*, the arrival of the Red Army—and everybody's life was suddenly transformed. This antithesis of before "Liberation" and after "Liberation" has become something like the watershed between heaven and hell in China to-day. Before "Liberation" there were suffering, despair, and brutality; after "Liberation" there were prosperity, smiles, and the milk of human kindness. What is no doubt true in many respects has been exaggerated so boundlessly that, in effect, a myth of a new Creation Day has been developed.

"Liberation" had meant freedom also for the suffering sisters—liberation from the bonds of marriage without love. A new marriage law had made it possible for them to obtain a divorce and, like thousands of other women who had been forced by parental authority into unwilling matrimony while hardly more than children, Sho-fang's sisters had hastened to shake off their fetters. They had since remarried, this time men of their own choice, and their unions were now blessed with offspring.

Mother Lan might have learned the lesson of her eldest daughters' marriages. But she failed to do so. Her mentality continued to be tied up in those concepts which in China to-day are called 'feudal'—among others, the belief that marriage is a matter, not for young people, but for their parents. Indeed, the children belong not so much to their parents as to the grandparents; continuity of the genealogical line is everything and the happiness of the individual nothing. As Sho-fang grew into a budding maiden her mother's reactionary mind began to look around for a suitable son-in-law, preferably another prosperous shopkeeper. But then happened what was bound to happen after "Liberation": Sho-fang fell in love. I found it difficult to picture those frogs' eyes in the flat face looking up soulfully into those of the young worker whom she had met at some trade-union meeting. Nor do I know what this young Apollo looked like. At any rate, it was a case of love at first sight, and love—*i.e.*, individual love by choice—was the fashion and all the rage in Communist China.

The young girl began walking out with her beau—likewise an unheard-of innovation!—while the reactionary mother suspected nothing. When at last the mother found her out and condemned her to house arrest the young people's decision to get married had been taken. Besides, the social prejudice of the rickshaw coolie's wife against an industrial worker, a representative of the new ruling class of China (at least in name), reflected such an absurd confusion that one might say the mother's 'feudal' prejudice was verging on lunacy.

As Flatface told me all these things I could not dismiss a faint suspicion that the young man may possibly have lacked qualities other than social standing to arouse such opposition from his future mother-in-law. But, whatever the merits of the case, workers are always right and 'feudal' reactionaries are always wrong. The two young people simply went to a registry office and declared themselves man and wife—so horribly simple has marriage become in the new China. The reactionary mother thereupon, somewhat 'feudally,' caught hold of her daughter's hair and pulled out a handful or so. The daughter appealed to the Women's Union, whose Executive specializes in the settlement of matrimonial and other conflicts, and they now tried to make the rickshaw coolie's wife see what a brilliant match the young worker was for her daughter, how times had changed, and how the new age favoured individual freedom. The old woman was no more than half convinced; but she stopped sulking when, nine months later (definitely not before!), she was made a grandmother.

Definitely not before: it is a strange fact that liberation from the old sex traditions has not by any means resulted in a leap into libertinism and promiscuity. The awakening of individual love by choice still has, among the young Chinese something tremendously shy and pure about it. In point of fact, the number of illegitimate births has not only not gone up following the liberation of the sexes, but has even declined. I recollect with much pleasure an evening I spent at the Railwaymen's Club in Peking. Once a week they had a dance there—not, by any means, some innocent folk-dancing, but the genuine Western article. The band was made up of railwaymen, and played foxtrot and waltz rhythms to tunes that were Chinese in character. The trade-union secretary, who was almost beside himself at the honour of welcoming a foreign guest to his club, had chosen the prettiest conductress as a partner for me. Unfortunately, since she spoke not a word of English, she had to confine herself to gazing at me silently from her well-shaped, slanting eyes beneath her tightly plaited pigtails. Chinese women have a wonderful sense of rhythm and, as a rule, make excellent dancers. But our common movement did not even for a moment result in that intimacy which arises invariably with a European woman. I felt as if I held an enchanting bicycle in my arms, and the same impression persisted when I passed on to other cotton-padded ladies. The entire new sexuality is still very much in an embryonic stage, and the trade-union secretary flung up his arms in horror when I told him that in the decadent capitalist West this kind of contact would occasionally be followed by greater intimacy. In China this is entirely out of the question, not only because nobody is ever alone anywhere, but also because there is a puritanical atmosphere pervading the whole country.

This atmosphere is in part a continuation of the old Confucian tradition, and in part has now received a new content by political propaganda. In the old days libertinism had been the privilege of the rich: with their money and their power they had been able to bend the daughters of the lower orders to their will. Hence in to-day's Communist China all free love is tainted with the political odium of 'feudalism.' That, at least, is the theory; but I honestly believe that it applies also in practice. It makes a colossal difference not having the continuous erotic stimulation provided in the West by loud-speakers, cinema posters, and Heaven knows what else. One's productive urges are almost automatically switched to another plane—from the nine-month plan to the five-year plan.

Also in another respect is the newly won individual freedom being rapidly curbed by a new type of discipline. The young couple whom I found standing—or, rather, sitting—before the Divorce Tribunal of the Peking Superior Court on the occasion of my visit there had married after "Liberation," and thus could not blame their troubles upon a wicked 'feudalist' order. Their case was simple enough: the husband, a schoolmaster, had married an exceedingly pretty young peasant girl in Shantung Province; now that he had been transferred to Peking she seemed to him uneducated and boring. He demanded a divorce, and, so as to lend emphasis to his application, had written out a lengthy list of offences, which he now read off with angry eloquence from a long strip of paper. The slut did not clean his clothes or shoes; she was fond of spending money (what woman isn't?); she was lazy and she was a liar. Worse still: whereas he liked to go to bed early and to rise early, the wife would come to bed only when he was asleep, and would then lie in till late in the morning. The wife was like a young dove: meek and sweet. She defended herself simply, without any oratory. Her husband, she said, was a devil; he beat her continually, treated her like a servant, cut off her housekeeping money, and so forth. The presiding judge was listening to her with patent sympathy. It was perfectly obvious that the smooth-tongued fellow simply wanted to rid himself of the simple country girl.

It was a wonderful divorce suit: without legal finesse, without tedious evidence, without expensive lawyers. The two young people sat in the middle of the room on separate chairs; facing them, below a gigantic portrait of Mao Tse-tung and red flags with yellow stars, sat the five lay judges who were trying the case—four men and a woman. They were not by any means the bunch of political tub-thumpers whom I had expected (for most of these judges have no legal training and are appointed by political organizations), but a group of very serious, decent people who would have been a credit to any Western jury. They listened patiently to the long lament of the husband and the complaints of the meek dove, and suggested, Solomonically, that the young people should think it over. They could have ten minutes, and then the court would see how things stood. After a ten-minute recess the two young people were still angry with each other. Thereupon the presiding judge rose to make a speech. It was not in the public interest, he declared, to dissolve marriages lightly. The husband should try to raise the simple girl to his own level by educating her. The young woman should try to provide a pleasant home for her husband and go to bed earlier. The whole bench of judges silently nodded their heads at each point, and after two hours the divorce case was over. And in fact, the wild orgy of divorces which broke out immediately after "Liberation" has now given way to the realization that excessive freedom in this respect would only open the door to frivolous and irresponsible behaviour, especially as the choice of a partner is governed no longer by parenta authority, but by an amorous whim. As a result it is again now very difficult to get a divorce in China.

The subject of love in China invariably brings back to me the features of Yang Gi-tsen, the Principal of the Reformatory for Fallen Girls. She was anti-eroticism personified: with a face like a spider, without even a spark of that maternal kindness which, surely, one might have expected from some one in her position. Frigid to the bone, she had borne no children and had left her husband, to devote herself to this task—the re-education of fallen girls. Indeed, there was no lack of fallen girls in Shanghai. Prior to the Communist "Liberation" Shanghai had been the sinful Babylon of the Far East, a city thick with brothels and kept women. Only a small part of the staff of the establishments had been willing victims of their fate; most of them had been victims of a society that saw nothing criminal in buying or stealing human merchandise from starving parents, and in ruining the girls through brutal compulsion or in extortion for unpaid debts by keeping them in the vile trade. All this sorry past formed part of that 'feudalism' which the Communists now take such pride in having liquidated. Yet it took the Red Government two years before it decided to wield the iron broom in Shanghai. In November 1951 all brothels were closed down and their inmates taken to that very Reformatory, which occupied the premises of a former retraining centre for vagrants.

It was a sad company which moved into the joyless brick barracks: 98 per cent. of them suffered from venereal disease, and some were incurably infected. The institution was almost indistinguishable from a prison—with its grey walls, the red star over the gate, its hermetic seclusion from the outside world and only twice-monthly visits by relatives. When I received an invitation to visit the place I had pictured it quite differently. After all, what tremendous scope was here for restoring the poor creatures! In the courtyard a board proudly proclaimed the aims of the institution in big Chinese letters: "We are fighting against the degradation of womanhood and are striving for the creation of a new human being."

But when I set out hopefully in search of that "new human being" I found nothing but the mixture as before: production targets as the supreme revealed truth, flags, portraits of Mao. Nowhere a flower, a bird, or anything that might have rekindled something like real gentleness in the downtrodden souls. I made no secret to Mrs Yang of my opinion of her inhuman institution. In the workshops the former prostitutes were sitting behind their machines as tightly packed together as sardines, knitting socks and gloves. Packed just as tightly, the night shift were dozing through the afternoon in their dormitories. There was an almost tangible desolation about the place. "Six months," was Mrs Yang's reply to my question of how long on an average the girls spent in this satanic mill.

Suddenly, among the thick lips, the coarse features, and the stringy hair of the rest of the women, I spotted a delicate rosy face which had preserved its gracefulness even under the prison uniform. A lock curled down over the forehead, and when I stopped before the girl she smiled and blushed at me like a teenager receiving her first declaration of love. This, Mrs Yang explained to me in a whisper, was an educated girl of good family, who had actually gone to high school, but had then, in order to get her impoverished parents out of financial difficulties, taken rich lovers. She had led a comfortable life, on soft feather beds and with champagne. And now she was here, among the common tarts. And not for a mere six months either, but for two years!

"She behaved in an unseemly manner," Mrs Yang remarked sorrowfully, "and her spirit is still not sufficiently reformed to justify her discharge."

The Principal's face looked even more spider-like at these words (like a spider consuming a fly), and I had no difficulty in discerning the evil triumph in her eyes, the triumph of an ugly woman who has been given power over a young, beautiful creature.

"But surely it is not surprising that a person of some sensibility should rebel against the straitjacket in this prison?" I protested. "Do you really believe you can reform the spirit of this intelligent girl by forcing her to do soul-destroying work in the company of cheap professional prostitutes? Is she regarded as a criminal?"

Mrs Yang only smiled maliciously. "Our results justify our educational methods," she observed simply. "So far we've had 3100 girls pass through our institution. At present we have 1400. Fewer than 1 per cent. are brought back as relapses. Most of them rejoin their families or become factory workers. Some have even married Heroes of Labour."

The poor sailors docking at Shanghai to-day! The whole atmosphere of gangsters and whores which used to swirl along the Broadway of the port has vanished like a phantom, and in the evening the footsteps of the lonely visitor re-echo from the closed shutters. Toby's Bar is the only dive that is left over from a glittering past. Toby is a Negro from the West Indies, a British national, and his business is so slack that he would pack up and cut loose then and there if only his Chinese wife could get an exit permit. He still has two hostesses lounging about in the neon twilight—a White Russian and a gipsy. White sailors, if they have to amuse themselves in a 'feudalist' manner, are at least not to sully any Chinese women. Altogether the night-club is only a grudging concession to the decadent customs of the West. At the Seamen's House, run by the Government, the sailors are offered more puritanical and more nutritious fare: steaks and beer at nominal prices, a wide selection of goods at a mere fraction of what the articles would cost outside, and free shows by artistes, jugglers, and other performers who conjure their audience's watches out of their pockets but do not keep them. But there is not a girl in sight: men serve even behind the bar. I have rarely seen more dejected fellows than the Dutch sailors whose ship was in port. They sat at the bar leafing disgustedly through the piles of Communist literature with their colour-print pictures of virtuous and victoriously smiling girl tractor-drivers.

Friends took me to the only place which had some of the old capitalist eroticism of the former Shanghai left. The Wing On restaurant was on the top floor of a house near the Nanking Road, and when I entered it still bore some of the garlands of the nationalization festival. The only things not nationalized were the charming young ladies who, looking like chaste schoolgirls, were sitting at the tables before inexpensive glasses of tea, glancing cautiously and furtively, almost with plumage ruffled in alarm, about the restaurant, as if waiting for somebody or something. Now and again a blue-clad man, in appearance every inch a good, progressive Communist, stepped up to a table and addressed one of the girls. Only then—without as much as the shadow of enticement beforehand—could she speak to him. The man would then make for the lift, with the lady unobtrusively following. No white man could risk such an adventure. A resident German who did risk it was disturbed in his love-making within ten minutes—by the police. The unfortunate lady was taken to the Reformatory. That is why the little singing birds behave in such an exemplarily virtuous fashion. They are there only on sufferance. On sufferance for whom? Who persuades the inexorably virtuous State to shut its eyes mercifully to human weakness? Could it be some Communists who have remained incurably reactionary below the belt?

Eros under police supervision: every European in China has a tale to tell about it. Above all the bachelors among the Western diplomats, many of whom in despair have asked for a transfer to some other post. Even a man enjoying the friendship of a European lady can be assured of the solicitous interest of the authorities. An elderly widower in Shanghai told me that on returning to his home one evening he had found a mysterious gentleman in his sitting-room; the man had explained that he was a secret policeman who had come for a little chat. This kind of informal conversation which, without ever assuming the unpleasantness of an interrogation, nevertheless touches easily upon all aspects of the life of the person questioned, is very popular with the Chinese police in their dealings with foreigners. In this particular case the conversation soon turned to the physical vigour of the old gentleman, whereupon the visitor abruptly put the question, "Why don't you marry again?" When my acquaintance parried this indiscreet question with a reference to his advanced age the visitor suddenly turned sharper. "And what," he asked, "is the business of the lady who visits you twice every week?"

"We play the piano together, if you don't mind," was the reply; "duets."

There are no secrets in Communist China. Even Cupid has to register his shafts as weapons liable to endanger the security of the State. Virtue is marching on, with step firm and unfaltering.

[CLARK, 108–110]

This is Shanghai 1959, once the lustiest city in the Orient, where "reason and persuasion," and a stern code of morality, or prudery, make it as exciting as a slumbering village. The pedicab coolie of 1949, riding his bicycle-propelled rickshaw, expected at least twice a day to receive a firm kick from a cop for some minor traffic violation. Now the undignified word "coolie" no longer is used, and the cop reverentially says, *"Tung-chih,* comrade, you should be more careful of the way you drive." And for a half hour the cop calmly chastises the pedicab driver for turning without a signal; the lecture is conducted with masterful aplomb. Maybe the pedicab driver who vividly recalls his hell-bent career as a private operator and the passengers who impatiently demanded to be ferried to Kiangsi Road, longs for the old days. A half hour wasted in listening to exhortation is worse than a boot in the pants. But then, on the other hand, what is the rush today? There are no restless passengers; there are no "street blossoms" on Kiangsi Road, or on the Bund, or, for that matter, anywhere in this metropolis of seven million five hundred thousand. Now the streets are deserted in early evening, and the "blossoms" (or, as *really* old China hands used to call them, "fallen sisters") have been uprooted and transplanted in greenhouses known as reformatories. As productive "flowers," they now toil on the docks, carting sheet steel and loading holds. Foreign sailors, even if they should, in desperation, be attracted to these unfeminine creatures, restrain any impulses to engage in polite exploratory conversation with them. While I was in Shanghai, two Yugoslav seamen were in jail for attempting to "demoralize" female citizens; and two Swiss businessmen, who tried merely to take a couple of ladies dancing, had just completed a four-month diet of rice and water. In the former case, some political motive may be suspected; Tito and Yugoslavs in general are in disfavor among Chinese Communists. But since Swiss were also arrested, it must be assumed that the new code of austere morality recognizes no neutrality. Foreigners as a whole are blamed for the decay that once marked Shanghai society and spread to other parts of the country.

But for frustrated foreigners there is always the Seamen's Club, formerly the exclusive Shanghai Club for British residents, on the Bund. Hundreds of Norwegians, Danish, and British sailors clutter the marbled lobby, gazing imperturbably past a huge plaster figure of Mao Tse-tung. Off the lobby is the longest bar in the Far East, one hundred and fifty feet of mahogany bearing the faint imprint of martini glasses of another day and the fresher stains of beer mugs. An old-timer, a Norwegian skipper, sips Shanghai Beer No. 1 without enthusiasm and murmurs, "Not like the old days, not at all." And in his saddened eyes is the image of old Shanghai, with its sophistication and scores of night clubs, now a dead relic of the "decadent bourgeois" past. At least, when they closed the lights of the night clubs and the brothels, the Communists had the courtesy to open the antiseptic Seamen's Club. Actually, very few of the old-timers are about. They prefer to stay aboard their ships, to read, to listen to the Voice of America on the radio, or simply to reminisce in privacy. It is mostly the youngsters, the Danes with crew cuts on their first night ashore, who, with no place else to go, show up at the club, looking bewildered in this previously wicked Babylon of the East. Finally, they resign themselves to an evening of "culture" and peer listlessly at the showcase of Ming vases or pick up English-language editions of Chinese magazines in the club's library. Not even a copy of *Punch* or *The Tatler* is in sight. The companionship of laughing ladies? This will have to await another time and another place. "Free love" (even if paid for) not only has been denied the foreigners, it is considered most distasteful (even if not paid for), and a crime, among the Chinese.

It is all rather strange, and terribly quiet, and yet oddly noisy in Shanghai. As I type these notes I can hear the clatter of cymbals and the loud beat of drums outside my hotel window. A procession of workers is passing by, no doubt proclaiming to the world that a local factory has discovered a new short-cut in the manufacture of ball bearings. And across the street I can see other workers on roof-tops, bending and stretching to some high-pitched calisthenics. The government has decreed that an hour's exercise each day improves productivity, and now all of China is bending and stretching. Eros is well under control; energy must be expended only in constructive directions.

> On either end of the springy carrying pole
> The girl balances two full water buckets.
> Lithely she moves ahead, not splashing a drop
> While the lad follows close behind.
> "Stop for a moment," he begs her,
> "Let me tell you the longing in my heart!"
> Without pausing, the girl laughs—
> "Look at the beads of sweat on your face!
> You can't even keep pace
> With a woman carrying two full buckets!
> What has your heart got to say about that?"

The above is described by *China Reconstructs* as a love poem for 1959. "Of course," says the magazine benevolently, "people still write love poems, but they have a new salty tang, very different from the wistful sentimentality of the old. This sparkling verse reveals two things about courtship in today's countryside—one, the sturdy independence of China's new young womanhood; the other, that neither lasses nor lads can get their heart's desire unless they prove themselves good workers. The lazy ones lose out in love as they do in the fields."

> Brother goes on winged feet, carrying baskets of earth.
> Close on his heels comes a girl, also with two full loads.
> "Even if you fly into the clouds," she says,
> "I'll not let you outdistance me!"

[GREENE, 89–91]

Chang Yung-tse's family came to Shenyang from Shantung province. He had been a studious boy and his family, who owned a hardware shop, were able to send him to college.

In the early summer of 1948 Chang was one of a group of students from the Northeast who made their way down to Peking to petition the Kuomintang authorities for promised school funds. This was at a time when Peking's students were protesting arbitrary arrests in the schools. One night—Chang's group was camped in an old Buddhist temple—the secret police rounded them up and took them all off to jail.

"How'd you get out?" I asked.

"My father got word of what had happened, and after a few months enough money was raised in Peking to buy me out of jail."

Chang remained in Peking—some of his friends crossed the lines into Communist territory—and after liberation he entered the Foreign Language Institute in Peking.

All this was said rather hesitatingly and seriously.

Liu Tien-yi was a blunter type. His family had been connected with the steel companies in this area. The father worked here under the Japanese, for a pittance.

"Sometimes my father brought back so little at the end of a week's work that we didn't eat. I mean my mother and the children didn't eat. Mother made my father eat, because if he lost his health and lost his job we would all have starved."

After the Japanese were defeated the works was taken over by the Kuomintang and things got worse. Many of the mills closed. There was no work. "My father was ingenious and became a street hawker selling small necessities which he often made himself out of metal scrap that he would go out and steal—things like small pots and frying pans.

"After liberation, of course, things picked up. As many as possible were put to work clearing the rubble and cleaning up the destroyed factories. At first for little wages, but just to be doing something again was a help. When the Metallurgical Institute was opened here, I applied, passed the examinations, and got a four-year training course—then was taken on almost automatically by the steel company. My father is still working here—he's too old to be in the furnace plants, he works in the tube mill."

We had more beer. The room was full of smoke, and the relating of these stories (so unusual for Chinese to be so outspoken about themselves) had brought a certain atmosphere of intimacy between us.

We were silent for a few moments. Why wouldn't young men like this be behind the regime, I thought. But such musings could wait. I wanted to make the most of the present atmosphere to ask questions that had always somehow been evaded.

"If a boy sees a girl that he takes a fancy to, how does he get to know her?"

They both smile at this sudden switch in conversation. Apparently he does what young men all over the world do—he might wait for her outside the factory gate, make some excuse for talking to her, ask her out to a movie.

"And if he wants to marry her?"

"I don't think he would ask her himself," Liu said. "A few might, but not most. Not right out like that. He would first get a friend to ask her if it would be all right for him to ask her to marry him . . . and in that way he wouldn't make it embarrassing for her to say 'no' if she didn't want to or embarrassing to himself to be rejected. Then, of course, there might be a good deal of discussion between the two families—but the decision is entirely up to the couple. If everything is all right, then they must both get a health certificate. Then they can get married."

"What ceremony is performed?"

"Usually none at all, except, of course, the families will come together to celebrate with a small dinner. Then the couple are given a three-day holiday with pay by way of a honeymoon."

"Of course," added the serious Chang, "the boy and girl would ask each other about their political views in order to be sure to marry someone who is politically mature."

And now an even more delicate question.

"What about boys and girls sleeping together before they are married? Does it happen often?"

"Oh yes, of course it does happen," Chang said. "But it's not against the law."

"No, no," said Liu, "it's not against the law, but it's frowned on. Not that we mind about people sleeping together from any old-fashioned moralistic ideas or religious notions—nothing of that kind; but if they sleep together they might have children, and anyway, isn't it better to get married?"

Mr. Liu, looking at his watch: "We better get going if we are to see the steel mills."

[CROFT, 95–97]

Of all subjects after Marx–Leninism, the one which I personally should have most avoided broaching with Little Wang was that of love; but the hot-blooded Abou felt no such constraint.

'There is one thing,' he said with troubled curiosity, 'which seems very wrong. I have never seen people making love in your country. I go to the Summer Palace, to Chungshan Park and to Coal Hill. This afternoon I come to the Ming tombs and there are thousands of people enjoying themselves. But there is never boy and girl together. What have you done to cause this? Why do young people never make love?'

For once Little Wang laughed; she thought Abou was joking.

'But it is not true,' she said. 'Boys and girls are often together, but they cannot always find time for making love. Even at the week-ends they have their work to do.'

'But I *never* see them together,' said Abou. 'In the gardens I have looked especially to find them, but they are always apart. And in the streets I see boys walking hand in hand together, but I never see them holding hands with a girl. It is unnatural for things to be so. It is terrible to keep them apart. You have done many wonderful things in your country, but this is something to your shame. You have forgotten love.'

Little Wang still could not take him seriously, but however hard she laughed and protested that boys and girls carried on together much the same in China as anywhere else in the world, it was difficult to believe her, for everyone coming to China comments on the same phenomenon. It is, no doubt, one of the direct products of female emancipation: the girls have not yet learnt to trust themselves with young men, nor have the young men, freed from the tyranny of the parentally arranged marriage, learnt the finer arts of courtship or the amorous advantages to be gained in public pleasure-grounds; where exactly they do their wooing, how the first move is made and how the pace is determined, would have been interesting to discover, but Little Wang did not venture to explain, and even the forthright Abou was too timorous to ask.

'It has been my greatest disappointment,' he repeated. 'All the time I have been in China I have seen no love. I have heard nobody talk about love. You tell me about your great industrial programme and your factories and health schemes and you show me your old monuments and your temples, but never do you show me love. I think your women must be afraid of love so they dress themselves in these terrible clothes deliberately. They try to look so awful that the boys will not be interested in them.'

At this point I suggested, with crude jocularity, that they were too concerned about production to have time for reproduction, which set Abou roaring and bouncing about in the car, but brought from Little Wang a withering glare of contempt.

She sat tight-lipped and sullen for the rest of the journey

back; and I felt doubly ashamed of myself because I knew I had deliberately meant to offend her.

[CROFT, 73–74]

For the long-term resident an insoluble problem is that of finding female companionship. It is physically impossible for an Englishman to enter into any form of private liaison with a Chinese woman without setting up a whirl of woe and worry all round. If he visits the lady in her home the matter will undoubtedly be communicated at the double to the leader of the Street Committee; if the lady visits him in his hotel, the room will be infested with a swarm of servicemen before she has had time to sit down. Percy Dryden once succeeded in escorting a woman unobserved, as he thought, over the threshold of his room in the Peking Hotel; but throughout the evening he was assailed at rapid intervals by a battery of servicemen irrepressibly eager to collect his laundry, brush his shoes, tidy his desk and, when the lady still remained, to replace one unwanted pot of tea with a succession of others. There seemed to be no sinister implications behind this curious carry-on; it was all based upon the not altogether facile assumption that any native woman consorting with a westerner would automatically be defiled—a belief inherited from associations in the earlier part of the century and systematically embodied in the prevalent puritanical dogma.

In any case, by accepting his invitation Dryden's guest had laid herself open to 'social rebuke'—or serious admonition from her Street Committee. She would undoubtedly be treated as one in need of correction, and if she persisted in the offence would be letting herself in for a torrent of criticism and self-criticism hardly designed to add to her enjoyment of life.

The social rebuke, or fear of it, has been the strongest police weapon in the campaign against vice and corruption. It has proved a more effective deterrent to prostitution than any system of fines and imprisonment, a safer keeper of the nation's chastity than any edict or promulgation, although, as Dryden told me, there was still a small black market in sex: 'But only the Japanese can break into it.'

[GREENE, 160–162]

This seemed like a good time to ask a question, one I asked in every commune I visited. "Have you ever," I asked Mr.

Chiao, "found it necessary, perhaps for a short period, to house husbands and wives in separate buildings?" Mr. Chiao asked the interpreter to repeat the question and the interpreter turned back to me. I repeated it.

The interpreter began to laugh and the director and the other members joined in. Mr. Chiao, still laughing, said something and the interpreter said, "Mr. Chiao wants to know if that's what they do in England." The widely publicized Party Resolution of December 1958 had ridiculed Mr. Dulles' speech in Seattle in which he had informed the world that Chinese families were being broken up. Cartoons of Dulles and Eisenhower were often painted on commune and factory wall boards. In all communes my question about family separation provoked mirth, except in one where the director said with a certain contempt, "You have been reading Mr. Dulles!"

"What do you do," I asked, "about a boy and girl who fall in love and have a child before they are married? Or before legal marriage age?"

The interpreter's translation of this question was followed by a rather lengthy silence. It was obviously an unusual question. The others at the table became very busy readjusting their notebooks and examining the points of their ballpoint pens. The girl who was picking up the wet towels paused to listen.

"There is no problem now about marriage," said Mr. Chiao. "Formerly, many could not afford to marry. But that is no hindrance now. Formerly also, the low level of education made some fall into wrong habits. That does not happen any more."

"But human nature is human nature," I insisted. "You just can't expect me to believe that babies are never born to unwed parents."

Mr. Chiao shook his head.

I pressed the point as far as I felt the traffic would bear. It would hardly do to dispute the director's accuracy; I could not go out, after all, and count the babies as I had counted the tractors in the tractor yard. And who knows?—he may have been right. I told him that officials in Peking and elsewhere, people at the university and in the health office, discussed these problems as a matter of reality. . . .

Mr. Chiao, however, stood his ground. "You may not believe me," he said, "but we really have none of these problems now."

I nodded and changed the subject.

China is today an intensely, almost compulsively "moral" society. Of the many communes I visited, all except one denied any knowledge of any children born out of wedlock. In the one exception, two cases were cited, both involving parents who were under the legal marriage age (twenty for boys and eighteen for girls). Both cases were resolved in the same way: by court orders permitting early marriage, "in the interest of the child."

11. Sport and Recreation

[CROFT, 98–102]

There is an extraordinary misconception amongst English people that, despite the strictures of Mao's regime, China is still a country in which, when evening comes on, all the vices in the calendar burgeon forth illicitly down sinister alleyways, in smoky dens and doss-houses, to the accompaniment of eerie, wailing music and mysterious oriental smells.

Anyone setting out with ambitions in this direction would be well advised to terminate his journey in Hong Kong or head straight for Tokyo instead, for since the Liberation China has been cleaned up with a truly comprehensive efficiency.

The high mark of this achievement is to be found in Shanghai, where later I took some pains to investigate the methods thought appropriate to the operation. In Peking I was content to examine the results, the most conspicuous being that night life in the western sense of the word has simply ceased to exist, or, to be more exact, is conducted with a propriety in comparison with which a Sunday night in Cheltenham would seem like a Neronian orgy.

To say that there are no bars, no cabarets, no dance-halls, no speak-easies, honky-tonks, clip joints or dives is only to hint at the complete social paralysis which grips the city after about eleven o'clock, when the theatres have emptied and the last overladen tram has gone clanking home. After that hour a walk through the streets is a darkling communion with yourself; you may stumble at street corners upon cigarette-sellers and vendors of chestnuts and noodles, vegetables and sesame cakes, or pedlars of soya sauce and biscuits and old clothes, but their wares have been packed up, their stalls shuttered, and they are preparing to lump their way home; or you may hear, from the building sites and factory yards, the endless *Wei-ho Wei-ho* of the labourers as they sway and bend in ghostly form beneath the great arc-lights that blaze all night long, beaconing the path to China's immeasurable destiny; but you will not encounter—unless it be a restless fellow-spirit from licentious foreign parts—a solitary prowler in search of nocturnal pleasures.

If you bear in mind that the first sign of aberrant activity by the local residents would almost certainly be spotted and re-

ported at once to the nearest Street Committee, it should not
be difficult to appreciate the aseptic thoroughness with which
the new morality is maintained. That it is a reformation of
phenomenal range and rapidity cannot be disputed, nor that
it is an entirely admirable improvement upon the vicious immorality it has replaced; but it seemed a pity that, in destroying the weeds of the old regime, the government should have
wiped out the garden altogether.

But if there is not much activity late at night there is a
wealth of it earlier on, although again it has little in common
with the fictional conception of the exotic and mysterious
orient.

The bazaars, of course, remain, and the brilliant fairs, and
the little street tables where families squat around, eating supper or drinking tea, but these no longer provide the centre of
social attraction. The focal point has shifted elsewhere: to the
huge department stores where, hour after hour, crowds of
workers wander enquiringly around, sometimes to buy, more
often just to look; to the Hall of Sino-Soviet Friendship where,
every night, people queue in their thousands for an exhibition
of Economic and Cultural Achievement in East Germany or
of Ten Years Socialist Construction in Bulgaria—does it
matter if they sometimes have no idea what they are queueing
to see?—it is something to do, a break from routine, a place
to go; or else there are the vast new gymnasiums, the festivals
of sport, the skating-rinks, the swimming-pools and stadiums.

The latest of these had just gone up when I arrived in
Peking. It was called, with characteristic exactness, The Working People's Palace of Sport, and its name did full justice to
the scale on which it had been built and the remarkable facilities it offered.

Compendious enough to incorporate the Empire Stadium
and Olympia together and still leave room for a tennis-court or
two in the wings, it comprised: eight indoor basket-ball
pitches; a recreation-room, where twenty-four games of table-
tennis could be played in comfort simultaneously; a central
arena, with a seating capacity of five thousand, for concerts,
wrestling, boxing and acrobatic contests; two gymnasiums; an
underground swimming-pool two hundred and fifty feet long;
and all the peripheral necessities of the modern games-player,
from rest and relaxation parlours to rooms for massage and
medical treatment.

Surprisingly I was given no statistics about the numbers of
people availing themselves of these facilities and no compari-
sons were made with recreational conditions under the Kuomintang; perhaps none were necessary because, as far as the
mass of the people were concerned, they did not exist at all

Although not myself a devotee of the sportsdrome, I would say without reservation that the Peking Working People's Palace of Sport is giving more pleasure to more sports-lovers per night than any similar institution elsewhere in the world.

Then there were the cinemas, where Socialist solidarity was further strengthened by the predominance of Soviet feature films. In Peking I saw only one home-grown product, an adaptation from an ancient popular romance, which had exquisite charm but moved at such a tortured pace that both then and subsequently, when I saw it again in Shanghai, its effect was so soporific that I never knew exactly what it was about.

More interesting were the coloured documentaries which preceded it, beautifully composed films showing the gardens of lilac and peonies in Fengtai, the autumn chrysanthemums in Peihai Park and the glistening brilliance of the goldfish ponds in Chung-shan Park. They had been specially dubbed, either for export or for the benefit of English-speaking visitors, and their enchantment was marred only by the commentator's continual reminders that, until the Liberation, the parks had been the private preserves of feudal landlords. When, in the last reel of the goldfish film, he smugly reiterated, 'So now you can see the people wandering at leisure among these beautiful ponds which after the Liberation were taken out of the hands of the reactionary classes,' Shakir sitting beside me growled under his breath: 'Maybe soon they will liberate the goldfish too!'

It is the theatres which stay open latest (even the last lights of the restaurants are dimmed by ten o'clock), and it is here that something reminiscent of night life may still be found, although the connection is largely tentative.

To the Chinese, the theatre does not denote merely an entertainment, still less a fashion parade or social jamboree; it is a functional necessity, a place where they spend a goodly part of their lives, may die or be born in, a joyous communion, a bedlam, a mystique, a mirror giving transcendent expression to the throbs and stresses of their collective soul. They do not simply go to see a performance; they go time and time again until they know every gesture, every inflexion by heart, until they have shed their own identities and become themselves participants in the action.

But while the play is so intensely the thing, the accessories pertaining to it have been shrugged aside. The audience sit packed closely together on wooden tip-up seats. The walls in most theatres have a barrack-like bleakness; the foyers are grey passageways, drably lit, starkly utilitarian. There are, of course, no bars. The thirsty spectator may help himself to a glass of hot water from one of the taps in the foyer or may even purchase a glass of orange-juice in the gloomy refreshment-room, but there the amenities end. Yet if the conditions seem a trifle Spartan by West End standards, to the Chinese, intent only upon enjoying the performance, they represent the height of upholstered luxury.

My first theatre visit was to see a Song and Dance Ensemble which had recently returned from a tour of the Middle East.

These ensembles are something of a communist speciality, but this one was more special than most. In the course of their tour the artistes had visited Egypt, the Sudan, Ethiopia, Syria and Afghanistan, and had taken the trouble on the way to study the folk culture of those countries and learn some of the national songs and dances. In honour of our delegation they sang Arabian love-songs in the original languages and performed complicated Egyptian dances with a precision and sinuosity which amazed the Arab delegates. 'Singing not so good as Egyptian,' declared Galal, deeply moved, 'but movement of dance altogether correct . . . all details exact.'

More surprising, however, than the apparent verisimilitude of the performance was the revelation it gave that Chinese women did actually understand the fundamentals of sexual allure.

For the Afghan folk-song 'You are so good that I have given my heart to you', they wore tight-fitting flowered dresses and vivid brocades, slashed generously down the sides; and in the plaintive Syrian lyric 'If I continue to love you it is sin But please let me look at you once more', their gently swaying hips conveyed a catalogue of tingling suggestion which, applied to their native opera, would have fetched out every Street Committee in Peking. This was demure modesty, however, compared with what they did to the Egyptian dances. In a moaning ecstasy, they abandoned themselves to the rhythms of the music, and their bodies swirled and vibrated as though in fevered anticipation of gaudy nights to come—or as though they had found at last a release for their own pent-up desires and yearnings.

[CROFT, 109–112]

For virtue-loving delegates the Peking night offered additional and peculiar attractions.

'A party is being thrown for you,' announced Shen in his most methodical English manner, 'by the young people of the city. All invited are invited to turn up for seven p.m.'

The party was held in the Hall of the People's Consultative Assembly; and the scene that ensued on our arrival was a convivial riot, a fantasy of real Peace and genuine Friendship, which defied the laws of ideological analysis and simply had to be taken spontaneously, uncritically, the way it was, precisely for what it was.

As the coach came to a halt outside the Hall hundreds of young Pekinese swept down the steps, shouting, cheering, clapping and leaping about in a rapture of enthusiasm. It was some minutes before we were able to force our way out of the coach and begin manœuvring up the steps. Eventually someone hacked a path through the welcoming throng, but suddenly the doors of the Hall jerked violently open and a battery of hundreds more young people raced frantically through them.

When comparative order had again been restored I proceeded to inch my way along. 'Ni-hao! Ni-hao!' shouted hundreds of jubilant voices. 'Ni-hao! Ni-hao!' I shouted back— and with that a kind of delirium came over the group surging round me. They grabbed my hands and bobbed feverishly up and down like boxers sweating off surplus weight on the morning of a big fight. Somebody identified me as English and the cry went up 'Hello-hello-hello! How-do-you-do! how-do-you-do! how-do-you-do!' In a tumult of shouting, skipping, jumping and heaving I was dragged, tugged, pulled, pushed and finally half-carried inside. Off went my coat. On came a chair. A dozen pairs of hands thrust me into it while beaming faces hemmed me in on all sides, but I could respond with nothing more constructive than a zany-like prolongation of the *Ni-hao* —*Ni-hao*—hello—hello—how-do-you-do theme.

Relief came with the arrival of a chunky, bespectacled girl who spoke excellent fourth-year student English: relief, at least, to the extent that I was able to communicate intelligibly with my expectant admirers—but what was there to say? What *can* you say on such occasions to a hundred different people at once which is not absurdly trite or utterly meaningless? You can, of course, tell them what you think about Marx–Leninism or, better still, ask what *they* think about it, but this did not seem the most appropriate moment for digging in that particular field. So there is nothing for it but to ask the first routine questions that come into your head and try to look interested in the routine answers. But I discovered that they were too shy or too polite—or just too plain curious—to do anything except pass the conversational ball back to me with the same enquiring clichés, until I returned to the point from where I had started and looked dazedly around, trying to seem as overjoyed at having made their acquaintance as they abundantly were at having made mine.

For the occasion, those who could afford it had shed their boiler-suits: the girls had put on flowered blouses, a few—especially daring—*cheong-sams*, slit to an inch above the knee; and the boys either high-buttoned tunics, grey, brown or blue —the Chinese equivalent of naval Number Ones—or double-breasted suits. They had also laid on a western-style dance band which manfully ploughed its way several times over through a repertoire of three Strauss waltzes, two Gershwin tunes—imported from Moscow after the visit of *Porgy and Bess*—and four or five foxtrots of nondescript origin.

The Dancing is notable for the spirit of determined optimism in which it is carried out rather than for any flashes of technical dexterity. The western style, of course, is completely alien to their own and they approach it on a principle of whimsical propulsion, whereby the feet of the female dancer are saved from permanent mutilation only because she holds her partner as far away from her as is physically possible without losing contact with him altogether.

From the Dancing we proceeded to the Entertainment in which the younger artists of the Peking Opera companies, together with student acrobats, jugglers, equilibrists and dancers, provided a magnificent impromptu cabaret. Not a word was said all night about productivity or the advancement of 'techniques', and nobody made any speeches about Peace and Friendship; until Tripp, tugging my sleeve during one of the songs, observed darkly, 'It worries me to see all this frenzied enthusiasm. If they can get so excited over this, what would they be like if the government wanted to prepare them for a war?'

It was impossible, of course, to say; but the question could never be ignored, a lingering hangover which hit you at the end of every delegation party. But there was no point in spurning the party for fear of the consequences; it was even possible that some little good might be done by going to it with a good grace.

'How does it come about,' I asked the chunky girl in the middle of the last waltz, 'that so many people are here?'

She laughed in surprise. 'But there are not many enough. There were only tickets for two thousand, so only a few could be allotted to each college. But thousands more were crying to come. All the youth of Peking would have come if there had been room.'

'Why,' I asked, 'should they be so excited by our visit?'

'Because,' she replied simply, 'they are happy to see you.'

[SCHMID, 31–33]

Away from the formal triumphal avenue which the regime has laid out before the Forbidden City, so that the rumble of the parading tanks might confirm the spirits of their ancestors in their imperial dreams, a strange spectacle could be witnessed on either side of the Tien-an-men Gate every morning. On a narrow platform between avenue and wall stood a number of young and not-so-young men, their arms raised and their bodies performing curious movements, half dance and half combat. Occasionally two of them would pair off: partner would become adversary, and the imaginary movements would gain meaning—evasion, feint, attack, withdrawal. Yet every movement remained slow, as if filmed in slow motion; there was none of that sudden violent resolution of tension between the bodies which usually marks the dramatic end of the Japanese jiu-jitsu. Even in his material presence the adversary remained like a shadow—not to be touched, or only quite softly. Hence the name given to the curious sport: shadow boxing.

It is related to jiu-jitsu; like it, it is a form of the art of self-defence, only much more complicated and involved in its drill. According to legend, Chang San-feng, its founder, one day watched a fight between a bird and a snake. He saw the bird plunge dynamically from the tree and violently attack the snake; the snake coiled itself into a ball and deprived its adversary of a target. Only when the bird had exhausted its strength by attacking and incautiously exposed itself did the snake strike and bite it dead.

In shadow boxing too—profound Eastern wisdom!—every attack is preceded by a withdrawal, calculated to tempt the opponent into a vulnerable position. There are thirteen elementary movements which the strange sportsmen practise outside the imperial palace: eight for the arms and five for the legs. The turns are performed towards the exact points of the compass, and each of them bears a pretty poetic name, such as "Return to the Mountain," "Carrying a Tiger," "Finding a Needle on the Bottom of the Sea." Shadow boxing, a Chinese well versed in the traditional arts explained to me, exercises and tunes up not only every single muscle in the human body, but also the mind. The heart is calmed and strengthened, and life is thereby prolonged. The mind gains such control over the limbs that a man's physical strength grows in proportion with his willpower.

Control over the body! Sometimes I hardly believed my eyes when I saw the queer contortions, worthy of a circus acrobat, which the acolytes of shadow boxing contrived to perform. Their ability to do the splits and at the same time touch their toes with their fingertips struck me as child's-play after I had seen a handsome, dark youth similarly perform the splits, then lower the upper half of his body backward, resting it, as if on a pillow, on the leg behind him, and finally grip that foot with his right hand—a contortion that made the beholder believe in some strange transformation in the anatomy of the human body.

Towards ten o'clock the beginners used to take up the rôle of humble spectators while the more advanced students tested their skill with sword, lance, and ball. They were in their third year, for three years are needed for learning the technique which makes the implement a living thing, and the body which wields it a weightless, whirling implement.

There are fifty-one movements in sword fencing. The fencer first lunges, "as if piercing three rings," and thrusts "as fast as a shooting star." The sword is then brought down "like a bee returning to its hive." A sideways lunge with raised arm is "like Phœnix spreading its wings." Only he who has seen this strange ballet of body and sword can understand that its realization requires two years of passionate devotion and that six months are spent solely on developing the sense of balance to the necessary degree of virtuosity.

The cult of shadow boxing by the Tien-an-men Gate is a significant symptom. During the first few years after the Revolution all emphasis had been on Western athletics as the most obvious and apparently most efficient method of producing a fine muscular specimen of humanity and a valuable soldier. Even to-day the official trend in sport still follows that universal people's-democracy pattern which finds its expression in the building of giant stadiums and other temples of the muscle. But the mere fact that shadow boxing is once more *permitted* and that this esoteric sport is again finding a growing circle of enthusiastic followers among the young people surely proves that the Chinese spirit has not been crushed by Communist vulgarity, but only buried, and that before long its young shoots will push up again through the covering of philistinism. This will take time, of course—but history and especially Chinese history, can only be viewed correctly in a perspective of centuries.

[WILSON, 185]

After we had dined, we set out to visit the Chinese circus. Professor Wang, Mr. Tien and I drove through the dark city. As we passed a modern market-place Mr. Tien said, "Formerly that was a place for prostitutes. There are now none in China. They have been abolished. So have drug addicts and beggars"; and indeed I never saw any, but I do not know what became of these unfortunate people.

The theatre, which held about a thousand people, was full of ordinary Chinese. Crowds always looked the same—there are no degrees of elegance in cotton work clothes. I noticed many children, only one soldier, and no other Occidentals. The only car outside the theatre was our own. Inside were many paper posters written both in Chinese and in English letters, for example, *"Maozhuxi Wansui!"* which literally means "Mao, Chairman—Long Life–" There was also *"Zhongguo Gonchandang Wansui!"* meaning "Chinese Communist Party—Long Life!"

The Chinese circus was a first-class vaudeville show with twenty acts, mostly juggling, and no animals at all except for a lion dance which proved as popular as a finale as had a similar act in Peking. Every kind of juggling, balancing, sleight of hand and trick bicycle riding was included, and I was especially impressed by the conjurer who stood alone in the middle of the stage and produced no less than seventeen glass bowls full of water, some with goldfish, from his mandarin cloak, and by two plump and cheerful middle-aged men, each of whom balanced a heavy earthenware crock sideways on his bald and polished head. These they rolled back and forth on their heads, spun and tossed from head to head as though is was the easiest thing in the world to catch a big pot on the top of one's head and have it rest there on its side without rolling off.

[CROFT, 194–197]

In the old brothel area of Fu Chou Road was the Great World.

Formerly, they said, although ostensibly a place of entertainment and refreshment it had functioned as an emporium of vice, notorious even in the east. Gang bosses ruled it; gambling, prostitution, opium were its stock in trade. It catered for every taste in the catalogue and attracted the scum of the China Seas.

It must have been a remarkable establishment then. It was even more so now.

You entered into a shadowy courtyard. Around it ranged a series of gaunt buildings with jutting galleries and grilled windows, connected together by gaslit arcades and stone stair-cases. In the yard itself a smiling, black-jacketed motor-cyclist rode the Wall of Death in a series of hazardous figure-eights, first by himself, then dragging a toy cannon behind him, then with two children sitting pillion fashion, a boy in front and a girl behind—and a flamboyant wave of his hand to the audience each time he reached the upper rim of the pit and began the thirty-foot dive to the bottom. The rickety bamboo enclosure swayed and shuddered to the roar of the machine; in the upper stand the spectators pressed close together, the back rows leaning precariously over the front; I, for one, was glad to get down to earth again; if the Wall did not frighten the rider, it certainly scared me.

But this was a diversion from the real business at hand, a shock absorber to the tumultuous medley of noise coming from all around. Within the Great World proper the most fantastic form of mass entertainment known to man was in full blast. To be exact, on one or other floor of the various buildings, to the clashing of gongs and cymbals, the beating of drums, the strident crescendoes of brass and the amplified screechings of the singers, five different kinds of opera were being presented at one and the same time, together with a puppet show, a display of juggling and acrobatics and a Soviet film commemorating the October revolution. Item by item, any one of these performances might reasonably have been compared with others seen elsewhere, but the total ensemble admitted no comparison with anything else on earth. It was shattering and fabulous, exhausting and exhilirating, appalling and irresistible. It began at twelve midday and went on non-stop till eleven at night. It was attended by twenty thousand people a day; it cost them sevenpence a head to get in, and they came and went as they liked with no such nonsense as booking offices, usherettes or commissionaries to worry about; the theatres even dispensed with the formality of doors.

It was indisputably, if not definitively, a people's theatre. They came in their boiler-suits and shawls, with their babies and baggage, from the morning shift and institute, the literacy class and self-criticism meeting, the barrack-room and building site. They sat on hard benches or leaned against grimy walls; young couples chewed wings of chicken; mothers fed their babies at the breast; old men and young boys cleared their throats with rattling ferocity. Children tagged each other down the aisles, climbed along the benches or stood almost on the feet of the musicians, gaping in solemn fascination at the spectacle on stage; while from the dark recesses of the pit rose the smell of steaming rice and the husky patter of the pedlars with their merchandise of nuts, melons, sesame cakes and sunflower seeds.

Tomorrow no doubt there would be the weary reality of the production drive, the sanitation campaign, the hygiene inspection, the lessons in Current Events. Tonight there was the escape into a world of fantasy and folly sublime: the thundering warlords and incredible emperors, the plaintive princesses and comforting concubines, the dragons and phœnixes, the grotesque masks and gorgeous brocades, the swishing swords and fearsome scimitars.

It would be a stony heart, I thought, that could not rejoice —but such was the case with my interpreter. As an ardent member of the local Youth League, he would, I thought, have taken some pride in the performance.

'The amazing thing is how no-one notices the noise,' I said. 'I suppose you grow up with it and take it all for granted the same as we do silence.'

'On the contrary,' he said, 'it is being greatly overdone. The new operas are far less noisy than these. But it is difficult to change people's tastes at once.'

On one floor a young man in a dinner-jacket was performing an extraordinary feat of juggling with a combination of a golf ball, a football and a large fruit-bowl, to the tortured accompaniment of *Good Night, Sweet Ladies* from the six-piece band. 'These are not Chinese players,' said the interpreter with obvious disdain. 'I don't know where they come from.'

'But the juggler is excellent,' I said. 'I have seen none better.'

'I shouldn't say so. He is not one of the top performers, but only good for popular playing.'

In the theatre below an all-female company from Chekiang were performing a love-story from Shao-Hsing opera, the style of which is subtle and delicate, the vocal inflections expressed in the fingers, the music soft and restful. 'Not so striking as the Peking,' I suggested, 'but perhaps it is more precise.'

'As a rule, yes, but not with this company. They have not the delicacy of the best players.'

We moved on to the puppet show, which was an imitation of the actual Peking opera being played in the theatre next door. The bearded Emperor fought with the benign General for possession of the wailing Princess. Their staves whirled and whistled; their heads twitched; they somersaulted and chased each other round the stage while the drums throbbed louder and the gongs were beaten stronger.

I asked to go backstage to see how it was done.

The performance there outdid the one in front.

In a space no bigger than a theatre dressing-room a company of ten people were at work. In one corner three musicians belaboured between them an assortment of drums, gongs, castanets, cymbals and strings. Opposite them, two female singers sang the choral parts into a microphone. Hanging in one wing was the Company's entire wardrobe; oil-stoves and kitchen utensils were stacked on the floor beneath; while in the centre space, under the imaginary floor of the stage, five young men manipulated the puppets. But—this was the astonishing thing—they were not mere manipulators. Instead of simply pulling the strings, they themselves, holding the dolls above their heads, acted in detail every move, gesture and expression of the character they were manipulating. They danced, shook, trembled, twitched, contorted and sang to themselves through every phase of the performance. They became, in fact, the puppets themselves.

If there is such a thing as surrealist drama, this, I felt, was it. I turned and whispered my admiration to the interpreter. 'It is not a particularly good example,' he replied frigidly. 'We have many similar companies with a more polished technique than these. I would rate this as a third-rate imitation of the real thing.'

He may of course have been right: he explained that he was a purist at heart; but in the Great World that night he sounded more like an arrogant young snob.

12. Art, Theatre and Architecture

[CROFT, 145–158]

Of all the relics of bourgeois frivolity, a copy of the *Yellow Book* was the one I should have least expected to find in the functional hinterland of Manchuria.

Yet there it was, solemnly and conspicuously displayed as 'An Interesting Volume of Lu Hsün's Youth' in an exhibition arranged to commemorate China's greatest modern writer. Beardsley, Burne-Jones, Gibbings, Dalgleish: what had these hot-house plants to offer to the dour apprentices of proletarian art? In which exotic corner of the hundred-flowered garden were they likely to be tended and admired?

The question was as incongruous as the presence of the *Yellow Book* itself in the bleak showroom of the Fine Arts Institute at Shenyang. It was just another freak, a bizarre manifestation of Chinese logicality, of the mental elasticity which persuades them to preserve even the most decadent ornaments of a despised society if by so doing they can illuminate some aspect of their own. Even the Dean, who knew something about western art and must have regarded the Beardsley crowd as ideologically beyond the pale, took the situation perfectly for granted.

I had not come, however, to gaze on the faded leaves of English romanticism, but to examine the communist claim to be sponsoring an artistic revival. What they were doing in Manchuria would be a pointer to the general rule—and undoubtedly they were doing a great deal.

The Institute had formerly been a comprehensive university which had undergone many shifts and changes during the Civil War and years of occupation. Since 1953 it had enjoyed a status of its own with departments of painting, sculpture and textile design. It was one of seven such institutes throughout the country and had its own secondary school attached, at which pupils could specialise in the Fine Arts from the age of twelve.

'Last summer,' said the Dean, 'a whole class graduated from the secondary school although competition was extremely

247

keen, with over one thousand candidates from a very wide area competing for eighty places.'

When I questioned the advisability of this kind of specialisation at school age, the Dean assured me that it was additional to and not in lieu of the general course of education.

'If the pupils fail to gain entrance to the Institute they can still take the University examinations, in most cases with successful results. The same principle has been applied to music, dramatic art and dancing, where most of the large institutes have their own secondary schools. This is a system which basically we have copied from the Soviet, although our teaching methods are entirely our own.

'Each institute,' he continued, 'has its own characteristic. Here we specialise in oil-painting and etching, with a special department in commercial design where the students produce all kinds of domestic requirements, including labels for bottles and canned goods.'

Surprised by the emphasis he placed upon the latter, I enquired how the serious student regarded work of this kind.

'It serves the people and gives enjoyment,' he replied abruptly.

'A painting will last forever—a canned beef tin is gone tomorrow.'

'But our students also learn to paint tea-sets and vases and other things of beauty for the home.'

'Even so,' I pointed to a portrait of Mao and a series of Increase Your Output Posters on the wall, 'it seems a pity they should have to expend their talents on this kind of thing. Don't they regard this as a decadent form of painting?'

'Our point of view,' he said conclusively, 'is that they should be trained to paint both things of beauty and household necessities.'

We were joined by the senior Professor of Sculpture, and I raised the question of Marx–Leninism dictating the artist's choice of subject.

Both Dean and Professor were taken aback. It seemed a possibility that had never occurred to them; but far from dodging the issue they were eager to pursue it.

'In class,' said the Dean, 'we teach the formal methods of painting. In his own work the student may paint as he likes.'

I mentioned such esoteric western forms as surrealism, cubism, dadaism. 'Are there any Chinese equivalents for these?'

'We have never had such forms here. Our artists want only to paint for the people.'

'But surely the artist paints to please himself. Look at Picasso'—I deliberately chose the one western artist whose name is revered in the People's Republic. 'Much of his work means nothing to the people.'

The shaft went home, for the Dean and the Professor went into an animated huddle, the outcome of which was the edifying statement: 'We agree that many people do not like some of Picasso's work, but we believe that there are many more who do.'

'On the contrary,' I said, 'I believe that very few of the people have any notion what most of Picasso's work is about —they complain that it means nothing except to Picasso.'

'Picasso's early work is of the highest quality. It has a universal meaning. He is a painter with diverse talents.'

With that statement I could hardly disagree, so I tried another tack. 'What are the prospects for a young painter who is entirely subjective, who insists on painting merely to please himself?'

My insistence on this theme sent Little Wang, my interpreter for the day, into a fit of giggling, and even the stern-featured Dean seemed momentarily amused. But he was not to be shaken into any original statement. Perhaps he had said what he thought; perhaps he didn't think; perhaps he didn't want to. 'The artist may paint as he wishes,' he said, while Little Wang went on giggling unaccountably to herself. 'We have adopted the policy, "Let flowers of all kinds blossom." The artist must choose for himself.' As though to prove his point, he led me into the library, where, in the well-stocked western section, almost the first books I saw were recent editions of illustrated works on Stanley Spencer and Henry Moore. 'You see, although we cannot afford to purchase many books like these, we like our students to know what is being done by the leading artists of our time—whatever their ideology. I presume that the same policy applies in your own country. The teacher is merely the guide, but it is left for the student himself to decide which way he wants to go.

'In China, at least, the young artist has no need to starve. He can work in publishing houses, in textile firms or for the government. If he is really talented and wishes to work for himself, his paintings will be reproduced and published in book form. He can earn from eight to thirty *yuan* for each reproduction—and there may be as many as a hundred paintings published in one book.

'For the sculptor,' said the Professor, 'the position is even better, for he is assured of work by the government. All the sculptural work in China is on a big scale—collective work on public buildings and monuments—and for a long time yet the demand will be far greater than the supply. When he has

gained some reputation in this way the young sculptor will
then be able to set up on his own.'

The Dean and the Professor were eminently practical men,
their feet firmly planted on the ground and their eyes fixed on
the future; only once did they make any reference to conditions in the past. This was after I had visited their museum
and admired their Ming vases and Ching urns and a collection of ivory and walnut boxes which had been carved, they
said, before the birth of Christ.

'In these you see our best traditions,' said the Dean. 'For
centuries they were shut away for the private enjoyment of
feudal owners, but now they are openly displayed to give
pleasure to all the people.'

In the main studio, in an atmosphere of intense quiet and
application, twenty students or more were at work on the head
of a bearded old peasant, while others worked individually on
paintings of beetles, birds and fish in the style of the great
classical master, Ch'i Pai-shih. In the etching-room another
group were laboriously fitting stone tablets into place on an
antique machine. And in the textile-design building students
who had come back in their spare time were executing original
and brilliantly coloured floral patterns for curtains, bedspreads
and clothing. I began to regret some of my earlier remarks.
There was no denying the liveliness and vitality of their work;
whatever its proletarian limitations, in terms of beauty and
craftsmanship the little I saw had more to commend it than
many of the peculiar creations I had seen masquerading as art
in the fashionable London galleries.

The Liaoning People's Cultural Institute stands about five
miles outside Shenyang, beyond the new housing estates and
grey-brick technical colleges, down a road so undeveloped
that driving along it became a feat of skilled navigation. My
visit had been arranged at short notice and, far from receiving
the red-carpet treatment, I was left mercifully free for the
early part of the evening to make my own way about while
the Director conducted a rehearsal.

In that wintry Manchurian night the bleak corridors, the
gaunt, concrete walls and broken windows—blocked up with
faded pieces of newspaper—gave me an initial feeling of having entered a singularly depressing provincial workhouse; but
the evening turned out to be as warm and refreshing as any
I had spent in the more spacious comforts of Peking. The
austerity of the dormitories—uncarpeted floors, sparse, shabby
furniture, shared kitchens with cold water only—contrasted
sharply with the radiant cheerfulness of the artists and their

families, whose intensity and dedication to their work were of a kind I had never encountered in the theatre before.

The Institute was one of eight which the government had set up in the major cities since 1951. It housed 470 artists, of whom over half belonged to the dramatic group, and the rest to the Song and Dance Ensemble. Different groups might be performing as many as five plays at a time, one in the town itself and the others in villages and factories in the Liaoning province.

After watching a rehearsal of Pa Chin's *Family* (where the acting was of a demonstrably higher standard than when I had seen the same play in Peking) I wandered down the corridor, and was suddenly arrested by the sound of a baby crying. Little Wang beckoned me after her into a nearby room, where we found the baby, only a few days old, lying beside its mother on a wooden bunk.

The mother gestured me to sit down. She explained that she was the wife of one of the musicians and was herself a singer in the Ensemble. She was a large, middle-aged woman with a handsome peasant face. She had never met an Englishman before, and she wanted to know all about the opera in London and the English singers and the 'national ensembles'.

I did my best to oblige until eventually her husband arrived. He was equally excited when he knew I was English, for he had just been rehearsing a Mozart opera with the Ensemble. I expressed my surprise at finding Mozart in Manchuria and he said that the musicians would like to play more western music but they found great difficulty in adapting themselves to the instruments.

A lean, bristle-haired young man looked in and asked if I would take tea with him and his wife on the floor below. He was leaving in the morning to join a company in a north-eastern village where they were to prepare for a play about life in an agricultural co-operative. He himself was primarily a stage manager, but he also acted occasionally and his wife was to play the leading part in the new play.

While his two children slept on top of a double-tiered bunk he and his wife urged me to tell them about the English theatre, in particular about Shakespeare. It would be wonderful, they said, to perform in Shakespeare's plays, but they did not yet understand how to act them. *Romeo and Juliet* had been produced recently in Peking, but it would be a long time before any of the provincial groups would dare to attempt such an undertaking.

It seemed they would have listened to my views on Shakespeare all night, but that was not the purpose of my visit. Eventually I turned the subject to their own work.

They had both been at the Institute since 1954, where they were paid comparatively high salaries, the wife earning 150 *yuan* a month and the husband 120. They paid five *yuan* a month for their room and ten *yuan* for their food—'and that is very good food'. They worked approximately an eight-hour day: 'When we are not performing we rehearse; when there is no rehearsal, we practise.' In the afternoons they relaxed or, if they felt inclined, could take lessons in Chinese ('Some of our older actors have difficulty in studying their parts because they are only just able to read'). A nursery was also provided for children up to the age of seven and soon the Institute was to have its own senior secondary school.

'How are actors recruited?' I asked.

'They come from many sources,' said Tsao, the husband. 'Many came from the old revolutionary base at Yenan, but there are a large number also from the former Kuomintang area, including workers, peasants and ex-army men.

'Most of our younger actors come straight from the universities or academies and are selected by examination. The first requirement nowadays is that they should be literate as well as talented.'

'What are the subjects of the examination?'

'They are tested in acting, dramatic appreciation, singing, dancing and Current Events.'

He threw in the last familiar item as unconcernedly as if he had been mentioning Verse Speaking or Skill in Deportment.

'What do you mean by Current Events?' I asked bluntly.

'In general it means world events as published in the newspapers.'

'Supposing,' I said, 'that a candidate was deficient in Current Events—or spent so much time on dramatic appreciation that he had little opportunity to study the newspapers—would that debar. him from entry if he was satisfactory in other respects?'

Tsao saw my point at once, so did his wife, but they both found it vastly amusing.

'The acting, of course, is the main thing,' he said.

'And in the case of a young actor with religious beliefs or with unorthodox political views—would he also be acceptable?'

'If the acting is good,' said Tsao, still laughing as though I had cracked a particularly potent joke, 'the candidate's chances will be good. He will be treated on the basis of the Constitution, which provides for freedom of religious thought. In our present Company, for instance, we have a number of Christians, Buddhists and Moslems, so you can see there is no religious discrimination.'

Which is not to say, I thought, that there is none of a political kind, but there was no point in pushing the matter further. The likeable Tsao was too wily or too naif to put a finger out of place.

Short, chubby and smiling, the Director suddenly appeared with lavish apologies for the necessity of having to rehearse while his guest was waiting. He led me down to the white-walled, blue-curtained reception room, where we were joined by the most sombre and striking figure I was to encounter across the length and breadth of China.

Dressed completely in black, with a thick black overcoat, black astrakhan collar, cropped black hair and magnificent black beard, Tien Yang looked unmistakably what he was, the leading actor in the Company—indeed, he might well have been the leading actor in the world. His black eyes were deep-set in a face which bore the marks and furrows of much suffering. In profile he looked like an Asiatic relation of the late John Barrymore, or as Barrymore himself might well have appeared had he ever been cast as Rasputin. You hardly needed telling that he had fought with the early revolutionaries; he looked like the father and patriarch of all revolutions.

He had acted, he said, in some of the early dialogue plays. 'Life was hard for the actor in those days. You lived on the run and depended on strangers to give you food and shelter. But the plays we performed expressed the soul of our people. The actors were voices and tongues crying out against the injustices of the time.' As a young man he had been whipped and tortured by landlords and government troops. Once, after performing in Ibsen's *A Doll's House*, he had been chained up and seen the leading actor shot before his eyes. Later he had made his way to Yenan and joined one of the communist-sponsored troupes. 'Since that day,' he brooded, 'and every day since then, I have had the joy of serving the people in the work which I chose to do when I was a child.'

'Do you believe,' I ventured timorously, 'that the people should only be shown plays which illustrate their own every-day problems?'

'In a good play,' he said, 'it is impossible not to illustrate the problems of the people.'

'What do you feel about Shakespeare?' I asked. '*Othello*, for instance? Or *Hamlet*? Those are plays universally considered of great psychological quality, but they can hardly be said to express the immediate problems of the people.'

'I would say,' he answered in his grave baritone voice, 'that they illustrate the problems of the English people.'

'Which people? Our Royal Family? Our Army leaders?

They certainly have little to do with the problems of the average working man.'

This threw Tien Yang and the Director into a lively argument with each other. It was impossible to know what point of view either was taking but, judging by Tien's fiery exclamations and the Director's rapid, high-pitched rejoinders, there was wide disagreement between them.

It was the Director who eventually replied. Ignoring the problem of Othello, he addressed himself to Hamlet.

'In his case, although he was a royal prince, and would not understand the everyday problems of the working people, the ideas he expresses are those of progressive people in a decadent society. He is in revolt against the tyranny of court and the feudal system of government.'

'But the English worker,' I insisted, 'would not agree. He would see him in a far different light, as a weak-minded, neurotic character so obsessed with self-pity that he is unable to deal with the problems confronting him.'

'That is not how we regard Hamlet. We believe that Shakespeare shows him as a fighter for his country's freedom, as an exponent of nationalism and revolutionary ideas. . . .'

This was too much. Throwing courtesy aside, I cut him short and launched into an elementary history lesson on Scandinavian politics in the thirteenth century and the conditions of the English theatre in the sixteenth. Tien Yang's black eyes flashed disbelievingly; the Director listened with mournful patience; and Little Wang scribbled furiously to keep pace with me. 'As far as the ordinary people were concerned,' I concluded, somewhat arbitrarily, 'they only understood Shakespeare when he was writing down to them—and what he wrote on that level constitutes some of the bawdiest bourgeois thinking of all time. In any case,' I added, 'the respect paid to Shakespeare by the people of his own country can be judged from the fact that nowadays only a few of them ever go to see his plays performed.'

Both Tien and the Director roared with laughter. 'We can learn the answers about Shakespeare from you,' they said, with a discretion that made further argument superfluous, 'but we cannot give them ourselves.'

So we changed the subject, and I got Tien Yang to tell me more about conditions in the old days and the Director to talk about the day-to-day problems of running the Institute, and late into the Manchurian night we sat talking theatre 'shop' without ideological references of any kind.

When at length my Molotova bumped and jolted its way back to the hotel, sometimes zig-zagging round pot-holes in the road, sometimes bouncing over them, I turned to tell Little Wang how admirable the evening had been—but she had nodded off to sleep on the seat beside me. I looked at her with a new respect; she had been working for over sixteen hours without a break, concentrating in two languages at once, and had uttered not a word of complaint.

The following day I was with the acting fraternity again, this time in the Changchun film studio.

It had been built in 1949 and was one of four owned by the State.

The film industry has lagged far behind the theatre in its development, partly because the Chinese have not yet mastered the 'techniques', but mainly because they have to pay ceiling prices for importing camera equipment and celluloid from Japan. The budget for a feature film must not exceed £15,000 and the whole process of production, 'including the time the actors spend in studying life on farms and factories', must be completed within a six-months' period.

In its short existence the Changchun studio had produced fifty-two feature films, among them the modern Chinese classics, *The White-Haired Girl* and *Chinese Women,* but it specialised mainly in dubbing foreign films into Chinese and Chinese films into the languages of the national minorities. At the time of my visit the dubbing department was busy on a series of French films which were shortly to be launched on a nation-wide basis, and three feature films were in production: a local opera; a children's film (showing how a rural branch of the Young Pioneers unearthed a gang of counter-revolutionaries); and a dialectical piece on marriage problems among co-operative members.

Compared with conditions in the Cultural Institute the actors lived in luxury. The studio had a permanent company of two hundred, housed in newly built flats, living on a salary of up to 350 *yuan* a month. Among the younger actors this unusual well-being was reflected in smartly-cut suits and a general suavity of appearance. They discussed their work with enthusiasim, but I missed the passionate simplicity of the actors at the Institute: playing before the camera had perhaps made them a shade sophisticated; the actresses even wore make-up outside the studio.

It would have been difficult to imagine a more perfect specimen of classical Chinese beauty than Wu Chi-yen, the heroine of the co-operative film. Her finely slanted features, silken complexion and heavy-lidded eyes would have compelled attention anywhere had she embellished her sinuous

figure with nothing more exotic than a padded boiler-suit.
I was told—and could well believe it—that she was one of
the most popular of the younger actresses.

'If you were in English films,' I told her, intending to flat-
ter, Chinese-fashion, 'you would be the dream-girl of all our
young men. Your picture would be pinned up in their coffee
bars and clubrooms. How would you fancy that?'

She did not fancy it in the least.

'I should consider such a thing very undesirable, both from
my own point of view and that of the public. I believe the
duty of the actor is to serve the people, not to be adulated
by them.'

'Surely,' I suggested, 'the one must follow the other.'

'It is true that the people should always take an interest in
their actors. Tien Hua, for instance, who played the White-
Haired Girl, receives many letters from the people. Some
praise her performance, but many are very critical and suggest how she could improve it.'

'Does she take them seriously?'

'She knows that people only criticise from a desire to help
her. It would be wrong for her to ignore them.'

When I told her of the kind of publicity given to English
actresses in theatre-gossip columns and fan magazines she
thought I was joking.

'Do you mean that your journalists are paid for writing
such things?'

I passed the matter off as just one of our national peculiarities: 'We always like to know how the other half lives. Don't
you yourself find that people are interested in your private
life?'

'On the contrary, they feel that acting is an exhausting
occupation. They would never think of intruding upon my
leisure.'

For no reason that I can remember we found ourselves
talking about the moral standards of the profession; and suddenly, as if recalling the lines of a drearily familiar speech, this
radiant and exquisitely beautiful girl treated me to a disserta-
tion on the mechanics of re-education in the primly impersonal
tone of an instructor in one of the Cadre training schools.

'The general public' (I think the phrase is one of my own
transposition: 'the People' was the epithet invariably used
and would have covered even this multitude of sins)—'the
general public consider that actors should have even higher
standards than the rest of the community. They are regarded
as the *engineers* of morals. They play parts which are moral
and instructive, and they would be denounced by the people
if they behaved immorally in their own lives.'

'Would you say that all your actors conform to this standard?'

'There have been only a few cases of actors failing in this respect, and they have been strongly opposed by the people.'

'With what results?'

'The actor is taken out of his role and re-educated.'

'What does that entail?'

'His immoral actions are analysed for him, both by the Director and the rest of the company. Their aim is not only to show him why and where he has committed wrong, but also to help him to understand the deep roots of his behavior. For example, if he has committed adultery, his whole relationship with his wife would be examined, and such factors as whether the marriage was arranged by their parents or made by their own choice would have to be considered.'

'And then?'

'If the re-education process is successful he is restored to his part.'

'Supposing it proves otherwise?'

'He would be allowed to play only minor roles, and in very bad cases he would not be allowed to act at all.'

Later I broached this subject with Vice-Director Chou Chan. He was in charge of the studio's production programme, but was also responsible for re-education—a chief executive with a roving commission in Marxist psychiatry.

A soft-voiced, sympathetic little man, he was greatly disturbed when I told him that English actors by and large took a more lenient view of their colleagues' weaknesses.

'But surely, if they behave immorally their fellow actors will want them to cure themselves.'

'Privately perhaps they might, but they would not tolerate any system of public re-education.'

'But what of the people? Surely they will condemn these actors and refuse to watch them perform?'

Patiently I tried to explain that the people would not be unduly disturbed by what the actors did off-stage if they gave good value on. 'Only recently,' I said, while he listened aghast, 'one of our leading actors behaved so immorally that he was punished by the State, but the people still applauded his performance when he returned to the stage.'

'It is a common saying,' he reflected at length, 'that our actors have much to learn from the English. But the things you have told me are not what we wish to learn. Even so, we have a great desire to see your actors, so please tell them we shall forgive all immorality if they come to visit us. Please convey to them our warm feelings of friendship and respect.

And that,' he added, playfully pinching my arm, 'is not said for propaganda.'

Over dinner that night Carl reported another aspect of re education.

He had been taken to an agricultural co-operative to meet a former landlord.

'But,' he said, groping through the jungle of his ultra-basic English, 'landlord not there. I talk instead to wife of land lord. She very glad he no more landlord. Since Liberation he learn to work in field, but she no mind. She smile all time. There sleep ten in one bed—landlord, wife of landlord, son, wife of son, children, landlord daughter, husband of daugh ter, children of daughter—all sleep in one bed—in bed like table. But since Liberation she no mind. She very glad. All family happy together in one bed. When one turn, all turn. All turn together since Liberation.'

[ESKELUND, 137–144]

Mao Tse-tung looked down fatherly at us from his tradi tional place of honour on the wall facing the door. Otherwise there wasn't a soul in the studio meeting-room where the in terview was to take place. I sat down in one of the easy chairs. My heart was hammering, for we had run to avoid being late.

"I told you so," I said to Chi-yun. "There was no need to hurry—film stars are never on time. I know them. We'll prob ably have to wait for hours . . ."

Just then there were footsteps outside. I jumped up and straightened my tie, but at the sight of the girl who entered sat down again, a little sheepishly. We were waiting for Miss Shih Wei, I said.

"I am Miss Shih Wei."

Chi-yun told me afterwards that the disappointment was written all over my face. You could hardly blame me for that. Here I was expecting a Chinese Marilyn Monroe, but the girl in the flat shoes looked more like a schoolteacher without her glasses. Even powder and lipstick could hardly have made her pale face glamorous, and if she had any excit ing curves they were well hidden beneath her loose blue trou sers and jacket.

What on earth can one write about her, I thought: she seems completely colourless. I doubt whether she would have minded much even if I had said it aloud. We had not talked with her for more than a few minutes before she said that an actor should not have too strong a personality.

"It is easier for the masses to identify themselves with a plain, ordinary type. The actor as a person should not attract too much attention. Individual performances must not overshadow the message of the film . . ."

She sat with her hands folded in her lap, very serious. Her name could hardly suit her better, I thought. Shih Wei means *Teacher of Virtue*.

What kind of message should a film have? She replied that it should first of all strengthen the class-consciousness of the people. "The audience must be able to distinguish clearly between its friends and its enemies. A film should also strengthen the masses in their belief in the new society—otherwise it has no justification."

Miss Shih Wei told us that twice a week she and her colleagues attended political meetings. "It is here we get our inspiration. We discuss the government's plans and try to coordinate our work with them. One must always maintain close contact with the problems of the nation."

When a Chinese script writer today gets an idea for a film, he first discusses it with the actors. If they think that it sounds promising from an ideological as well as a political point of view, they go out among the people and live in the milieu which the film is to depict. They try to find the right "types" and study them at close hand. Miss Shih Wei had once spent six weeks in a coalmining town in North China. She had also lived among farmers and factory workers.

"From the people, to the people," she quoted from Mao Tse-tung, looking reverently up at his picture.

I had heard that she had played a street girl in one of her latest films. She nodded.

"But how could you find a model? After all, there are no longer street girls in China."

"No, that was quite a problem, but then I got hold of a comic-strip from before the liberation. There I found the right type."

The Chinese Communists have often said that one of their aims is to get rid of all class distinction. Everybody must learn to feel and think like workers. Miss Shih Wei was a living proof that they have succeeded in some cases. "My work," she said, where European actors would have talked about their art. Every morning she came to the studio at eight o'clock and stayed until four, with an hour off for lunch.

"But what if they are shooting a film—don't you stay longer then?"

"No, we never work overtime."

Despite the "Miss", she was married and had three children. Two of them she saw only during weekends; they were at a government nursery. The third one was only a year old and lived with her and her husband, who was a government official. "My beloved," she called him. This expression has been introduced by the Communists who consider it more "progressive" than the old-fashioned way of addressing one's spouse. Not many Chinese women can say "my beloved" without wincing, however.

We learned that Chinese film actors are divided into sixteen different categories whose salaries range from nine pounds sterling to forty-five pounds a month. Miss Shih Wei was in the tenth category and earned slightly more than ten pounds.

"Can one say that this is a measure of an actor's popularity?"

"No, it depends just as much on seniority and effort. We try to avoid building up stars. We do not want a few to get all the attention—that is undemocratic . . ."

The Communists have also tried to distribute the star-lustre more evenly within the theatre. They made a point of replacing a popular actor with his understudy without notice. The people must learn to appreciate the idea behind a play rather than an individual performance, they said.

But the public rebelled. When the understudy entered the stage the audience would boo and whistle and demand its money back. It did not help that the press started a campaign against such outbursts of "obstinate and undemocratic individualism". The authorities finally had to discontinue the practice.

Miss Shih Wei, who was twenty-eight, had only been working in films for a few years. Before that she had performed in Chinese operas. This had been very tiring work, she said, as the performances usually began at four in the afternoon and continued until midnight . . .

Europeans find it hard to understand why the majority of Chinese prefer opera to the cinema. I recently met a Danish salesman who was on a business trip to China. Some Chinese acquaintances had invited him to the opera.

"There was no scenery or anything," he told me. "The actors ran around on the stage, screaming and yelling, and the orchestra sounded like boys banging away on tin cans. I didn't want to be impolite to my hosts, but after an hour or so I just couldn't stand it any more, my ears ached."

No wonder the performances are so noisy. There are really not supposed to be walls or a ceiling to hurl the sound back at you. When the first operas were shown—that was under the Mongols in the thirteenth century—there were no theatres in China. The performances took place in the open air, so the actors had to shout to make themselves heard, and the musicians had to bang away at their instruments. They still do.

When an actor first enters the stage he announces his name and role. This is really unnecessary, for the audience already knows all about him from his dress and make-up. If he carries a fan he is a scholar. A peasant feather in the hat signifies a general. Those dressed entirely in black are invisible. Crafty officials have their faces painted white. Generals have red faces—a custom from the Sung dynasty, when military leaders used make-up to hide their unwarlike paleness.

I vividly remember the first Chinese opera I attended. Chi-yun was with me. She had promised to explain the plot to me, but even so I could not understand much of it.

"Why is that fellow waving a whip?" I asked.

"Because he is on horseback."

"Why does the general suddenly step on a chair?"

"He is mounting the city wall . . ."

A while later the actors sat down on the floor and began making funny movements with their arms. What on earth was the idea of that?

"Have you no imagination?" Chi-yun asked. "Anybody can see that they are rowing."

One of the rowers began waving a black flag with white stripes. The waves became higher, they were drowning—everybody knew this except me, and I no longer felt like asking, I did not want to be accused of being unimaginative . . .

Thanks to the opera, even the poorest Chinese farmer knows the more dramatic episodes from his country's long history. During our conversation with Miss Shih Wei I asked whether all the popular old operas were still being performed. No, she said. After the Communists came to power, the opera companies had been given a list of the plays that were "desirable".

"Of course we do not want to perform plays which are in the old, feudalistic spirit," she explained. "If you make a virtue of servility and submissiveness, the people will learn to think incorrectly."

Miss Shih Wei said that even some of the "approved" plays had been altered a little—the bad characters had been made worse, the good ones better. Otherwise the audience might easily be bewildered. The message of the play should be as clear and simple as possible.

"We have reformed and developed the various national arts," she said. "But this national inheritance can only serve the people after it has been re-evaluated from our new ideological point of view."

Much of China's literature has also been discarded or "simplified". When the Communists took over, one of the largest publishing houses in the country had eight thousand eight hundred titles in stock. When the directors of the company had been "re-educated", they were told to compile a list of those books which were suitable for new China. Of course they wanted to play safe, so the list which they finally handed in contained only one thousand two hundred titles. The rest of the books went back to the papermill.

A Yugoslav journalist whom I know recently interviewed Lao Sheh, the author of *Rickshaw Boy*. The journalist told Lao Sheh that he would like to translate this book into his own language.

"Better wait a few months," the famous old author said. "Then there will be a new edition of the book in Russian." He explained that the old central figure had not been sufficiently "positive" in his attitude—he had laughed at his troubles and not taken up the struggle. Lao Sheh had therefore changed him a little, and it would be better for the Yugoslavs to be introduced to the new, class-conscious *Rickshaw Boy* . . .

Miss Shih Wei thought that it was perfectly justified to make such alterations. In her opinion, the main purpose of art was to serve the State. Other Chinese Communists share her opinion, or at least they say so—all except one.

That one is Hu Feng. When you mention his name in China, people become silent or quickly change the subject. Once I asked an official from the Foreign Office to tell me something about Hu Feng. He was usually very helpful, but on this occasion he stiffened. "No comment," he said.

Hu Feng is a writer and literary critic who made a name for himself after the liberation. Everybody considered him a good Communist, but about two years ago he wrote an essay on a classical Chinese novel called *The Dream of the Red Chamber*, hinting that there could be other views on art than the strictly Marxist one.

The article caused a stir in literary circles throughout the country. Nobody had dared to say such a thing before. The authorities ordered Hu Feng to write a denunciation of his own views, and so he did—but most of his self-criticism turned out to be a subtle defence of liberalism and individual freedom.

Only after this "self-criticism" had been published did the Communists discover that they had walked into a trap. Now the Chinese have always had a special ability to hide their innermost feelings, to nod and smile when the situation demands. Perhaps it is this knowledge which makes the Communists so sensitive about traitors within their own ranks. Hu Feng was arrested and a nation-wide campaign started against him. The authorities insisted that there was a Hu Feng conspiracy among the intellectuals. Thousands were arrested.

When Hu Feng's earlier writings were examined, they turned out to be studded with ambiguous statements. The life-histories and confessions of a large number of people were examined for signs of similar "hidden obstructionism". Newspapers and books published since the liberation were also gone through by patriotic committees—a kind of Chinese "Un-American Activities Committees".

Many public institutions were closed for weeks while the investigations were going on. At Yenching, my old university, they also seached for "traitors". All they found was an anti-Communist slogan on a wall in one of the toilets.

One student was accused of being a secret admirer of Hu Feng and of having exchanged letters with like-minded people. When he denied this, his progressive schoolmates decided to lock him up in his room until he confessed. Three-quarters of a year passed before he broke down.

The authorities called Hu Feng all the usual names reserved for enemies of Communism. Even so, many came to realize what he stood for. He was against blind imitation of the Soviet Union. He desired an independent Chinese Communism and greater academic freedom.

The authorities must finally have realized that the attacks on Hu Feng had the opposite of the desired effect. I have been told that many people who had never felt the lack of freedom began to wonder. There might be something to what Hu Feng had said, since everyone was so excited about it—perhaps it would be better with a little freedom . . .

The campaign against Hu Feng was dropped as suddenly as it had started. Some months later the government introduced many of the reforms which he had indirectly advocated. Scientists were permitted to criticize Soviet methods and theories, professors were exempted from attending so many meetings, students were encouraged to study other languages than Russian, and a campaign was started to make people express themselves without fear.

"Let a hundred flowers bloom, let a hundred different families speaks their minds", was the name of this campaign which was in full swing when Chi-yun and I arrived in China. Every time we said to a Communist that there was a lack of freedom, he would cite the flower-slogan.

One day we talked to a high official from the Ministry of

Education. It was a good thing, I said, that the government had started this campaign—it proved that they wanted to give the intellectuals more freedom of expression.

"Well, it actually isn't so much to please the intellectuals," he replied. "We realize that we were beginning to stagnate in the field of science for want of fresh ideas. The real purpose of the campaign is to achieve better scientific ideas."

Was it Hu Feng who caused a change-over to a more liberal course in China? Or was it Stalin's death? Probably a combination of both. Hu Feng is still locked up, but he is expected to be released soon. It is whispered that the Communists now recognize his talent and that he will be offered a high post when the episode is no longer so fresh in the minds of the people . . .

I did not mention Hu Feng during my conversation with Miss Shih Wei. Why should I embarrass her? The government no longer attacked him, but neither had he been restored to favour, so people hardly knew what to think.

She told me that being a foreigner, it would be hard for me to understand the change in the Chinese people since the liberation. Their way of looking at life was different—one could also tell this by their taste in movies.

"We Chinese do not care much for pure entertainment any more," she said. "The foreign films which were so popular before the liberation would not be appreciated any more. They belong to the past—now the people demand a more positive line . . ."

On our way home we passed a cinema. Outside was the longest queue we had ever seen. There was an English film on the programme—the first one to be shown in China after the liberation. The ticket window would not be opened for several hours, but the people did not seem to mind waiting.

[BOYD ORR, 43–48]

Imagine a large, crowded theatre, where the audience sits on hard seats and attendants go up and down the aisle offering packets of melon seed and dried beef, pots of tea to be drunk through the spout (on the back of each seat is a tray on which to put the pot, and the attendants regularly bring boiling water), and hot towels—very refreshing in a crowd. People talk loudly, call out to friends. Behind the curtain marked "Safety" in large Chinese characters the band is warming up—a shrill and brassy, almost barbarous sound, enlivened by some wind instrument that drones like a bagpipe. The lights dim.

The safety curtain rises. The stage is bare of all scenery, and only an embroidered backcloth gives it an exotic look. Half hidden in the wings, the members of the orchestra, dressed in blue-cotton uniforms, bend over their instruments —cymbals, drums, castanets, flutes, two- and three-stringed violins. And suddenly, as the musician who rests his short two-stringed violin on his knee begins to draw the bow across the strings, an actor, his face painted and his eyebrows pencilled black and lengthened, wearing a black hat, a brilliant-blue silk robe with long white cuffs, and high white-soled boots like buskins, comes on stage. He walks with studied step in time to the music. He gives an elegant flick to his cuffs, halts, announces himself in a high, nasal voice, gives his name, tells the audience what he is about—he is, in fact, a scholar-official going to take the civil service examination—and passes across the stage. Cymbals clash. Woodwind wails. The play has begun. And after him come equally astonishing figures in costumes derived from those of the Ming dynasty (1368-1644) but heightened and extravagantly theatrical—a clown with white butterflies painted on his face who tumbles and trips over his clothes; a general, long pheasant plumes in his headdress, whose face is painted red to show his honesty and martial qualities; a girl, dressed in an embroidered blue gown, mincing and swaying as she walked.

"Opera" is a misnomer. The West has broken down the ancient unity into sung drama, ballet, the variety hall, and the circus ring. Here all are blended—speech which breaks into song when passion mounts; dance—in the way the actors follow the directions of the band, and the battle scenes, when the stage becomes a swirl of men thrusting with pike and sword in ordered rhythm; the tricks of clowns, whose task is to make the audience laugh; and above all, mime.

There are few props. A chair does duty as throne, bed, or mountain. Crossing a river, the boatman and his passenger mime the whole action: there is no boat or paddle. Mounting a horse, a General picks up his whip, lifts his right leg in a splendid gesture, and behold! he is mounted. It also preserves something of the "type" rather than the "individual", as did Greek drama and the Medieval moralities. The colours of faces, the dresses, even gait and the exquisite gestures, of hand and arm, indicate qualities of social standing;—white is for cunning; black for ferocity and treachery; Emperors wear yellow; flirtatious girls—green. To appreciate it to the full the symbolism must be known by heart, and it was extraordinary, watching the capacity audience, to see how intimate they were with all the details of the performance as the actors played out an incident from history, a thousand years old, of love between a young scholar and a patrician's daughter. At each well-executed aria or acrobatic feat they shouted, *"Hao! Hao!* Good! Good!"

As it happened we made our acquaintance with Chinese opera not at one of the time-honoured playhouses but at a modern theatre, complete with picture-frame stage, orchestra pit, stage, lighting equipment, and excellent dressing rooms for the actors, which was only a year or two old. The Government is encouraging this most popular of all Chinese art forms (added interest in folk art and national arts is a feature of several resurgent Asian countries), and as if to emphasize this the theatre is built plumb in the middle of the one-time matshed quarter called Bridge of Heaven where hucksters, entertainers and pedlars used to jostle each other for a pitch.

The theatre has a permanent company. That night they were performing an historical drama, *The Emperor Bids Farewell to His Favourite,* which tells how a brave general was outwitted by a cunning rival who despatched a spy to his camp to give a false report on his master's intended strategy. The general accepts the tale at face value, in spite of his commander's suspicions, falls into the trap, and is surrounded. The enemy troops, scenting victory, sing folksongs of the hero's native land and fill his troops with longing for home. As he wavers between surrender and defiance, his favourite concubine enters and exhorts him to fight to the death. To raise his spirits she performs a sword dance. (At this point, while she turned and pirouetted, the two swords she wielded flashing above her head, the old-fashioned audience would have shouted "Good! Good!"; this one, which had a good sprinkling of civil servants, clapped.) Then, lest she should be a burden to him, she thrusts a sword into her breast. Distraught the hero rushes out of his tent to give battle, but is defeated, and finally kills himself by plunging with his horse into a river, calling out the name of his beloved as he dies.

The piece had something of the quality of an Old Testament story. Nor was it far out in date. Based on a play written more than three hundred years ago, the event it described took place in about 100 B.C. "You see why someone called Chinese drama 'the history book of the illiterate'," remarked a playwright a few seats away from us. "You know the itinerent story tellers?" We had seen them reciting to attentive crowds in the parks and teashops. Some of them were blind. Inevitably, we had thought of Homer. "The stories they tell," he went on, "are first these stories, about history, China's Robin Hoods, sad businesses about girls who couldn't marry the men they loved, the wiles of politicians—this was how illiterate peasants and city people learnt their history.

Many, you'll find, know the popular plays by heart. Not all are history. There are fairytales, folk tales, and a lot of feudal themes, which we've had to alter. You won't see much history in the next item."

And nor we did. It was sheer virtuosity, acted by Mei Lan-fang, King of China's actors. Perhaps one should say "Queen", since he plays only female parts. Until recently impersonators played all the female parts, since an ancient edict had banned women from playing in the company of men on the score of "immorality". Now female parts are coming to be played by women. There is, however, a type of drama in the South which reverses the roles, women playing both male and female characters—one of their theatres in Shanghai is called "Theatre of the Cats".

Mei Lan-fang has been acting since he was twelve. Off stage he looked the sixty-year-old, portly, well-preserved gentleman he is. On stage he acquired the delicacy and grace of a girl as he played the part of an Imperial concubine, neglected by her lord, who drowns her sorrows in drink. For an hour he was the fading courtesan in all her moods, passing from melancholy and bitterness to a maudlin dignity as she refused the help of her servants to get to her bed.

"You liked it?" said the playwright as we left. It was impossible not to admire it. This was the tour de force of a great artist. But we were disturbed by that earlier remark of his— "things which we've had to alter." It sounded like censorship. This was his explanation: "This government is encouraging the arts. They're particularly interested in reviving declining folk arts, like shadow puppets. But the real Chinese drama is the most popular art form here. It has a huge following. On the other hand it reached its perfection in a 'feudal era'. With us, however, the texts have never been sacrosanct. Actors, managers and Imperial officials have altered them at will. Governments or dynastic officials have suppressed some that seemed too liberal, or altered them out of all recognition. Now we've revived these, and cut out the passages that praise landlords. We've also taken out vulgarities, some of the most superstitious incidents, and some of the ghosts. A European audience doesn't believe in ghosts very strongly. Here, millions of people are only just emerging from a real belief in ghosts and evil spirits. To emphasize them on the stage could be harmful."

"How," we asked, "do audiences react to these changes?"

"Often they have the last word," he said. "I'll give you an example. In one favourite play two lovers are reunited in Heaven by crossing a bridge formed by magpies. An overzealous editor of plays decided that peace doves would be much more in keeping with the times. But the audiences wouldn't have it. So out came the doves, and back went the magpies."

[SCHMID, 50–55]

The actor's art is ephemeral. Every night he cleans off his greasepaint and becomes an anonymous person again. The stage sets are painted over and made to serve another purpose. But there is another art form which is of frightening endurance, which enables beauty to be perpetuated for many centuries and, by the same token, allows lack of taste to mar the aspect of a city likewise for many centuries—architecture.

Here the struggle between tradition and progress has flared up in a much more real and ruthless way than in the æsthetic make-believe world of the theatre. Peking, that sleepy museum city which used to be described as the most beautiful town in the world and chosen as their spiritual home by romantically-minded dreamers—this city has now become the capital of a China that is rapidly modernizing itself. Shanghai, the city of international commerce and industry, is no longer the pulsating heart of China—indeed, it is not even its workshop any longer. In the interior of the country, at Lanchow and in Sinkiang, safe from imperialist invasion and close to the wealth in the earth, China's new production centres are being set up. And the hub of this new State-guided and State-organized reconstruction is Peking, the awakened sleeping beauty, with its Ministries and scientific institutes, which are springing up on the outskirts like mushrooms after rain.

It is obvious that the capital of a modern Chinese State is incompatible with a museum city: it must be the one or the other. True, one group of Chinese architects believed that the dilemma could be solved by the construction of a modern city outside the walls of ancient Peking, rather like the French in Morocco, who succeeded in preserving the character of the old native quarters by building separate European districts. But this trend is now on the retreat before a more radical school of thought which does not really consider the narrow little streets and gateways worth the fuss that is made over them by sentimental traditionalists. After all, they are exceedingly difficult to negotiate in a motor-car, and the old houses leave a lot to be desired in the hygienic field. Sometimes entire districts are without running water. Therefore: away with them! Only 'valuable monuments' are to be preserved, such as the restored temples, the imperial palaces, and the city gates. Whether the crenellated city walls are to be spared is still under discussion.

All these matters were explained to me by Mr Fong Khe-chiung, the Director of the City Planning Office. He was surprisingly young—only thirty-one—and when I asked what qualifications he had for his high office he replied that he had acquired his experience in the revolutionary struggle without ever attending a university or even a secondary school. He was not even a native of Peking, but the son of peasants from Manchuria.

He had a cheerful, chubby face with shrewd, humorous eyes, and it was instantly obvious that it would be futile to expect from this hard-boiled Party member any sentimental or æsthetic inhibitions whatever. Quite the contrary: the entire lay-out of the imperial city was a horror to him. "In the old days," he explained to me, "the Emperor was everything and the people nothing. That is why he built his Forbidden City right in the centre of the town, its long, massive, gilded roofs towering high above all other buildings. The single-storey habitations of the people all around it are in a way an expression of their inferiority and their underprivileged status. Now that the people have assumed power they shall have tall modern buildings in their turn—blocks of six, eight, or ten storeys, with wide avenues and thoroughfares. To-day we are for the most part still building in brick, which we make from the loam soil outside the city, but we are already thinking of erecting skyscrapers of concrete and steel."

The simple man told me all this with evident pride. He was one of those naïve reformers who see indisputable merit in tearing down something old and out of date and replacing it by something new that will stand as a testimony of our progress to future generations. We were driving north, down one of the exit roads along which workmen were just then busy with picks and shovels levelling down an earth rampart that used to serve the defence of the city. Presently we found ourselves in a vast district of brand-new buildings, whose general lay-out looked most impressive, but whose architecture betrayed rather too obviously the misunderstood monumentality of their Russian models to reflect any element of Chinese tradition, let alone Chinese æsthetic sense. This was the district of the Institutes. There were masses of them. Behind us was the Institute of Medicine; to our left was the Institute of Aeronautics, and a little beyond the Institute of Geology. In front of us the Institute of Metallurgy enclosed a spacious forecourt with its two great wings; and farther down the Mining Institute was followed by the Oil Institute. It was simply spectacular: all these buildings had sprung up within a space of a few months.

"All this used to be one big burial-ground," Fong explained. "We dug up the bones and took them elsewhere, and since the Liberation we have built thirty institutes here."

I asked if I could go up to the roof of the Institute of Metallurgy so as to get a better view of the site—and got a curious surprise. Time and again, on previous sightseeing trips, I had found myself barred by janitors from entering not only the buildings, but even the forecourts of schools, hotels, and administrative blocks, and even my Press card had been useless unless accompanied by an official pass from the Foreign Ministry. And such a pass took a very long time to obtain. In Peking you need a pass even to visit a friend at a hotel, and when you leave this must be handed to the porter, duly signed by the person you have visited. Now I found that even the City Architect enjoyed no privilege in this respect, and had first to make a humble application to the Comrade Director of the Institute before being allowed into his sacred precincts.

Not only the northern exit road, but also the western outskirts of the city are one gigantic building site, with veritable armies of workmen digging foundations with only the most elementary mechanical equipment, carrying the soil in baskets at the ends of the thousand-year-old shoulder-pole, and ramming it down by means of tree-trunks flung into the air with ropes and allowed to fall back. In this western district, in addition to the big hospital for children and the Ministry of Planning, a vast settlement of workers' flats was built immediately after the "Liberation." Eight years later the buildings were in such a state of dilapidation that there was some talk of tearing them down and rebuilding them. The third big development area is in the east of the city, but the industrial enterprises to be erected there are still in the planning rather than the building stage. To this day Peking is the somewhat inflated administrative nerve-centre of an organism which is industrially still at a very low level of development.

On our return to the City Architect's office I had another big surprise. I expressed the wish to take a picture of the City Architect in front of a big plan of Peking, on which the new districts would be marked. But in the whole town-planning office there was not a single town plan—apart from a small pocket plan which the City Architect carried on him. I asked, therefore, to be allowed to see the surveyor's map of a certain district. Again there was no such thing—or perhaps it was that they did not want to show it to me, since the whole of Peking lives in permanent fear of spies who might show 'imperialist' bombers the way to their city.

Short as the history of Chinese architecture since the "Liberation" is, it has nevertheless passed through a turbulent development. After an uncertain start it came under the influence of the traditionalist architect Lian Su-cheng, who published a learned article in the *Journal for Architecture* for 1953, demonstrating that the Chinese style of the timber frame skeleton had proved solid and durable over the centuries, and was, in fact, easily applicable to the modern constructional method of steel and concrete. Under his leadership the Chinese architects suddenly began to adorn their buildings with huge curving roofs of glazed tiles, which cost three to four times as much as ordinary tiles. In 1953-54 an Official Guest-house was built in this manner in the north-west of the city—to-day it is inhabited chiefly by Russians—requiring about 300,000 such tiles. Critics have calculated that, in this and other buildings, the mania for glazed tiles has meant a waste of some 6,000,000 yuan. But, oddly enough, it took a speech by the Russian Khrushchev to achieve an about-turn in China. When on December 7, 1954, he criticized the extravagant historic-revival style of the Russian architects the course was abruptly altered in China too.

One official building within the complex of the Winter Palace reflects the suddenness of the reversal: one of the wings still has a Chinese roof, while the other has a plain flat one. But the new course has not brought a real turn towards genuinely modern businesslike design. True, there is a lot of talk in Peking nowadays about 'structuralism,' which seems desperately similar in essence to the functionalism of the Dessau Bauhaus—condemned until recently as a bourgeois aberration—but the architects still lack the courage of simple design without pointless ornamentation; or where they do achieve it the result is an ugly, boxlike concrete cube.

[SCHMID, 28–31]

Today the Forbidden City is forbidden no longer. On the contrary. Even under the Republic it had still been confined to the fortunate few who could afford the high admission fee, and hence it had been deserted most of the time. Today for a mere five sen—which is less than a penny—the coolie can partake of the splendour and the marvels of his former rulers. For, although it was built by the "feudal" rulers with the sweat of their subjects, the new rulers are nevertheless proud of this splendour as a manifestation of the national genius, and every moron is invited to stroll about the For-

bidden City, feeling himself as a fellow-creator, as part of
that inspired collectivism which has created these treasures.
And thus every Sunday a swarm of blue-clad ants descends
upon the enormous site, losing itself in the vast courtyards,
crowding on the steps: blue termites, male and female, with
funny little children (who are still allowed colourful clothes)
held by their hands or carried pick-a-back. The visitors are
welcomed by young girls who act as eager guides, and everybody listens and learns.

The Chinese spirit is strangely reflected in these edifices.
Europeans strive for variety: they try, whenever their buildings are grouped together, to invest them with individual
features. Every little Gothic church and every Renaissance
palace seeks its own physiognomy. But here the law is a
cosmic symbol: axes and symmetries impose their strangle-
hold on every building, and there is no room even for a
tower. The vertical is avoided as though it were sacrilege.
Breadth is everything, massively horizontal halls. In the Tai
Ho Tien the Emperor used to hold his New Year reception;
the Chung Ho Tien was used for religious ceremonies; the
Pao Ho Tien was the scene of a vassals' banquet on New
Year's Eve; in the Chien Ching Kung the highest officers of
the State were received. And thus it continued, with grandiose
generosity: one sacred place for every Imperial function, and
every one of them—no matter whether used for banqueting,
praying, sleeping, or merely passing through—almost totally
identical with every other. Yet, with all its monotony, the
Forbidden City is one of the world's greatest architectural
wonders. Beauty is created here not by any originality of
forms, but by their interrelation, just as one spider's web is
much like another, without any special individual distinction
and yet beautifully and wonderfully devised. Wherever one
stands in this city of golden roofs one feels embedded and
included in a harmony of carefully attuned proportions. The
gentle curve of the double roofs, the cadence of the columns
which bear them, the marble balustrades whose white posts
rise up like stalagmites to meet the descending wood—all
these are just right and could not be otherwise, just as each
golden vessel, every shrine, and every fabulous beast occupies
in this secret system of co-ordinates the place where it be-
longs.

Whereas the Forbidden City is situated, as a meaningful
hub, right amid the homes of the common mortals, I had to
have myself pedalled a long way through the streets of the
Tartar City before reaching the remote neighbourhood of the
Temple of Heaven. While the Imperial City is dominated by
the red hue of active, throbbing life—the red of its walls and

the rust of its timbering—the Temple of Heaven is lifted by the blue and green of its dome into a more abstract, spiritual world. From outside, the gate through which the sacred precincts are entered glows rose-coloured. But the moment you have passed under its arch you are part of a different world. You feel, upon entering the numinous, that you want to halt at every step, retrace it, and advance more slowly, so as to savour to the full the harmony of the proportions of this symphony in space. The Temple of Heaven, of course, entirely lacks the impressive ostentation of the Forbidden City. On its white, circular base, surrounded by quadruple balustrades, it towers so high above the surrounding buildings as to become a symbol of loneliness. Of the loneliness of the Most Exalted, the Emperor, who used to repair here for prayer to Shang Ti, the highest god, in times of drought and famine. As in the pyramids of the Egyptians and the Mayas, this encounter is woven about with a mystery of numbers. The floor is composed of nine marble circles, the innermost consisting of nine and the outermost of eighty-nine slabs, around the circular block on which the Emperor would kneel, girdled, as an ancient sage has put it, "by the circles of the terrace and beyond it the circle of the firmament."

But, alas! little is felt to-day at this spot of those mysterious cosmic bonds of power. The Temple of Heaven, too, has become an historical monument, the object not so much of devotion as of national pride. The endless stream of blue-uniformed visitors is, moreover, channelled into a useful purpose: the adjoining buildings now house exhibitions illustrating the country's economic development and the queue of those waiting to be admitted never comes to an end.

13. Population

[CHANDRASEKHAR, 24]

Babies are now arriving in Communist China at the rate of some 55,000 a day. At this rate, China's population soon will be increasing each year by more than two Australias, and in a dozen years may have added the population of a United States of America.

In the past, a serious analysis of China's population was hazardous, if not impossible, because no one knew for certain its size and composition. Since China had never had regular scientific censuses or complete and continuous vital statistics, there were as many estimates and "guesstimates" of China's total population and birth and death rates as there were writers on China.

This guessing game came to an end when the Communist Government conducted China's first modern, nationwide scientific census in 1953-54, revealing a total mainland population, as of June 15, 1953, of some 583 million. The figure was surprising even to the Communist Government. It meant that all previous analyses of China's economic and demographic positions were misleading, since they had assumed a population of about 450 million.

How valid is this Chinese Communist figure? Statistics under communism have definite strategic value; they are not readily divulged, nor abundant when given out. This does not mean that the Government does not have them, for large-scale economic or social planning is impossible without dependable statistics. But the Government does not always choose to release them, and when it does there is always the suspicion that they may not reflect the true state of affairs.

A major objective of my rather extensive travels in China at the end of 1958 was to study China's population problems and policies and evaluate her population statistics. I met numerous economists, statisticians, medical workers and other officials connected with the census, the Statistical Bureau and the Ministry of Health. I inquired into the operation of the Vital Registration Law, passed in January, 1952, in every city, town and village I visited. Despite Peiping's recent confession of falsified statistics in certain sectors of China's econ-

274

omy, I believe that the 1953 census figures, by and large, are correct.

What is the demographic picture of China today? Projection backward on the basis of the 1953 census placed the 1949 population at 540 million. Today the number has increased to about 680 million. The annual rate of increase has risen from 2 per cent in 1950 to 3.5 per cent last year.

The birth rate per 1,000 has fallen slightly, from 37 in 1952 to 34 in 1959. The death rate per 1,000 has registered an impressive decline, from 18 in 1952 to 11 in 1959. Barring major war or internal revolt, famine or epidemic, China could reach the billion mark within about three decades.

Regional food shortages and floods in 1955 sharpened the Government's awareness of China's population problem. Excessive and ill-spaced births also were clearly depriving the country of real wealth in terms of womanpower for fields and factories. A number of planners argued that a breathing spell was imperative to give the economy time to catch up.

As a result, the Government decided to adopt a policy of population control. In 1956, a "great debate" on birth control was launched—one of those official debates whose outcome is determined in advance.

To silence orthodox Marxist critics, no less a man than Liu Shao-chi, the party theoretician and pamphleteer, now Chief of the State, convened a birth-control conference. When Premier Chou En-lai visited India in November, 1956, one of his first requests in New Delhi was for information on India's experience with family planning. Throughout 1957, the Government waged a determined campaign.

"An ideal family," every newspaper, poster, journal, and loudspeaker affirmed, "should have three or four children in a planned manner."

Family-planning exhibitions and technical guidance centers were opened in many Chinese towns and villages to explain the official policy of population control. Newspapers and magazine articles, radio talks, films, traveling exhibits, official instructors and singing guides were utilized all over the country to hammer away on the need for limiting family size, the advantages of doing so and the means of doing it.

The realism of the approach startled many visitors to China during this period. Complete details were shown in what amounted to animated diagrams, and anything which was not clear was explained by formidable women guides without prudery or squeamishness. The authorities were leaving nothing to chance: the most illiterate peasant left an exhibit knowing exactly what to do to prevent a large family.

However, when I visited China late in 1958, the birth-control policy had been reversed, the exhibits closed down and the films withdrawn. This remains the present state of affairs. Everybody assured me that the outside world had misunderstood the birth-control campaign, that it had not been designed to reduce the population but to protect the health of China's mothers.

All over the country, everyone I met insisted that China was not only not overpopulated, but actually underpopulated and facing an acute labor shortage! There is no greater wealth —so went the new party line—than that represented by human beings, all of whom are primarily producers and only secondarily consumers, and there is nothing the Chinese people under communism cannot achieve; in view of the work to be done and the targets to be achieved, 650 million people are not nearly enough. However, I was assured that all this did not mean that birth-control advice and contraceptives were no longer available.

I received the most authoritative statement of the new policy from the Vice Minister for Health, Mr. Wu Yun-fu. "There seems to have been some misunderstanding on this question abroad ever since the campaign was called off at the beginning of the year," he said. "We don't call it family planning or birth control or planned parenthood. These terms as used in capitalist countries have an entirely different connotation. We call it in China *planned births.*"

"This looks to me like a distinction without a difference," I said.

"No, no. There is a difference. Planned births are for the sake of the mother's health. Too many births have a bad effect on work, production and study."

Mr. Wu went on to explain that too many pregnancies meant a woman's frequent absence from factory or farm, which interfered with production. Besides, too many children would leave no leisure for the mother, or the father, for that matter. Since Communist China wants everyone to study intensively during leisure hours, a large family can be a handicap.

"We don't encourage contraceptives, for contraception is not the end of our policy," he continued. "Two births may be considered too few and six children may not be considered too many. The Government has not laid any restriction on the number of children a couple can have. They may and should have as many children as they can, so long as the health of the mother is not impaired."

"Can a mother resort to contraception on economic grounds —that is, for reasons of poverty?" I asked.

"But there is no poverty today, thanks to our cooperatives

and communes. All children are taken care of. So there is no question of poverty being a reason for controlling the size of the family."

Since visiting China I have tried to disentangle the complex reasons why the birth-control campaign was called off. One was undoubtedly the deep-rooted Chinese tradition and sentiment in favor of large families, a tradition which many doctors—mostly gynecologists and obstetricians in city hospitals—believed would take at least a generation to overcome. As might be expected, this sentiment is stronger among peasants than among industrial workers.

I also gathered indirectly that the family-planning campaign had been launched at an inauspicious time—that is, during the collectivization of farms and on the eve of introducing communes, when the Government was relatively unpopular in the countryside. The peasants apparently suspected some devious motive and therefore did not take to family planning. Had the movement been launched in the wake of the early and popular, but short-lived, land-redistribution program, the peasants might have accepted the innovation.

Another, and perhaps more important reason for abandoning the birth-control campaign was ideological. All Chinese discussions of population are prefaced by an ardent rebuttal of the "bourgeois and reactionary" Malthusian doctrine that improvident fertility and overpopulation are the causes of poverty.

According to Marx, overpopulation is impossible under socialism, for the poverty of the peasant and worker grows from feudalism and class exploitation, underproduction and maldistribution, and quickly vanishes under communism when the nation's resources are fully exploited. Malthusianism and its modern variant, neo-Malthusianism, or birth control, were devised by the capitalists to delude the workers into believing that they were responsible for their own poverty.

This view has been dinned so thoroughly into the population that everyone, from the Government guide and rural school mistress up to responsible officials, recites it at the mere mention of China's population problems. Even while the family-planning campaign was in full swing sporadic articles upholding the traditional Marxist viewpoint continued to appear in Chinese journals. Thus the campaign was ideologically embarrassing.

Furthermore, Russia's view is that a big population is good in itself and, while China is not a satellite of the Soviet Union, there is obvious need for a united front on ideological questions from Peiping to Warsaw. When Russia honors mothers who bear many children, China can hardly deplore her own large population—especially when it also gives her a certain added importance in the Communist camp.

In fact, the Chinese Communists seemed to delight in the sheer immensity of their numbers. The fact that China alone accounted for one-quarter of the human race, and all the Communist countries for a third, was a matter of intense pride.

But the most important reason for scrapping the birth-control campaign was probably a local political one. The feeling gained ground that the birth-control drive would be interpreted as a confession of failure, an admission that Peiping was incapable of delivering the goods. And so, in typical Communist fashion, there was a sudden and complete reversal.

There may be yet another switch some day. The Chinese Communists are said to have told recent visitors that when their population reaches 800,000,000 they expect to reinstitute an intensive birth-control program.

What is the likely consequence of this meandering population policy? Extensive public-health programs, maternal and child-health services, free medical aid and similar measures are reducing the death rate in all age groups, while the ambivalent birth-control policy is not helping to reduce the present high birth rate. As a result, China's potential for future population growth is enormous.

Is China's huge population an asset or a liability? The answer cannot be a simple yes or no, for it depends on too many factors. For example, if the young (under 16) and old (over 60) age groups are disproportionately large, the working population will be hard put to it to support them; but the advantages of an ample working group are obvious. Also, if the people are healthy, trained in modern skills and have access to the needed resources, a large population will certainly be an asset. But a large, illiterate population, in poor health and without adequate resources, hampers a country's efforts to advance.

In underdeveloped countries with democratic governments a large and growing population is a liability. This is because any increase in output tends to be eaten up by population increases, leaving no surplus for capital formation or higher living standards. One has to run fast merely to stand still.

But that is not true in a totalitarian country like Communist China, where the Government has complete control of the nation's material and human resources. China's construction and production methods today are primitive, based almost entirely on human labor. The vast areas of China which the Communists propose to colonize are marginal land, mountainous and near-desert, requiring incredible amounts of human labor to become habitable. Thus, it seems to me, Peiping is encouraging the masses to multiply so that they can be harnessed to do the work of the beast and the machine.

China's huge population also can be a military asset for its rulers. The likely pattern of future war would deny the military value of mere numbers divorced from industrial potential and advanced technology, but for the present Communist China can at least hope to make up in quantity what she so obviously lacks in quality.

Despite these apparent advantages, however, China is bound sooner or later to face the old Malthusian dilemma. Already she finds the task of feeding, clothing, housing and educating her people one that strains all her resources. No matter how loud her reiterations of Marxism, as her millions increase the ghost of Malthus will continue to haunt China.

In this setting China's mounting numbers cannot but alarm her neighbors, especially in view of her lack of emigration outlets and her expansionist Communist ideology. It is in this sense that China is likely to become a demographic danger spot in Asia.

SOURCES

Lord Boyd Orr and Peter Townsend, *What's Happening in China?*, Doubleday, 1959. Lord Boyd Orr, a British citizen, is a Nobel Peace Prize winner. Peter Townsend lived in China from 1942 to 1951. He learned to speak and read Chinese, and was Special Correspondent for the BBC in Shanghai during the Communist takeover.

Sripati Chandrasekhar, *Red China: An Asian View*, Praeger Paperbacks, 1961; and "The Population Explosion in China," *The New York Times Magazine*, December 6, 1959. Mr. Chandrasekhar, an Indian citizen, is the author of several books on Asian demography. He is Director of the Indian Institute for Population Studies, and editor of the *Population Review*. He has also been in charge of demographic research for UNESCO in Paris.

Gerald Clark, *Impatient Giant: Red China Today*, David McKay, 1959. Mr. Clark, a Canadian citizen, is Chief Foreign Correspondent for the *Montreal Star*, and co-writer and narrator of CBS's "The Face of China," which won both the Emmy and the Sylvania awards for the best television documentary of the year.

Michael Croft, *Red Carpet to China*, St. Martin's Press, 1959. Mr. Croft, a British citizen, founded the National Youth Theater in England. He visited China as a member of a Youth Delegation.

Karl Eskelund, *The Red Mandarins*, Alvin Redman, 1959. Mr. Eskelund, a Danish citizen, is married to a Chinese he met while a student at Peking University in 1936. He is the author of several travel books.

Felix Greene, *Awakened China*, Doubleday, 1961. Mr. Greene, a British citizen, has lived and worked in the United States for twenty-five years. He has been a commentator in Canada, New Zealand, and South Africa, and a senior official of the British Broadcasting Company. His book is based on visits to Red China in 1959 and again in 1960.

Liu Shui Sheng, "Life in a Chinese University," *The Atlantic Monthly*, December 1959. Liu Shui Sheng is a pseudonym which means "foreign student"; it is used by the author to conceal his real identity and nationality. He studied at Peking University for three years as a foreign exchange student.

Robert Loh, "Setting the Stage for Foreigners," *The Atlantic Monthly*, December 1959. Robert Loh, a graduate of the University of Shanghai, studied political science at the University of Wisconsin. Then he returned to China and worked as a mill manager and personal assistant to the biggest Chinese industrialist under the Communist regime.

Peter Schmid, *The New Face of China*, George G. Harrap, 1958. Mr. Schmid, a Swiss citizen, has been a theater critic, literary editor and special correspondent for a number of periodicals. He is the author of books on Japan, Spain, South America and Southeast Asia.

J. Tuzo Wilson, *One Chinese Moon*, Hill & Wang, 1959. Mr. Wilson, a Canadian citizen, is Professor of Geophysics at the University of Toronto, and President of the International Union of Geodesy and Geophysics.

Louis Wiznitzer, "I Saw Red China from the Inside," *U.S. News & World Report*, June 15, 1959; and "Paper Tiger," from a CBS broadcast, May 6, 1959. Mr. Wiznitzer, a citizen of Brazil, has been foreign correspondent for a number of Brazilian newspapers. He is Latin-American editor of *Atlas* magazine in New York.